The Image of the Unseen God

Catholicity in an Evolving Universe
Ilia Delio, General Editor

This series of original works by leading Catholic figures explores all facets of life through the lens of catholicity: a sense of dynamic wholeness and a conscious awareness of a continually unfolding creation.

Making All Things New: Catholicity, Cosmology, Consciousness
Ilia Delio

A New Heaven, A New Earth: The Bible and Catholicity
Dianne Bergant

The Source of All Love: Catholicity and the Trinity
Heidi Russell

CATHOLICITY IN AN EVOLVING UNIVERSE

The Image of the Unseen God

Catholicity, Science, and Our Evolving Understanding of God

Thomas E. Hosinski, CSC

ORBIS BOOKS
Maryknoll, New York 10545

ORBIS BOOKS
Maryknoll, New York 10545

Fathers and Brothers
MARYKNOLL™

Founded in 1970, Orbis Books endeavors to publish works that enlighten the mind, nourish the spirit, and challenge the conscience. The publishing arm of the Maryknoll Fathers and Brothers, Orbis seeks to explore the global dimensions of the Christian faith and mission, to invite dialogue with diverse cultures and religious traditions, and to serve the cause of reconciliation and peace. The books published reflect the views of their authors and do not represent the official position of the Maryknoll Society. To learn more about Maryknoll and Orbis Books, please visit our website at www.maryknollsociety.org.

Copyright © 2017 by Thomas E. Hosinski

Published by Orbis Books, Box 302, Maryknoll, NY 10545-0302.

All scripture quotations are taken from the NRSV unless otherwise noted.

Manufactured in the United States of America.
Manuscript editing and typesetting by Joan Weber Laflamme.

Library of Congress Cataloging-in-Publication Data

Names: Hosinski, Thomas E., 1946– author.
Title: The image of the unseen God : Catholicity, science, and our evolving understanding of God / Thomas E. Hosinski, C.S.C.
Description: Maryknoll : Orbis Books, 2017. | Series: Catholicity in an evolving universe | Includes bibliographical references and index.
Identifiers: LCCN 2017005223 (print) | LCCN 2017023827 (ebook) | ISBN 9781608337248 (e-book) | ISBN 9781626982598 (pbk.)
Subjects: LCSH: God (Christianity) | Philosophy and religion. | Catholic Church and philosophy. | Religion and science.
Classification: LCC BT103 (ebook) | LCC BT103 .H68 2017 (print) | DDC 231.7—dc23
LC record available at https://lccn.loc.gov/2017005223

To the memory of
my ordination classmate, colleague, and dear friend
Rev. Jeffrey G. Sobosan, CSC, ThD
(1946–1999)
and my colleague and dear friend
Becky Abildskov Houck, PhD
(1950–2009)

Life's journey was too short for both,
but their extraordinary lives and persons
graced this earth beyond measure.

Contents

Foreword   xi

Preface   xiii

Acknowledgments   xvii

1. God in the Teaching and Life of Jesus   1
   God in the Teachings of Jesus   2
   Jesus' Actions as Clues to Understanding
       Divine Action   16

2. God in Early Christianity   23
   The Cosmic Christ   23
   Universal Salvation   25
   The Trinity and the Divinity of the
       Incarnate Word   29
   The Humanity and Divinity of Jesus Christ   36

3. From the Middle Ages to Modernity   41
   Anselm and Existence as Participation
       in the Divine Being   41
   Thomas Aquinas and Secondary Causes   44
   Nicholas of Cusa and the Coincidence
       of Opposites   46
   Luther and the "Crucified and Hidden God"   51
   Friedrich Schleiermacher and Religious
       Experience   54

4. **What We Can Learn from Contemporary Physics
   and Cosmology**   63
   Relativity Theory   64
   Quantum Theory   68
   Implications for Theology   75

5. **What We Can Learn from Biological Evolution**   81
   Darwin's Discovery   81
   The Roman Catholic Response to Evolution   86
   DNA and the Relation of All Forms of Life   88
   The Origin of Life and Complexity Theory   89
   The History of Life and Mass Extinctions   93
   Implications for Theology   97

6. **The God of Possibility and Empowerment**   105
   The Doctrine of Creation out of Nothing   106
   How Might We Understand God's Creative
       Activity?   110
   God's Restraint, Humility, and Self-Limitation   117
   Existence as Participation in the Divine Life   119

7. **How Does God Act?**   123
   Criteria for a Theory of Divine Action   123
   The Religious Ground of the Theory and
       Types of Divine Action   125
   How God Influences Events   127
   The Test against the Religious and Theological
       Criteria   133
   The Test against the Scientific Criteria   140

8. **The God Who Heals and Saves**   149
   God's Reception of the Universe into God's Own
       Experience   150
   The Divine Attributes   152
   The Complementarity of God and the World   158
   Divine Knowledge and Divine Judgment   161
   Universal Salvation   164

The Problem of Evil   168
The Uniqueness of the Work of Jesus Christ   171

9. **The Trinity and Christology**   175
    The Trinity   175
    Christology   186

**Conclusion: Eschatology and the Incomprehensibility
    of God**   193

Recommended Reading   199
Index   201

Foreword

ILIA DELIO

The twentieth century bore witness to profound theological insights in light of the new scientific age. Thinkers such as Alfred North Whitehead and Pierre Teilhard de Chardin grappled with a new understanding of God in a world of change. Despite their prodigious writings on divinity and materiality, there is still doubt and confusion as to why such bold new theologies emerged in the first place. Is it necessary to come to a new understanding of God? Should our understanding of God depend on the new advances in science? Or is divinity independent of materiality since there are no real relations in God, as Thomas Aquinas maintained? The essentially dynamic view of physical reality ushered in by modern physics became a recurrent motif of early twentieth-century philosophical thought. Alfred North Whitehead described "the creative advance of nature . . . which we experience and know as the perpetual transition of nature into novelty." The same belief in the genuine novelty in nature underlay Henri Bergson's discussion of time in *Creative Evolution*. "The universe endures," he wrote. "The more we study the nature of time, the more we shall comprehend that duration means invention, the creation of forms, the continual elaboration of the absolutely new."

In this illuminating new book Thomas Hosinski takes up the questions of change, novelty, and future in a deeply profound and engaging discussion on God and evolution. A disciple of Whitehead, the author provides a thorough background to his ideas and then systematically unfolds his vision of God in a world of change and complexity. This is an important book because here we have a theologian who deals with the philosophical shifts rendered by the new science while grounding his insights in scripture and tradition. He shows us that a viable doctrine of creation demands a type of cognitive consonance between science and theology.

Hosinski's book contributes to a new understanding of God in an evolving universe. Whereas Heidi Russell's book on the Trinity (*Source of All Love*, the third volume in this series) shows divine love at the heart of cosmic life, this book takes us into the heart of God philosophically and theologically. Whitehead's process theology strives to articulate the divine mystery in a world of deep relationality and change. How we understand God in a world of change is still a divisive issue. Does God remain unchanging while the world changes? Is God the source of change, and if so, does God change? These questions cannot be addressed by theology alone and must rely on a renewed philosophical understanding of nature. Following Whitehead, Father Hosinski treats evolution as normative of nature and hence as a basis of philosophical and theological reflection. Again following Whitehead, he maintains that God is not to be treated as an exception to all metaphysical principles, invoked to save their collapse; rather, God is their chief exemplification. Viewed as primordial, God is the unlimited conceptual realization of the absolute wealth of potentiality. In this aspect, God is not *before* all creation but *with* all creation.

This is the type of theology that can forge new horizons of insight, as Christian faith and life struggle to find their way in an expanding universe. I urge you to read this book carefully and reflect on God at home in a world of change. For a God who is not related to the world is ultimately not a God for the world.

Preface

"He is the image of the unseen God."
—Colossians 1:15 (NJB)

God is the ultimate mystery, our term for the infinite and unknowable source of all things. In the above quotation the author of the Letter to the Colossians expressed the fundamental Christian experience of Jesus Christ as the clearest and deepest revelation of God. The word *image* has several meanings. *Image* can mean an exact likeness or even an incarnation of something else, in the sense of a tangible or visible representation of it. But *image* can also mean a mental picture, an idea, or a concept of something. It is with all these senses in mind that I have chosen the title of this book. Jesus Christ is indeed the incarnation of the unseen God; because of that we have our surest clues to forming an idea or concept or understanding of God in Jesus Christ. In this book I have tried to serve these convictions.

This book is part of a series, Catholicity in an Evolving Universe, under the direction of Ilia Delio, OSF. "Catholicity," Delio has said, "reflects divine incarnational energy at the heart of cosmic evolution."[1] God truly dwells in the universe, gives the universe its energetic drive toward the future, and lures the universe to new possibilities beyond the accomplishments and tragedies of the past. The universe lives out of this divine energy. For Christians, what has made us aware of this wholeness, this fundamental relationship between God and the cosmos, is the

---

[1] Ilia Delio, *Making All Things New: Catholicity, Cosmology, Consciousness* (Maryknoll, NY: Orbis Books, 2015), xiv.

experience of the incarnate presence of God in the person of
Jesus Christ. If catholicity, in the original sense of that word, is
an awareness of wholeness, of being part of the cosmos, then,
for Christians, catholicity is "a consciousness of the whole centered in Christ."[2] In this book I have tried to present an image
of God, centered in Christ, as the "divine incarnational energy
at the heart of cosmic evolution." That energy is the unfathom-
able Love at the heart of the universe: a Love that empowers all
things, gathers, enfolds, and saves all things; a Love that makes
us whole and calls us to love in response.

I have tried to honor the heart of the Christian tradition
regarding the understanding of God. But what we have come
to know of the universe through science must also inform our
understanding of the God revealed in the person of Jesus Christ.
This, in my judgment, requires a different philosophy than the
one used through most of the history of the Christian tradition
to assist the understanding of God. The ancient Greek systems of
metaphysics, even as revised by Christian theologians of the past
in order to serve the Christian faith, were based on a far different
understanding of the physical world and, to put it bluntly, are
outmoded. If we are to speak of our faith to our contemporary
world, we need to think in terms compatible with what we know
of the universe through empirical science. Christian theology
needs to experiment with alternative metaphysical categories for
expressing the Christian understanding of God. There is, after
all, no revealed metaphysics.

For this reason I will employ a revised version of the process
metaphysics of Alfred North Whitehead, which I believe to
be compatible with the contemporary scientific understanding
of the universe. Process thought is often rejected by Christian
theologians, sometimes without even being given a fair hearing,
because many theologians assume that it is incompatible with
the Christian tradition. The principal reason for this rejection, I
believe, is that many of the most prominent process theologians
have been quite radical in their willingness to abandon traditional Christian positions on God, going so far, for example,
as rejecting the doctrine of creation from nothing (*creatio ex
nihilo*) and questioning the traditional doctrine of the Trinity.

---

[2] Ibid., 10.

In contrast, I will use process metaphysics, but with some major revisions. In this way I hope that the riches of the Christian tradition and its most cherished convictions about God can be expressed in ways that mesh with our contemporary scientific understanding of the universe while remaining faithful to Christian religious experience.

Science and philosophy, however, are neither the source nor the ultimate criteria of our knowledge of God. For Christian theology Jesus Christ, who is the fullest revelation of God, must be both the source and ultimate criterion for what we claim to know of God. And so I begin the book with a study of what Jesus' teachings, actions, suffering, death, and resurrection teach us about God. The first chapter serves as a touchstone for developing an image or understanding of God. I will return to it throughout the book.

Ultimately, love is the key to our knowledge of God. We know God best through our love, which is born of being loved. As the author of the First Letter of John said:

> Beloved, let us love one another, because love is from God; everyone who loves is born of God and knows God. Whoever does not love does not know God, for God is love. . . . God is love, and those who abide in love abide in God, and God abides in them. (1 John 4:7–8, 16)

We can know with our minds and with our hearts. Blaise Pascal's famous dictum in his *Pensées*, that the heart has its reasons which reason does not know, may seem to imply that reason and feeling are opposed and unknown to each other. But in truth, reason and feeling are related. We *know* the deepest truth when we *feel* the deepest truth, and this is love, the Love at the heart of the universe and the love which that Love enables and evokes in us. The mystery that is God is best known with the heart, in love.

Acknowledgments

I would like to thank those whose support has been important in enabling me to complete this project. First, my thanks to Rev. Mark L. Poorman, CSC, president of the University of Portland, and Dr. Thomas G. Greene, provost, for their support and encouragement. The University of Portland is blessed to have such outstanding human beings as its leaders. My thanks as well to the members of the Congregation of Holy Cross at the University of Portland, my daily companions in an extraordinary religious community. Finally, I wish to thank Lara Shamieh, PhD, for her unfailing interest and support during the writing of this book. She is a true blessing and gift to me. Words can never properly express how I value her gracious presence in my life.

Chapter 1

God in the Teaching and Life of Jesus

It may seem strange to begin a book on how our understanding of God has developed because of contemporary science with a discussion of God in the teachings and life of Jesus. But we must do so for two very important reasons. First, science is neither the source nor the ultimate criterion for the Christian understanding of God. The source of that understanding is in revelation, the living encounter with God, put into words and recorded in the biblical tradition and in the subsequent tradition. And its ultimate criterion must be the teachings, life, and person of Jesus Christ, whom Christians believe to be the Word of God made flesh, the ultimate and incarnate revelation of God. If we are to speak of the Christian understanding of God, this is where we must begin. The second reason for beginning with Jesus is that Jesus' teachings and ministry present us with an expressed and incarnated vision of God that in many significant ways is in tension with customary assumptions about God based on the traditional doctrine. This rather unusual understanding of God may be much more consonant with what science reveals about the universe than we might expect. Both of these reasons, I believe, account for why many theologians today are appealing to the teachings and life of Jesus as support for their revised interpretations of the Christian doctrine of God.[1]

---

[1] As just one recent example, see John B. Cobb, Jr., *Jesus' Abba: The God Who Has Not Failed* (Minneapolis: Fortress Press, 2016).

God in the Teachings of Jesus

What Jesus has to say about God ought to carry great weight in our understanding of God, most especially given the Christian conviction that Jesus Christ is the incarnation of God. Jesus' view of God is expressed in a few direct statements, in the implications of many of his parables, and in his teachings about how we ought to live and act. Jesus' own experience of God is the foundation for all of these and for his actions as well.

God as Abba

Contrary to the dominant image of God as King of Israel and the universe, Jesus consistently speaks of and addresses God as Abba. This is an Aramaic word used by children of all ages to address their fathers, thus having strong connotations of respect, reverence, and familial intimacy. Some scholars argue that in Jewish family life at the time of Jesus the father was mainly an authority figure concerned with family honor and proper behavior, and not so much a figure of intimacy and loving support.[2] If this is accurate, then Jesus' use of the term was transformed by his own experience, for he most often depicts his "heavenly Father" as tender, merciful, compassionate, and loving: a "motherly father," if you will. Undoubtedly it was Jesus' experienced intimacy with God that led him to address God as Abba in his prayer (a practice unique to Jesus in the history of Judaism). We see this sense of God's character reflected in Jesus' teaching and in the imagery of his parables.

God as Merciful, Forgiving, and Compassionate

One of the most striking of Jesus' teachings is found in Matthew's Sermon on the Mount:

You have heard that it was said, "You shall love your neighbor and hate your enemy." But I say to you, love your

---

[2] See Bruce J. Malina, *The New Testament World: Insights from Cultural Anthropology*, rev. ed. (Louisville: Westminster/John Knox Press, 1993), 125–26.

enemies and pray for those who persecute you, so that you
may be children of your Father in heaven; for he makes his
sun rise on the evil and on the good, and sends rain on the
righteous and on the unrighteous. . . . Be perfect, therefore,
as your heavenly Father is perfect. (Mt 5:43–45, 48)

This teaching exhibits three important aspects of Jesus' understanding of God. First, it clearly points to God's mercy, forgiveness, and compassion in stating that God gives what humans
need to grow their food (the sun and the rain) to the evil as well
as to the good. The "evil" are God's "enemies," as it were, but
God mercifully gives them all that is necessary for life. Second,
though this is not the direct concern of the teaching, it is obvious
that Jesus sees God acting in and through natural processes, a
theme I consider in detail later in the book. And finally, we can
see here the source of all of Jesus' teaching about how we ought
to act. If we are to be children of God our Father, then we ought
to love even our enemies and show mercy and compassion to
all: "Be perfect, therefore, as your heavenly Father is perfect." In
the Gospel of Luke this saying is rendered "Be merciful, just as
your Father is merciful" (Lk 6:36).

While Jesus certainly drew this understanding of God as
merciful, forgiving, and compassionate from his Jewish tradition,
especially from the classical writing prophets, his own experience
of God reinforced it and accounts for why this vision is so central
to his teachings about God. Abraham Heschel, in his classic study
The Prophets, characterizes the prophetic experience as sympathy with the feelings (or pathos) of God, including the feelings
of compassion, tenderness, and love. For the prophet, Heschel
argues, it is God's compassion and love that abide forever, presid-
ing over anger and judgment.[3] Jesus certainly found this vision
of a merciful, compassionate, loving God in the prophets, but
he also certainly *felt* this directly in his own experience of God.
Jesus is not simply presenting an abstract *idea* of God that he
draws from his tradition; he understands and *knows* God to
be this way because this is how he *feels* God in his experience.
Bernard J. Cooke has pointed to a closely related aspect of Jesus'

[3] Abraham Heschel, *The Prophets* (New York: Harper and Row, 1962), 23–26, 219–31, 287, 289–91, 297–98, 307–23.

experience. He argues that Jesus experienced *his own* sympathy and compassion for the afflicted and the outcast as a revelation of *God's* sympathy and compassion: "In a sense, Jesus is constantly saying, 'If I think and feel this way, certainly my Father does also.'"[4] Jesus' understanding of God, then, is influenced by his tradition; by his own experience of God as beautiful, merciful, and compassionate; and by his own feelings of compassion for the afflicted and outcast. These are closely related elements in the vision of God he presents.

The parable of the Prodigal Son (Lk 15:11–32) communicates this vision of God as a merciful and compassionate Father in a most moving way. In the story the younger son asks for his inheritance, thus deeply insulting and hurting his father since in that culture one inherited only upon the death of one's father. In effect the younger son has said to his father, "I wish you were dead." The father was not obliged to give the younger son what he demanded, but he did. The young man then goes away, squanders it all, and finds himself impoverished and hungry. He realizes that his father's servants enjoy conditions much better than his own and decides to return to his father and ask to be hired as a servant. He prepares a humble speech of repentance, acknowledging his sin against his father and stating that he no longer deserves to be called his son, and sets off for home. Meantime, his father has been watching for him and "while he was still far off, his father saw him and was filled with compassion; he ran and put his arms around him and kissed him" (Lk 15:20). The young man goes into his confession of sin but his father isn't even listening; he issues orders to his servants to bring the best robe for his son and to prepare a special feast, "for this son of mine was dead and is alive again; he was lost and is found" (Lk 15:24).

The father in this story clearly represents God, and one would be hard pressed to find a more moving depiction of God as a merciful, forgiving, compassionate Father who loves beyond any hurt or offense. There are many interesting implications of this parable, but for my purposes I wish to focus on only two:

---

[4] Bernard J. Cooke, *God's Beloved: Jesus' Experience of the Transcendent* (Philadelphia: Trinity Press International, 1992), 97; see also 55–56, 91, 95–98, 101.

judgment and power. In the Middle Eastern culture in which Jesus lived, God was understood to be a just Judge and all powerful. It was seen as the duty of a just judge to impose some punishment or penalty for an offense in order to do justice to the offended and to reestablish proper balance and harmony. In the context of the story a human father who had been so deeply hurt by his son would think it necessary to judge his errant son and impose some sort of punishment, as the son expected, so that the honor of the head of the family would be restored. But Jesus depicts the father as ignoring all these conventions. The father's love and compassion rule, and the offense is ignored in the joy of having the son back: "he was dead but is alive again; he was lost but is now found." Likewise, Jesus implies, God does not judge and punish but welcomes all us errant children back into God's loving arms. We learn how deeply we are all cherished and loved.

But reflecting on this parable a bit more deeply, it seems fairly obvious that what Jesus has done is to transform the story of Israel's national history of sin, punishment and exile, and the prophetic promise of restoration into a story of a father and his sons. Just as Israel "went away" from God, then suffered punishment and exile, and through the prophets heard God's promise of enduring love and restoration, so the younger son goes away from the father, squanders his inheritance, and suffers the terrible consequences; but when he returns to his father he is met with great mercy and love and is restored to his inheritance. We should note that in his parable Jesus has transformed the traditional understanding of divine judgment and punishment. Traditionally it was believed that *God* in judgment sent punishment on wayward Israel because of her sins; it was *God* allowing Israel's enemies to conquer her. But in the parable the father does not in judgment punish his son; rather, the horrible conditions suffered by the son are the natural consequences of his own choices and decisions. The parable depicts God as the healer, the redeemer, the one who restores to life, not some transcendent Judge who punishes, however justly. Like the father in the story, who empowers his son and then heals and restores him after his failures, God uses God's power to empower us, not to control, and to heal us, not to punish. We will later see that this transformed understanding of divine judgment and divine power appears in several of Jesus' parables and teachings.

The second part of the parable contrasts this understanding of God with the self-righteous and merciless response of the elder son. When the elder son in the parable learns of his younger brother's return and his father's gracious reception of him, he grows angry and bitter. The righteous, those who have followed the Law and tried to live virtuously, do not respond well to God's compassionate generosity toward "sinners." They feel cheated somehow; they want to have harsh judgments passed on those who have not lived as faithfully as they have, and they want to see sinners punished. When we realize that initially we sympathize with the complaints of the elder son, we, the religious ones who have tried to follow God's will, experience the final challenge of the parable. We are forced to recognize that we are not at all like God; we are not moved by compassionate love for our wayward brothers and sisters. Instead, we have allowed our righteousness to mutate into self-righteousness. Ironically, then, we too find ourselves in the situation of the younger son; that is, we too need God's compassionate mercy and forgiveness for our self-righteousness and lack of compassion.

The same point is made in Jesus' parable of the Vineyard Workers (Mt 20:1–16), in which Jesus compares the "kingdom of heaven" to a landowner hiring laborers to work in his vineyard at all hours of the day. At the end of the day he starts with the laborers hired in the eleventh hour of the twelve-hour workday and unexpectedly pays them a full-day's wages. When the laborers hired first come up to receive their pay, they expect more, but they too are given a full-day's wages (which is what they had agreed to work for), and they start complaining that the owner has "made them equal to us who have borne the burden of the day and the scorching heat" (Mt 20:12). When we first hear this story, we tend to sympathize with these laborers, because we too live in a culture with conventional expectations regarding justice. It doesn't seem fair that those who have worked so much longer get no more than those who have hardly worked at all. The owner's response in the story is, "I am doing you no wrong; did you not agree with me for the usual daily wage? . . . Are you envious because I am generous?" (Mt 20:13, 15).

Since this is a parable of the kingdom of God, it is probable that it intends to teach us something about God's judgment from the actions of the landowner. The symbol kingdom of God refers to God's "rule" or reign, and one of the traditional expectations regarding the coming of God's kingdom involved divine judgment and final justice, the punishment of sinners and the reward of the righteous. If inclusion in God's kingdom is salvation or redemption, then this parable seems to imply that God gives salvation to all, including those who do not appear to deserve it. Interpreting the parable this way makes clear how misguided is the response of the "righteous." If "payment" for living in accord with God's will is salvation or redemption, how could we be "paid" any more than this? If we resent God giving salvation even to those who do not appear to deserve it, we see once again that we lack compassion for those we, in our self-righteousness, judge more undeserving than ourselves. Once again we learn how unlike God we can be, how unworthy to be called children of God, and how deeply we too rely on God's generosity, mercy, and forgiveness. The same points emerge from Jesus' parable of the Forgiven but Unforgiving Servant (Mt 18:23–35).

God's Will to Save the Lost and Redeem Even Evil

One of the central themes of many of Jesus' parables is finding the lost, often associated with the theme of completion. The parables of the Lost Sheep (Lk 15:4–7; Mt 18:12–14) and the Lost Coin (Lk 15:8–10) not only focus on the finding of the lost but also on completion: the shepherd wants *all* the sheep; the woman wants *all* the coins. The parable of the Great Banquet (Lk 14:16–24; Mt 22:1–10) in the Lucan version ends with the master of the house saying, "Go out into the roads and lanes, and compel people to come in, so that my house may be filled" (Lk 14:23). The parable of the Dragnet (Mt 13:47–50) compares the kingdom of God to a dragnet. Most scholars agree that verses 49–50, which apply the parable to the final judgment, are an addition by the evangelist. Without these verses the parable reads in this way: "Again, the kingdom of heaven is like a net that was thrown into the sea and caught fish of every kind; when it was full they drew it ashore, sat down, and put the good into baskets but threw out the bad." The point made by comparing the kingdom of God to a dragnet is precisely that it gathers *everything*. The sorting of the fish in verse 48 *could* be interpreted in accord with the overt reference to final judgment in verses

49–50 to mean the separation of the "just" and the "wicked" at the final judgment. But one might also interpret it to mean that God saves all and makes use of whatever is good. The parable is much more subtle without verses 49–50.

The same is true of the parable of the Wheat and Tares (Mt 13:24–30). Although often interpreted as a parable about final judgment, in accordance with the allegorical interpretation given in Matthew 13:36–43, it is actually much more subtle. The comparison of the kingdom of God to the decision of the landowner confronted with weeds in his wheat field actually puts the focus on the tolerance of the landowner in the present ("Let both of them grow together until the harvest") and his intention to make use even of what appears to be evil or disastrous: he will gather the wheat into his barn and bundle the weeds to be burned. This latter act, so often interpreted as punishment for the evildoers at the final judgment, actually carries a different symbolism. The plant identified as the weeds in this parable is most likely darnel, an annual grass closely related to bearded wheat (the variety grown in Palestine at the time of Jesus). Darnel is virtually indistinguishable from bearded wheat until the plant sets grain: darnel is shorter than wheat at fruition, and its grain is darker in color than wheat. Darnel's grain is toxic to humans and cattle but can be used as chicken feed. Also, it is important to know that at the time of Jesus there was a shortage of firewood in Palestine, and bundled darnel stalks, somewhat like our pressed-wood fireplace logs, were used as fuel for cooking and baking.[5] Hence far from symbolizing punishment, the burning of darnel shows the landowner's intention to save everything and make use even of what appears to be evil: perhaps he will use the darnel to heat his oven to bake bread from his wheat. If this parable symbolizes divine judgment, then it points to divine tolerance, salvation of all, and the divine transformation of earthly disasters and sorrows and evils into a divine victory. This interpretation of this parable could be extended, but we have seen enough for my purposes. Alfred North Whitehead, who alludes to this parable at least twice in his writings, was inspired by it, I believe, when he wrote this about

---

[5] See Joachim Jeremias, *The Parables of Jesus*, trans. S. H. Hooke, 2nd rev. ed. (New York: Charles Scribner's Sons, 1972), 224–25.

God's judgment: "It is the judgment of a tenderness which loses nothing that can be saved. It is also the judgment of a wisdom which uses what in the temporal world is mere wreckage."[6]

The parables we have briefly considered seem to imply not just that God has a universal salvific will, but that God intends to save all, no matter what conventional notions of justice expect. God's mercy and forgiveness know no limit. We are to love even our enemies because that is how God is, making the sun shine and the rain fall on the evil and the good. We are to welcome all our wayward brothers and sisters because that is what God does. God saves even what appears to be unlovable and unredeemable. Finally, I would note that Jesus' teaching on forgiveness supports the view that God saves all.

> Then Peter came and said to him, "Lord, if my brother sins against me, how often should I forgive? As many as seven times?" Jesus said to him, "not seven times, but, I tell you, seventy times seven." (Mt 18:21–22)[7]

The "seventy times seven" is a way of saying that one cannot calculate the limits of forgiveness, that one ought to forgive indefinitely. If this is how we are to act to be under God's "rule," then this teaching clearly implies that God forgives infinitely. Jesus teaches forgiveness without limit because he knows that God is forgiving without limit.

God's Care for Nonhuman Life

The evidence in the Gospels for Jesus' view of nonhuman life is slender, but what is there is richly suggestive. There are three sayings of Jesus, considered authentic by the vast majority of scholars, that are important for this topic. The first two of these occur in the context of Jesus instructing his disciples not to be anxious about food and clothing.

---

[6] Alfred North Whitehead, *Process and Reality: An Essay in Cosmology*, corrected ed., ed. David Ray Griffin and Donald W. Sherburne (New York: The Free Press, 1978 [1929]), 346.

[7] I have modified the translation from the NRSV to follow the original Greek.

Look at the birds of the air; they neither sow nor reap nor gather into barns, and yet your heavenly Father feeds them. . . . Consider the lilies of the field, how they grow; they neither toil nor spin, yet I tell you, even Solomon in all his glory was not clothed like one of these. (Mt 6:26, 28–29)[8]

In the saying about the birds, Jesus affirms the traditional Jewish theology that all good things come from God and expresses the belief, naive to the modern mind, that God provides food for the birds. As anyone who has observed birds knows, birds work hard at getting enough food each day for themselves and their young. Jesus would have known this fact. He would have known that God does not pour grain and insects from heaven into the open beaks of birds. But his point is that the food for the birds is there in nature. Once again we see Jesus affirming the providential action of God in and through the normal workings of nature.

The saying about the flowers also expresses basic trust in God's providential care for all creatures. "Lilies of the field" is probably a reference to the wildflowers of Judah (and perhaps of Galilee as well).[9] It is clear from the saying that Jesus thought flowers were beautiful, so beautiful that not even the richest display of kingly vestments—for which Solomon was legendary—could compare. God lavishes such extraordinary beauty on the quickly passing "grasses" of the field. But there is something more implied by this saying. The beauty of the flowers is a reflection of God's loving care, and thus, by implication, Jesus is saying that God cherishes *all* of God's creatures, even the wildflowers to which so many people pay no heed at all. This is quite in keeping with the theological implications of the first creation narrative and its antiphonal statement, "And God saw that it was good" (Gen 1). From Jesus' simple statement about the wildflowers we may draw the conclusion that in his view God cherishes all the creatures of the world and cares for and about them.

---

[8] See also Luke 12:24, 27–28.

[9] See Bernd Heinrich, "Of Bedouins, Beetles, and Blooms," *Natural History* 103, no. 5 (May 1994): 52–59. Heinrich studied the wildflowers of the Judean desert and the Jordan valley east of Jerusalem.

This same view is expressed in the third saying related to this topic, though the Christian tradition usually has overlooked its implications: "Are not two sparrows sold for a penny? Yet not one of them will fall to the ground apart from your Father" (Mt 10:29). Older English translations often rendered the last part of the saying "without your Father's knowledge," or "without your Father's will," assuming that the statement concerned divine omniscience or the divine "permission" necessary for all events in nature or history to occur. But the Greek text simply says, "apart from your Father," and implies a fundamental and enduring *relationship* between God and the nonhuman creatures of the world. The parallel saying in the Gospel of Luke renders the saying this way: "Are not five sparrows sold for two pennies? Yet not one of them is forgotten in God's sight" (Lk 12:6). This saying communicates more than simply God's interest in even the lowliest of creatures (judged by usual human standards). To be remembered by God is the equivalent of being valued by God; and being valued by God, when connected to the belief in God's universal salvific will, suggests salvation by God. If not even a sparrow dies "apart from the Father," if not even a sparrow is "forgotten" by God, does this not imply that God saves all God's creatures? I realize that it is dangerous to argue anything from only one or two sayings, but at the risk of reading too much into it, I believe this saying suggests that Jesus thought God's universal salvific will is not restricted to humans alone but extends to all creatures.

Such a statement seems almost shocking to most people's ears today, so accustomed are we to a Christian tradition that has assumed and taught that only human beings have immortal souls and that only humans would be present in "heaven." But I submit that it would not have been strange to a first-century Jew. While both the prophetic and the apocalyptic traditions could be vague about the final nature of God's kingdom, both of them seem to have expected a "this-worldly" kingdom, not some transcendent, ethereal, non-earthly condition. They expected God's kingdom to be established on earth—no matter how radically transformed from present "sinful" conditions. The presence of animals and plants would quite naturally be expected in a "this-worldly" eschatological vision. One need only think of Isaiah's famous vision of the Messianic age to understand this:

> The wolf shall live with the lamb,
>   the leopard shall lie down with the kid,
> the calf and the lion and the fatling together,
>   and a little child shall lead them.
> The cow and the bear shall graze,
>   their young shall lie down together;
>   and the lion shall eat straw like the ox. (Is
>   11:6–7)[10]

To believe that God would save animals and plants as well as humans is not out of the realm of possibility in first-century Jewish thought, and I think it probable that this is what Jesus believed. The Father's compassionate love knows no limits—it is universal—and the Father's will to save all would not restrict itself to humans alone.[11]

God's Action in the World Is Hidden

Several of Jesus' brief parables express a conviction that God works in the world in hidden ways and through quite ordinary processes. God's presence and action need not be some overwhelming, supernatural interruption of natural processes; God's kingdom can come about quietly and gently behind the scenes, as it were. The parable of the Mustard Seed is one of these.

> He also said, "With what can we compare the kingdom of God, or what parable will we use for it? It is like a mustard seed, which, when sown upon the ground, is the smallest of all the seeds on earth; yet when it is sown it grows up and becomes the greatest of all shrubs, and puts forth large branches, so that the birds of the air can make nests in its shade." (Mk 4:30–32)[12]

---

[10] See also Isaiah 65:25; Ezekiel 47:9–12; Jeremiah 31:12.

[11] See Wisdom 11:24–12:1, which states that God spares all things "for your immortal spirit is in all things."

[12] See also Matthew 13:31–32; Luke 13:18–19.

Mustard is an annual plant in Palestine that is noted both for its extremely small seeds and for the tremendous size it can achieve in a single growing season, up to ten feet tall. It is sometimes a cultivated plant but is quite invasive and can take over a garden if not restrained; in its wild form it can be a rampant weed. Jesus' parable makes at least three related points. First, in comparing the kingdom of God to a mustard plant, a weed, Jesus seems to be saying that the coming of God's kingdom is not something supernatural or exotic but is already all around us in the common, the ordinary. Second, the growth of the plant, while very fast, is taken for granted because it happens all the time and is quite common; yet to the Jewish mind at the time, growth from "dead" seeds to living plants is miraculous, an action of God.[13] In short, God's activity is hidden within the common and the ordinary, easily overlooked because of what we take for granted. Finally, the image of growth is important: the kingdom of God *grows*. It is not something that will arrive by means of some supernaturalistic intervention in history, but is already growing all around us, obscured by its hiddenness within the ordinary.[14]

The one-sentence parable of the Leaven or Yeast makes exactly the same points: "The kingdom of heaven is like yeast that a woman took and mixed in with [the Greek actually says 'hid in'] three measures of flour until all of it was leavened" (Mt 13:33).[15] This parable would have shocked Jesus' listeners for several reasons, including that Jesus compared the kingdom of God to the action of a woman, a challenge to a very patriarchal culture. But even more shocking, Jesus compares the kingdom of God to yeast and the resulting leavened bread. Leavened bread is the ordinary, everyday bread, not the sacred bread; matzah, the sacred bread, was and is unleavened. But to compare God's kingdom to yeast is really shocking. In Jesus' day women couldn't run down to their local grocery store and buy a cube of yeast; they had to make their own. They did this by taking a piece of bread, covering it with a damp cloth, and placing it in a dark corner, where the yeast would grow on the bread and they could harvest it as they needed it. This process seemed "unclean," not fit for sacred times and observances. So at Passover women had

---

[13] See Jeremias, *The Parables of Jesus*, 148–49.
[14] See also Luke 17:20–21; Mark 4:26–29.
[15] See also Luke 13:20–21.

to remove all yeast from the house. Yet Jesus compares the sacred kingdom of God—a euphemism for the very presence and action of God—to the yeast in the ordinary, everyday bread. So God and God's action is hidden within the ordinary and everyday. And God's kingdom grows, observable only by its effects.

God Does Not Act through Coercive Force

It is well known that Jesus taught nonresistance to evil and rejected the use of force.[16] I said above that Jesus' ethical teachings have their source in his experience of God and his understanding of how God is and acts. The teaching against the use of force has the same root as the teaching on the love of enemies: this is how we ought to act in order to be children of our Father in heaven, for God does not act upon us or the world with coercive force. As stated in the Beatitudes, "Blessed are the peacemakers, for they will be called children of God" (Mt 5:9). Jesus experienced and knew a God who suffered the evil done in the world without retribution, a God who turned the other cheek and went the "extra mile" in relating to the world: Jesus' God deals with the world in peace.

If this is how we are to act in order to be under God's "rule" and to be children of God, and if this is how God is and how God relates to the world, then we are dealing here with an unusual understanding of God's power. It is not that Jesus doubts God's power; rather, from his experience of God (and in conjunction, I believe, with his observation of the fact of human freedom), Jesus has reconceptualized God's power. He is not thinking of its exercise as absolute omnipotence, though he surely believed that God possesses absolute power. He seems to be thinking that God has freely chosen to limit God's power so that we might freely embrace and live under God's rule, just as the father in the parable of the Prodigal Son freely empowers his younger son so that eventually he might freely come home. For if all things are possible for God,[17] then it is possible that God,

---

[16] See, e.g., Matthew 5:38–41; Luke 6:29.
[17] See Mark 10:27: "For mortals it is impossible, but not for God; for God all things are possible." See also Matthew 19:26; Luke 18:27.

being as God is, freely chooses not to use the absolute power God possesses. A passage from *The Wisdom of Solomon* shows how one could combine the ideas of God's absolute power and all things being possible for God to think of God as restraining God's power:

> For it is always in your power to show great
> strength,
> and who can withstand the might of your arm?
> Because the whole world before you is like a
> speck that tips the scales,
> and like a drop of morning dew that falls on
> the ground.
> But you are merciful to all, for you can do all
> things. (Wis 11:21–23)

When humans have faith, when they freely align their wills to the will of the Father, then God's power acting in and through human cooperation[18] can bring about the unexpected: "For truly, if you have faith as a grain of a mustard seed, you will say to this mountain, 'Move from here to there,' and it will move; and nothing will be impossible for you" (Mt 17:20).[19] But humans clearly have the power to oppose God's will, to prevent forcibly the presence of God's kingdom in their own hearts, wills, and actions, and in the social structures and norms they create together; and God does not combat force with force. God is like the father in the parable of the Prodigal Son, who does not use his power to dominate his son, who subjects himself to his son's choices and decisions, and who uses his power not to control but to heal and restore.

Further clues to Jesus' understanding of how God exercises God's power are evident in Jesus' own actions.

---

[18] The parable of the Talents (Matthew 25:14–30; Luke 19:12–27) seems to support the view that God desires human cooperation in building the kingdom of God.

[19] I have restored the original Greek: "as a grain of" instead of "the size of." See also Luke 17:6; Mark 11:23; Matthew 21:21.

Jesus' Actions as Clues to Understanding Divine Action

As is true of his teachings, Jesus' actions are clues to his understanding of God. By enacting the kingdom of God in his own life and ministry, Jesus reveals his understanding of how God acts and what God is like. As the Gospel of John in particular argues in its presentation of Jesus, Jesus does the works of the Father. Therefore, most especially for those who hold the orthodox Christian faith claim that Jesus is the incarnation of God, Jesus' actions have enormous significance for understanding God.

Jesus' Acts of Mercy, Forgiveness, Healing, and Compassion

Virtually all scholars affirm that Jesus was known as one who could heal, one who could exorcise demons, one who associated with "sinners" and shared meals with them, and one whose treatment of women was quite unusual in his culture.[20] Healing, including the "spiritual" healing of exorcism, is a classic manifestation of God's life-giving power. The Jewish tradition has a long history of healers and exorcists who were understood to be able to heal because the Spirit of God worked in and through them. Likewise, this healing power was understood to be a manifestation of the divine compassion and mercy. Because of this, Jesus understood his healings and exorcisms as manifestations of God's compassionate power working in and through him; they are an actualization of God's "rule," a making present of the kingdom of God.

---

[20] See, e.g., John P. Meier, *A Marginal Jew: Rethinking the Historical Jesus*, vol. 2: *Mentor, Message, and Miracles* (New York: Doubleday, 1994), 509–1038; Gerhard Lohfink, *Jesus of Nazareth: What He Wanted, Who He Was*, trans. Linda M. Maloney (Collegeville, MN: Liturgical Press, 2012), 128–52; John Dominic Crossan, *The Historical Jesus: The Life of a Mediterranean Jewish Peasant* (San Francisco: HarperSanFrancisco, 1991), 303–53; John Dominic Crossan, *Jesus: A Revolutionary Biography* (San Francisco: HarperSanFrancisco, 1994), 66–101; Marcus J. Borg, *Jesus: A New Vision* (San Francisco: Harper and Row, 1987), 57–75; E. P. Sanders, *The Historical Figure of Jesus* (London: Allen Lane/The Penguin Press, 1993), 132–68.

In one healing narrative we see Jesus rejecting the traditional idea that physical disabilities or illnesses are God's punishment for sin:

> As he walked along, he saw a man blind from birth. His disciples asked him, "Rabbi, who sinned, this man or his parents, that he was born blind?" Jesus answered, "Neither this man nor his parents sinned; he was born blind so that God's works might be revealed in him." (Jn 9:1–3)

In Luke 13:1–5 Jesus is reported to have rejected the idea that death by human violence or accidents occurred as punishment for sin. Jesus' exorcisms as well were understood as the manifestation of God's power and healing and are connected by Jesus himself to the presence of the reign or "rule" of God: "But if it is by the finger of God that I cast out the demons, then the kingdom of God has come to you" (Lk 11:20). God's power and rule manifest themselves by healing, by freeing from bondage (illness, disability, or possession), by giving life.

One might also regard the forgiveness of sins as another kind of healing activity: spiritual healing. In some cases the Gospels record that Jesus performed a physical healing and declared a person's sins forgiven in the same incident (Mk 2:3–12; Mt 9:1–8; Lk 5:17–26). Frequently Jesus manifests God's merciful compassion toward those deemed sinners by announcing that their sins are forgiven, or by refusing to condemn them as the "righteous" do. A particularly moving example of this is the narrative of the woman caught in the act of adultery and Jesus' forgiveness of her (Jn 8:3–11). The Gospels consistently portray Jesus as showing this compassionate mercy and forgiveness toward sinners, just as he preaches a God who has compassionate mercy upon sinners and forgives them.

The same forgiveness and compassion are also manifest in the well-attested fact that Jesus associated with "sinners" and ate meals with them.[21] This practice not only ignored but reversed the conduct expected of a "righteous" Jew and most especially a

---

[21] See, e.g., Mark 2:15–17 (parallels in Matthew 9:10–13; Luke 5:29–32); Matthew 11:16–19 (parallel in Luke 7:31–35); Luke 15:1–2; 19:1–10.

religious teacher, who was to shun such social contact with tax collectors and other "sinners." Jesus clearly felt his inclusive or open table fellowship to be an enactment of the kingdom of God, of how God is and what God wants. Jesus reaches out to all who need healing: "I have come to call not the righteous but sinners" (Mk 2:17). Eating with "sinners" is a particularly effective way of communicating a God who embraces all; it symbolizes the fact that God withholds neither care, nor food, nor companionship from anyone. Just as God sends sun and rain on the evil and the good alike, so God gives nourishment, life, and acceptance to all. The refusal to eat with someone is a refusal of acceptance, a refusal to share life with them; and Jesus clearly judges this to be un-Godlike.

Jesus also ignored and reversed some commonly accepted cultural (patriarchal) norms and expectations regarding the treatment of women.[22] He spoke with women in public, he discussed theology with them, and he welcomed women among the disciples traveling with him—all actions that went against the dominant patriarchal expectations of holy men and rabbis. One can argue that Jesus judged the patriarchal view and treatment of women dominant in his culture to be oppressive and not in accord with how God is toward us, male and female. Patriarchy is another form of bondage, and Jesus acted in several ways to free women from this bondage, just as he acted to free the ill and disabled from physical bondage and "sinners" from spiritual and social bondage. His own practice was an implicit criticism of the un-Godlike character of patriarchy and a manifestation of God's compassionate love for all equally. The kingdom of God, as Jesus lived it, presents us with a radical egalitarianism, because that is how Jesus understood God to be in God's relationship to us.

Jesus' Ministry, Death, and Resurrection

The kingdom of God as Jesus preaches and enacts it in his ministry involves both explicit and implicit criticism of all usual

---

[22] See the classic work by Elisabeth Schüssler Fiorenza, *In Memory of Her: A Feminist Theological Reconstruction of Christian Origins* (New York: Crossroad, 1983), 105–59; also idem, *Jesus: Miriam's Child, Sophia's Prophet* (New York: Continuum, 1994), 67–96.

social, political, and religious assumptions, expectations, structures, and institutions. It calls people to a complete revaluing of all aspects of individual and social life, including conventional understandings of religious and moral "righteousness." It asks for the objective, external transformation of social and religious institutions, not by overt political process or by social, military, or religious revolt. Instead, it holds before us an ideal of overwhelming beauty and asks us freely to revolutionize ourselves, to give ourselves over to God in the subjective, internal transformation of our individual hearts and minds, issuing in altered conduct. Jesus asks us to place ourselves under God's "rule," to use our freedom and our power as God uses God's freedom and power: with mercy and compassion. And he acts this way himself, with compassion, not coercion; he seeks to persuade, not to force and control.

He asks us to recognize the infinite beauty and holiness of God, our Father, and he asks us to treat each other the way the Father treats us. The two great commandments, which Jesus quotes from the Books of Deuteronomy and Leviticus, are the heart of the Jewish tradition for Jesus, because they capture what it means to be under God's "rule":

One of the scribes . . . asked him, "Which commandment is first of all?" Jesus answered, "The first is, 'Hear, O Israel: the Lord our God, the Lord is one; you shall love the Lord your God with all your heart, and with all your soul, and with all your mind, and with all your strength.' The second is this, 'You shall love your neighbor as yourself.' There is no other commandment greater than these." (Mk 12:28–32)[23]

To be completely in love with God—to truly *feel* God's infinite beauty—must express itself in loving one's neighbor as oneself. The symbol kingdom of God captures that beauty, the beauty of how God is and how God deals with the world, the beauty of how the world could be if we loved God enough to treat one another that way, too. This is the ideal that Jesus holds before

[23] The first commandment is from Deuteronomy 6:4–5 and the second from Leviticus 19:18. See also Matthew 22:37–40; Luke 10:25–28.

us in his teaching and his action, and the power of ideals is precisely their power to attract and persuade us in our freedom. One cannot force anyone to accept an ideal and live up to it; one can only challenge and invite people to let the ideal seduce their hearts and minds and conduct. Jesus acts with the power of persuasion, not coercion, as he experiences God acting in the world. And he holds before us his vision of how beautiful God is and how beautiful the world could be if only we would give our hearts and minds and strength to that God and if only we would strive to love as the Father loves.

Jesus exercises power in his healing ministry as he experiences God acting: through persuasion, the attraction of an ideal, the lure of beauty and holiness, truth and ultimate value. He rejects the use of coercive force, control, and dominating power. We see this mode of action carried through in the narratives of his arrest, trial, and execution. He is unresisting at his arrest, hearings, and execution, incarnating his teaching that one ought not resist evildoers, but rather turn the other cheek (Mt 5:38–41; Lk 6:29). The gospel narratives tell us that when he was arrested, Jesus explicitly rejected the use of violent force on his behalf (Mt 26:51–52; Lk 22:49–51; Jn 18:10–11). He makes himself "powerless" in the hands of those who used coercive force against him, choosing the course of nonresistance and suffering leading to death. This, I submit, tells us what Jesus believed God to be like in the hands of the world: nonresistant, suffering, choosing to be "powerless" when faced with human choices for evil, choices that resist God's "rule." Especially for Christians, who believe that God was acting in Jesus, his conduct in his passion and death must be seen as a profound revelation of God's character and response to the world.

The Christian tradition from the outset has proclaimed that God raised Jesus from the dead. This surprising act of God, which was not expected even by Jesus' closest disciples, fits exactly with the mode of God's action implied by Jesus' parable of the Wheat and the Weeds, discussed above. In the parable the landowner is confronted with an agricultural catastrophe: his wheat field is full of darnel, the work of an enemy. His surprising response is to accept the presence of the darnel, and he overcomes the evil with a plan to save and make use of the darnel in the end. He thus transforms a catastrophe into a victory by means of a surprising response. Likewise, Jesus' execution, legitimated by the highest political and religious authorities of his time and place, apparently marked the harsh end to this dreamer's life and to all the hopes of his disciples, plunging them, no doubt, into a state of hopeless remorse felt for the world and for themselves. Yet the apparently permanent evil of Jesus' execution—and of our sin—did not defeat the creative, forgiving, and loving power of God. From the evil and wreckage of Jesus' execution God brought new life and new hope by raising Jesus from the dead. God must suffer the evil, but God can redeem and transform it into a higher victory, a redemptive act. Jesus' life, death, and resurrection incarnate God's mode of interacting with and saving the world. That is why the cross, forever a symbol of the deepest human evil and of human and divine suffering—and thus a symbol of God's judgment upon us—became for Christians the ultimate symbol of divine forgiveness and God's victorious transformation of all the evils of our lives, the symbol of our salvation and our hope.

Chapter 2

God in Early Christianity

The development of the early Christian understanding of God is quite complex. The adoption and adaptation of various Greek philosophies assisted Christian thought in developing a more refined and technical doctrine of God. But they also introduced certain assumptions about deity, implicit in Greek philosophy, that produced enduring difficulties or tensions in Christian thought about God. I will mention some of these, but I wish to focus primarily on certain aspects of early Christian thought about God and Jesus Christ that demonstrate what Ilia Delio means by the "catholicity" of the Christian tradition as "a consciousness of the whole [cosmos] centered in Christ."[1] I believe that these aspects of the catholic Christian vision of God and Christ are quite compatible with the understanding of the universe we gain from contemporary science, as I hope to show. We can see this holistic catholic vision of God, world, and Christ already expressed in the New Testament.

The Cosmic Christ

The Christian community from very early in its history understood Jesus in a cosmic context. The Jewish roots of the Christian community prepared the way for such an understanding. In the Jewish tradition God always dealt with the world through God's

---

[1] Ilia Delio, *Making All Things New: Catholicity, Cosmology, Consciousness* (Maryknoll, NY: Orbis Books, 2015), 10.

word: God created the universe through God's word (Gen 1); God's word addresses Abraham; God's word comes to Moses, through whom God reveals to Israel God's "Ten Words" of the Law; and the word of God spoken through the prophets predicts the coming of the Messiah as having cosmic consequences, not just nationalistic ones. The Gospel of John begins by speaking of the Word of God made flesh (Jn 1:1–3, 10, 14, 16–18), situating the story of Jesus in the context of creation, ultimate revelation, and salvation.

Paul also interprets the meaning of Jesus Christ in such a cosmic context. The famous passage in his letter to the church in Rome says that "the whole of creation has been groaning in labor pains until now" (Rom 8:22), not only seeing the salvific event of Jesus Christ as the salvation of the whole world, but also anticipating its completion or consummation in the future. The Letter to the Colossians quotes what is likely an early Christian hymn that makes very clear how early Christians thought of the comic significance of Jesus Christ:

> He is the image of the invisible God, the firstborn of all creation; for in him all things in heaven and on earth were created, things visible and invisible. . . . All things have been created through him and for him. He himself is before all things, and in him all things hold together. . . . For in him all the fullness of God was pleased to dwell, and through him God was pleased to reconcile to himself all things, whether on earth or in heaven by making peace through the blood of his cross. (Col 1:15–17, 19–20)

This reconciliation of all things to God in Christ and the consummation of God's plan is echoed in the Letter to the Ephesians: "He [God] has made known to us the mystery of his will, according to his good pleasure that he set forth in Christ, as a plan for the fullness of time, to gather up all things in him, things in heaven and things on earth" (Eph 1:9–10). The Letter to the Hebrews also interprets Jesus Christ in such a cosmic context (see Heb 1:1–3).

The early Christian community understood Jesus as the Christ, the Messiah, fulfilling God's promises to Israel. But going beyond what was expected in Judaism, early Christians also understood

Jesus to be the very incarnation of God's eternal Word.[2] Far from seeing the salvation won by Jesus Christ as restricted to some particular group of people, early Christians believed that it truly had and has cosmic significance. One of the implications of this cosmic victory over sin and death could be that God not only *wills* to save all, but that in Christ, God will actually "gather up all things" (Eph 1:10); that is, salvation could be seen as *universal* salvation. Several important theologians in the early centuries of Christianity defended such a speculative view.

Universal Salvation

Universal salvation is a minority teaching in the history of Christian thought, but it can claim some of the greatest early Christian thinkers as its advocates and it has never been condemned by the church. One of the first to present such a view was Irenaeus of Lyon (d. ca. 200). The central idea of Irenaeus's theology is his notion of "recapitulation."[3] For Irenaeus, God's salvific plan involves Jesus Christ's progression through birth, suffering and death, resurrection, coming again, and last judgment. In this process Christ recapitulates not just the whole of humanity but of all creation, restoring it to the initial purity and perfection intended by God in creation. The salvation won by Christ restores the whole of creation, bringing new life to a world lost in sin. Irenaeus believed that in the final consummation of God's plan, Christ would overcome all sin and death and bring salvation to all. Yet he also seems to have thought, on the basis of some statements in scripture, that some would not

---

[2] For an intriguing argument that the historical roots of the Christian belief in Jesus Christ as the incarnation of God may be found in Jesus' own intention to incarnate God's presence and return to Israel, see N. T. Wright, *Simply Jesus: A New Vision of Who He Was, What He Did, and Why He Matters* (New York: HarperOne, 2011), esp. 167–76. See also idem, *Jesus and the Victory of God* (Minneapolis: Fortress Press, 1996).

[3] For a detailed discussion of this idea, see Gustaf Wingren, *Man and the Incarnation: A Study in the Biblical Theology of Irenaeus*, trans. Ross Mackenzie (Edinburgh: Oliver and Boyd, 1959), 79–90, 122–32, 170–80, 192–201.

accept God's salvation and that consequently some would suffer eternal punishment.[4]

Irenaeus further believed that Christ's salvation is truly universal in the sense that it will extend to all of creation, not just humans. He writes:

> Neither the substance nor the essence of the created order vanishes away, for he is true and faithful who established it, but the pattern of this world passes away [cf. 1 Cor 7:31]. . . . But when this pattern has passed away, and man is made new, and flourishes in incorruption . . . then there will be new heavens and a new earth. . . . That this state of things will remain without end, Isaiah says [see Is 66:22].[5]

Basing his hope partially on Isaiah 11:6–9, Romans 8:19–23, and 1 Corinthians 15:28 ("that God may be all in all"), Irenaeus did not limit salvation to human beings but took seriously the notion of *universal* salvation, the salvation of all creation. I believe Irenaeus's hope also involved an intuition that Jesus' teaching implied such a view. But in any case the Christian tradition has for far too long ignored the great truth Irenaeus felt but could not express with consistency and persuasive power: that God's salvation is meant for the entirety of creation, not just humans.

A more influential version of belief in universal salvation was proposed by Origen (d. ca. 254), the great third-century theologian of Alexandria.[6] Origen resolved the apparent contradiction in

---

[4] For a discussion of this ambiguity, which Irenaeus never tried to resolve, see Wingren, *Man and the Incarnation*, 192–201.

[5] Irenaeus, *Against Heresies* V.36.1, trans. E. R. Hardy, in *Early Christian Fathers*, ed. Cyril C. Richardson, The Library of Christian Classics, vol. 1 (New York: Macmillan, 1970), 396. For analysis and other citations, see also Wingren, *Man and the Incarnation*, 184–86, 197.

[6] Later Gregory of Nyssa (d. ca. 395) and Gregory Nazianzus (d. 389) developed and modified Origen's version of universal restoration. See Brian E. Daley, *The Hope of the Early Church: A Handbook of Patristic Eschatology* (Cambridge: Cambridge University Press, 1991); John R. Sachs, "Apocatastasis in Patristic Theology," *Theological Studies* 54 (1993): 617–40; Henri Crouzel, *Origen*, trans. A. S. Worrall (San Francisco: Harper and Row, 1989), 257–66; John Clark Smith, *The*

scripture that Irenaeus could not, and he did so in an ingenious way. He believed that God would restore all human beings to God in the end, but he knew that scripture also speaks of eternal divine punishment. His solution was to reflect on what purpose divine punishment could have and what the word *eternal* means. Following Clement of Alexandria (ca. 150–ca. 215), Origen held that God would not punish to be vindictive; God's punishment would only be for educational and purifying purposes.[7] God would punish to persuade away from evil and toward the divine will, just as teachers in the ancient world might punish students to turn them toward proper behavior and learning. Second, divine punishment is like the process of purifying gold ore: the ore must be subjected to "punishment," crushing and intense heat, in order to separate the pure gold from the dross. In a similar way God might punish to purify humans of their sin. The purpose and aim of divine punishment, then, is education, purification, and healing.[8]

But is punishment eternal? Origen points out that the word *eternal* (Greek: *aion, aionios*) can have two meanings.[9] It can mean duration without end (the sense we usually give to the word if we are using it technically). But it can also mean a very long time, as, for example, in the student's complaint that this professor's class seemed to go on for eternity. Origen held that only God can be eternal in the first sense of the word. Creatures can be eternal in that sense only by being united with God through Christ. It follows that neither sin nor death can be eternal in this sense of the word, since neither have a share in the divine nature. And since God's punishment purifies, heals,

---

Ancient Wisdom of Origen (London: Associated University Presses, 1992), 41–60; and Jaroslav Pelikan, *Christianity and Classical Culture: The Metamorphosis of Natural Theology in the Christian Encounter with Hellenism* (New Haven, CT: Yale University Press, 1993), 311–26.

[7] See Sachs, "Apocatastasis in Patristic Theology," 618–20 on Clement and 623–26 on Origen's interpretation of divine punishment. Many commentators have seen the roots of the doctrine of purgatory in this understanding.

[8] For analysis and references, see Smith, *The Ancient Wisdom of Origen*, 48–51.

[9] See Crouzel, *Origen*, 244; Sachs, "Apocatastasis in Patristic Theology," 626–27.

and ultimately saves, then neither can punishment be eternal in this strict sense of the word. This allows Origen to reconcile the apparently contradictory statements we find in scripture. There is divine punishment that will go on for a long time, but its intention is not punitive; rather, it is part of the process by which God purifies all human beings so that, in Christ, they will be restored to union with God and eternal life in the strict sense of the word. In short, God will save all, and scripture's use of the term *eternal punishment* does not contradict this.

However, this doctrine of universal salvation seems to call into question human free will. If God will save all, are we really free? What if I choose not to be saved? It is hard to imagine that anyone who truly understands what this would mean could actually desire not to be saved. Nevertheless, Origen had a solution to this apparent problem, and once again the educational or pedagogical function of divine action was the key. The following statement was written in another context, but it captures Origen's idea.

> God does not behave as a tyrant, but as a ruler, and when he rules, he does not coerce but encourages, and he wishes that those under him yield themselves willingly to his direction so that the good of someone may not be by compulsion, but according to his own choice. . . . In a sense then God seeks a way whereby a person should want to do voluntarily what God wishes.[10]

God will not save humans against their will or force them to accept the gift of salvation. Instead, based on his reading of 1 Corinthians 15:23–28, Origen was convinced that Christ "will subject all rational creatures to himself through *persuasion*, not through constraint, and thus bring their freedom to fulfillment in obedience to the divine will."[11]

Some readers will no doubt be thinking of objections to the doctrine of universal salvation, and later I will respond to them. But for now, I simply want to show that important early Christian

---

[10] Origen, *Homilies on Jeremiah* 20:2, in Smith, *The Ancient Wisdom of Origen*, 48.

[11] Sachs, "Apocatastasis in Patristic Theology," 628; see also Origen, *Against Celsus* 8:72, and Crouzel, *Origen*, 264.

thinkers understood God, Jesus Christ, and salvation in a cosmic or universal context. In this sense early Christianity was truly catholic in its understanding of the significance of Christ.

The Trinity and the Divinity of the Incarnate Word

Christianity shares much in common with Judaism and Islam, but it makes some unique claims about God based on its understanding of the cosmic Christ. These uniquely Christian claims about God, as they came to be doctrinally defined, resulted from serious controversies within the Christian community in the fourth and fifth centuries. I have no intention of entering into the details of the extremely complex debates and disagreements of this period.[12] I want to focus, instead, on the doctrinal results of these controversies and their implications for the understanding of God.

It is worth remembering that Christianity was not a legal religion within the Roman Empire until 313 CE. When the Emperor Constantine legalized Christianity, Christians for the first time could enter into public debate about doctrinal issues. While everyone in the Christian community believed that the Word of God (Greek: *Logos*) was incarnate in Jesus of Nazareth, the relation of that Word to God was understood in different ways. Arius (d. ca. 336), a presbyter (priest) in Alexandria, who was a powerful preacher, held that the Word of God could not be understood to *be* God, despite the statement in John 1:1, because

---

[12] There is a huge literature on the history of these controversies. For reliable discussions of the entire period, see J.N.D. Kelly, *Early Christian Doctrines*, 2nd ed. (New York: Harper and Row, 1960), 223–343; Jaroslav Pelikan, *The Christian Tradition: A History of the Development of Doctrine*, vol. 1: *The Emergence of the Catholic Tradition (100–600)* (Chicago: University of Chicago Press, 1971), 172–277; and Leo Donald Davis, *The First Seven Ecumenical Councils (325–787): Their History and Theology* (Wilmington, DE: Michael Glazier, 1987), 33–80, 134–206. For a very readable summary of the history and arguments leading up to the Council of Chalcedon (451), see Philip Jenkins, *Jesus Wars: How Four Patriarchs, Three Queens, and Two Emperors Decided What Christians Would Believe for the Next Fifteen Hundred Years* (New York: HarperOne, 2010).

this would compromise the proper understanding of God. Everyone in these disputes accepted certain attributes or characteristics of God based on the assumptions of the Greek philosophies they were using to help in the technical discussion of God. Among these are the attributes of immutability and impassibility; that is, God cannot change and God cannot suffer, feel emotion, or be affected by anything outside of God. To the Greek mind, change is a mark of imperfection, as is being influenced in any way by something else. Therefore, since God must be perfect, God cannot change. If God is perfect and *could* change, this could only mean that God would move *away* from perfection. And if God could suffer, feel emotion, or be affected by anything outside of God, then God would be dependent on something other than God, which would compromise God's perfection and absoluteness as the source and sustainer of all things. Therefore, God must be impassible. Arius argued that since the Word of God became incarnate in Jesus and underwent change, suffering, and death, this Word (Logos) could not be identical with God. He apparently envisioned the Word as the first of God's creatures, immeasurably greater than any other creature because that Word had accomplished the works of creation and redemption. But he could not be God. Arius believed he had both scriptural and philosophical support for this interpretation.

Despite the fact that they shared the same assumptions about the nature of God, Arius's own bishop and many other Christians could not accept Arius's interpretation of the Word (Logos) for two basic reasons. Christians believed that *God* had saved us in Jesus Christ, and Arius seemed to be arguing that we were saved by a creature. Even worse, Christians from the beginning had been *worshiping* Jesus Christ. If the Word incarnate in Jesus were merely a creature, no matter how exalted, then Christians could rightly be accused of idolatry, since worship ought to be directed only to God. Arius's opponents, therefore, thought it was clear that Arius was wrong and that the Word incarnate in Jesus must be thought of as divine. But among Arius's opponents there were different ways of conceptualizing the Word's divinity, and they were not easy to reconcile.

In the Western or Latin-speaking part of the Christian Church there had long been a stress on the absolute oneness of God, but also a willingness to say that this one divine Being eternally constituted itself in three "Persons" *(personae)*. Tertullian (d. ca. 220), a North African theologian who was the first to use the word *Trinitas* ("Trinity") of God in Latin, presented such a view. He argued that the inner or intrinsic being of God was threefold or triune (which came to be called the *immanent Trinity*). The Father eternally generates the Son, and the Father and the Son eternally generate the Spirit within the Godhead. But these three Persons are substantially one without division; that is, there is only one divine Being. In God's dealings with the world (the mystery of the economy—God's creative, providential, and redemptive action), God distributes or extends God's Being into the Trinity of Persons; we experience God's action as Creator, Redeemer, and Sanctifier. This comes to be known as the *economic Trinity*. In short, the economic Trinity reflects the immanent Trinity, the inner triune character of God; our experience of God reveals what God really is. One group of Arius's opponents used this conceptual framework and held that the Word of God incarnate in Jesus is the second Person of the Triune God and must be understood to be God. I will call this group the One Substance party for reasons we will soon see.

In the Eastern or Greek-speaking part of Christianity, a dominant way of conceptualizing the divinity of the Logos drew its inspiration and vocabulary from Origen. Origenist theology was also trinitarian but stressed strongly the distinction among the Persons *(hypostases)* of the Trinity while affirming the oneness of God. The term *hypostasis* could have several meanings. In its basic meaning it was considered a synonym for *ousia* ("being") and was translated into Latin as *substantia* ("substance"). But it could also be understood as connoting an "externally concrete independence,"[13] a distinct objectivity in relation to other objects, and this is the sense in which Origen used the term. Origen conceived of the Son or Word of God as distinct from the Father and also as subordinate to the Father; the Son is eternally *begotten*

---

[13] G. L. Prestige, *God in Patristic Thought*, 2nd ed. (London: SPCK, 1952), 169; for a thorough discussion of the various senses of *hypostasis*, see 162–78. According to Kelly, *hypostasis* came from Stoicism and *ousia* came from Platonism, and they were originally synonyms "meaning real existence or essence, that which a thing is" (Kelly, *Early Christian Doctrines*, 129).

from the Father (which he distinguished from *created*). In that way the Son is derivative from the Father.[14] Yet, being *eternally* begotten, the Son participates and shares in the divine nature and is truly divine, not created. An analogy drawn from middle Platonism supported this view.[15] The sun generates light without itself undergoing change; in an analogous way, God the Father can eternally beget the subordinate Word without undergoing any change. Likewise, just as sunlight—derived from, subordinate to, and not identical with the sun—nevertheless participates in the nature of the sun, so too could the Word or Son of God be derived from, subordinate to, and not identical with the Father and yet participate in the one divine nature. The Origenist theologians of the East differed in exactly how they expressed it, but they shared the view that the Word of God incarnate in Jesus was divine, not a creature, and subordinate to (not identical with) the Father.

The dispute between Arius and his supporters and these other theologies caused so much turmoil that Emperor Constantine called the Council of Nicea (325 CE) to resolve the conflict. The problem facing the council was to craft a creedal statement that would satisfy both the Origenist and the One Substance parties in their condemnation of Arius's view. They eventually agreed on the following creedal statement:

> We believe in One God, the Father almighty, maker of all things, visible and invisible;
>
> And in one Lord Jesus Christ, the Son of God, begotten from the Father, only-begotten, that is from the substance [*ousia*] of the Father, God from God, light from light, True God from True God, begotten not made, of one substance [*homoousios*] with the Father, through Whom all things came into being, things in heaven and things on earth, Who because of us men and because of our salvation came

---

[14] According to Kelly, Origen based this not only on scriptural passages (such as Proverbs 8:22), but also on the middle Platonism that influenced his thought (Kelly, *Early Christian Doctrines*, 131–32).

[15] This analogy reflects the scientific beliefs of the day and, of course, does not hold up given our current understanding of stars.

down and became incarnate, becoming man, suffered and rose again on the third day, ascended to the heavens, and will come to judge the living and the dead;

And in the Holy Spirit.

But as for those who say, There was when he was not, and Before being born he was not, and that He came into existence out of nothing, or who assert that the Son of God is from a different hypostasis or substance [*ousia*], or is created, or is subject to alteration or change—these the Catholic Church anathematizes.[16]

There are two terms in the creed that allowed Arius's opponents to sign the creed. There is first the strong distinction between *begetting* and *making*: the Son of God is "begotten not made" as all creatures are. This was the exact term the Origenist theologians used to speak of the Son's relation to the Father and clearly implied the derivation and subordination of the Son that they were used to speaking of. Their favorite analogy is also in the creed: "light from light." When taken together with the statement that the Son is "from the substance of the Father," affirming the Son's divine nature, the creed states a view most Origenists would have no trouble affirming.

The other term, insisted on by the One Substance party, is *homoousios*, "of one substance with the Father." Arius denied that the Son was of the same *ousia* or substance as God, and so the creed affirms the exact opposite, which satisfied the One Substance party. This term, however, was not exactly defined at the council, and differing interpretations of it helped to fuel continuing controversy after the council. Even though Arius was condemned at Nicea, those sympathetic to him and those holding "semi-Arian" views on this topic exploited the ambiguities of the Nicene Creed and the controversy continued.[17] Nicea, then, did not end the controversies, and in the confusion Arianism maintained a hold on many Christians, including a number of bishops.

---

[16] Kelly, *Early Christian Doctrines*, 232.

[17] For a summary of these controversies, see Pelikan, *The Christian Tradition*, 1:206–10.

The resolution of this controversy took place at the Council of Constantinople in 381 CE.[18] This council defined the relation between the one being of God and the three Persons in the formula: one *ousia*, three *hypostases*. That is, God is to be understood as one "substance" or being, in which three truly distinct objective manifestations can be distinguished. This technical definition of God as three *hypostases* in one *ousia* was taken to be identical with the long-established Latin formula of three Persons *(personae)* in one substance *(substantia)*, and this became the central dogmatic teaching on God. However, differing interpretations of the meaning of this formula are possible. The definition of *hypostasis* endorsed by the council means that real distinctness and individuality must be affirmed of the three Persons, but this must be maintained without sliding into tritheism; God is only one being, not three distinct entities or beings.

Theologians tried several ways to protect the unity of God and to avoid tritheism.[19] One of these was to stress the unity of divine operations or actions: the Persons of the Trinity never act alone; all three Persons are involved in any divine action. Although piety attributed the work of creation to the Father, redemption to the Son, and sanctification to the Spirit, this could not be correct or it would compromise the unity of God. Gregory of Nyssa (d. ca. 395) developed the classic way of stating the unity of divine actions: "Rather does every operation which extends from God to creation . . . have its origin in the Father, proceed through the Son, and reach its completion by the Holy Spirit."[20] In any action of God all three Persons are acting; none of the Persons ever acts alone, because in truth there is only one God acting. Another way of stressing the unity of God is to speak of the mutual indwelling or coinherence *(perichoresis)* of the three Persons: the Son and Spirit dwell in the Father; the Spirit and the

---

[18] For a detailed discussion of this council, see Davis, *The First Seven Ecumenical Councils (325–787)*, 81–133.

[19] For a detailed summary of this topic, see Kelly, *Early Christian Doctrines*, 263–79.

[20] Gregory of Nyssa, "An Answer to Ablabius: That We Should Not Think of Saying There Are Three Gods," trans. Cyril C. Richardson, in *Christology of the Later Fathers*, ed. Edward R. Hardy, The Library of Christian Classics, vol. 3 (Philadelphia: Westminster Press, 1954), 262.

Father dwell in the Son; the Father and Son dwell in the Spirit. God is one because the three Persons are always together and cannot be separated. Yet another way of stressing divine unity is to say that whatever is affirmed of God must be affirmed of all three Persons; there is only one undivided substance or being in God and the real distinction among the Persons does not divide the simple unity of God's being.

Practically every theologian in the fourth and fifth centuries, and ever since, ends the discussion of the Trinity by invoking the mystery of faith, that is, the inability of the finite human intellect to grasp and comprehend the infinite, transcendent God. Even the famous analogies of Augustine (d. 430) can only take us so far in comprehending the doctrine of the Trinity.[21] Starting from the statement that "God is love" (1 John 4:8), Augustine suggested that in analyzing the phenomenon of love we can distinguish the lover, the beloved, and the love that unites them, and that this is an analogy for the Father (the lover), the Son (the beloved), and the Spirit (the love that unites them). Or, an analogy that is perhaps easier to grasp: we understand that we are one being, yet within ourselves we can distinguish among our intellect, our memory, and our will. These are truly distinct from one another, yet they are all ours, united in the oneness of our being. Even though these analogies can give us some sense of how we might distinguish three distinct things within one reality or being, Augustine himself acknowledged that they ultimately break down and that the Trinity is ultimately a mystery we cannot comprehend.

Although at times the doctrine of the Trinity can sound like a word game, its essential points are extremely important for the expression of Christian faith. The doctrine of the Trinity affirms that what was and is incarnate in Jesus is truly God, not a creature or some intermediary form. This doctrine affirms the Word of God incarnate in Jesus to be the Son, the second Person of the Trinity, and thus it affirms a direct divine immanence or presence in the human Jesus. Equally important, the doctrine of the Trinity also affirms the direct immanence or presence of God as Spirit in the world at large. The Holy Spirit is at work everywhere, in

---

[21] See the summaries of Augustine's analogies in Kelly, *Early Christian Doctrines*, 276–78.

everyone, guiding and sanctifying the cosmos. Once again we see early Christianity thinking of God in relation to the whole of things, the cosmos, and seeing all centered in Christ.

The philosopher Alfred North Whitehead considered these affirmations of God's presence in Jesus and the universe very important in the history of human thought. He remarked of the Christian theologians who developed these doctrines that they "have the distinction of being the only thinkers who in a fundamental metaphysical doctrine have improved upon Plato."[22] The advance is that in place of Plato's secondary image of God and pale reflections of the divine Ideas in the world, these theologians insisted on a doctrine of direct divine immanence.[23] Despite being influenced by a philosophical vision that stressed God's radical transcendence, and despite holding to the divine attributes of impassibility and immutability, the theologians of this period insisted on God's actual presence in Jesus and in the world. In this they were being faithful to Christian religious experience, the experience of God present and acting in the person of Jesus Christ and in Christ's gift of the Spirit in them and in the world. Early Christian theology, then, despite its adherence to a philosophical conception of deity in strong tension with the implications of Christian religious experience, presents us with a view of God as both transcendent and immanent and pushes this affirmation to a new level of intensity in the history of human thought about God.

The Humanity and Divinity of Jesus Christ

Once the Arian controversies seemed to be settled, a controversy that had been developing for quite some time began to cause great conflict in the Christian community. The technical theological question concerned how the divine Word of God incarnate in the human Jesus is related to his humanity; more

---

[22] Alfred North Whitehead, *Adventures of Ideas* (New York: Macmillan 1933), 214–15.

[23] Whitehead also judged that Christian theology failed to follow up on this discovery in its thought about God and God's relation to the world (see *Adventures of Ideas*, 216–17).

simply, how are the divinity and humanity related in Jesus Christ?[24] The representatives of the two great Eastern schools of theology, Alexandria and Antioch, took very different approaches to speaking of this relationship. To simplify, Alexandrian theologians began with God and asked how God became human. Antiochene theologians, in contrast, began with the human Jesus and asked how God came to be present in him. Alexandrians stressed the unity of the person of Jesus Christ and thought of the incarnation as the divine Logos/Son assuming humanity, uniting it to the divinity in a "hypostatic union" and thereby transforming or "divinizing" it. The real identity of Jesus Christ in this view is the divine Person, the second Person of the Trinity; his humanity is attenuated. Antiochene theologians, in contrast, stressed the humanity of Jesus Christ and thought of the incarnation as the divine Logos/Son coming to dwell in him through the human Jesus' perfect obedience to God's will. These two approaches came into bitter conflict in the persons of Cyril, patriarch of Alexandria (d. 444), the leading Alexandrian theologian, and Nestorius, patriarch of Constantinople (d. ca. 451), who supported the Antiochene view. These two bishops bore profound personal antipathy for each other.

The controversy between them led to the Council of Ephesus (431). At this council Cyril used his influence to have Nestorius condemned as a heretic and deposed as patriarch of Constantinople. This caused the Nestorian Church, which exists to this day, to break away in support of its patriarch. But Ephesus resolved nothing and satisfied no one. After Cyril's death, an older form of Cyril's theology was revived by the abbot of a monastery in Constantinople, insisting that after the incarnation Jesus Christ had a single nature, that of the divine Logos/Son. This is known as the Monophysite ("one nature") controversy, which was the most immediate reason for calling the Council of Chalcedon in

---

[24] For thorough discussions of this conflict, leading to the Council of Chalcedon (451 CE), see Pelikan, *The Christian Tradition*, 1:226–77; Kelly, *Early Christian Doctrines*, 280–343; Davis, *The First Seven Ecumenical Councils*, 134–206; and most exhaustively, Aloys Grillmeier, *Christ in Christian Tradition*, vol. 1: *From the Apostolic Age to Chalcedon (451)*, 2nd rev. ed., trans. John Bowden (Atlanta: John Knox Press, 1975).

451. This council sought to affirm the truth it saw in both the Alexandrian and Antiochene ways of thinking about Jesus Christ. It hoped in this way to correct the error of the Monophysite heresy and to restore harmony to the Christian community. It produced the following creedal statement—definition of faith—which has the force of dogma for virtually all Christians.

> In agreement, therefore, with the holy fathers, we all unanimously teach that we should confess that our Lord Jesus Christ is one and the same Son, the same perfect in Godhead and the same perfect in manhood, truly God and truly man, the same of a rational soul and body, consubstantial [*homoousios*] with the Father in Godhead, and the same consubstantial [*homoousios*] with us in manhood, like us in all things except sin; begotten from the Father before the ages as regards His Godhead, and in the last days, the same, because of us and because of our salvation begotten from the Virgin Mary, the Theotokos [Mother of God], as regards His manhood; one and the same Christ, Son, Lord, only-begotten, made known in two natures without confusion, without change, without division, without separation, the difference of the natures being by no means removed because of the union, but the property of each nature being preserved and coalescing in one *prosopon* and one *hupostasis*—not parted or divided into two *prosopa*, but one and the same Son, only-begotten, divine Word [Logos], the Lord Jesus Christ, as the prophets of old and the Lord Jesus Christ Himself have taught us about Him and the creed of our fathers has handed down.[25]

The dogmatic affirmation of the Council of Chalcedon is usually summarized as the "one person–two natures" theory concerning Jesus Christ. The definition of faith equated the two terms that the disputing parties used for the unity of Jesus Christ's person: *prosopon* and *hypostasis*. It insisted that Jesus Christ was both truly God and truly human, having two natures (divine and human), and it insisted that these two natures were united in the oneness of the person of Jesus Christ without in

---

[25] Kelly, *Early Christian Doctrines*, 339–40.

any way being changed, mixed together, divided, or separated. It used the title Theotokos [Mother of God], a favorite title for Mary used by the Alexandrian party, but immediately qualified it by saying that Mary is the Mother of God "as regards his manhood" to satisfy the Antiochene insistence that God cannot have a mother. In these and other ways this is a compromise statement affirming what was most precious to the disputing parties.

On the other hand, one of the enduring difficulties of this definition of faith is that it is not clear how these assertions can be coherently made while holding to the impassibility and immutability of the divine nature. It is difficult to understand, for example, how the properties of each nature can "coalesce" or "combine" in the one Person or *hypostasis* of Jesus Christ. Is it the one Person who is the subject of suffering and crucifixion? And if so, does this not imply that the impassible divine nature undergoes suffering and death? Or are we to think that only the human nature of Jesus somehow suffered and died, while the divine nature remained impassible? And if this is the case, does this not in fact separate the natures, which the definition of faith says is not the case? And if one brings trinitarian dogma to bear here, does the mutual indwelling of the Persons of the Trinity mean that the one God suffered and died on the cross? How many divine Persons, if any, died on the cross? If none, what happens to the unity of Jesus Christ? And would not the limitations of the human nature in Jesus Christ be lost because of the infinite character of the divine nature? For example, how would the omniscience of the divine nature interact with the limited and fallible knowledge of the human nature in Jesus Christ? Would not the union with the divine nature so change the human nature that Jesus Christ would no longer be "like us in all things except sin"? These and similar problems have continued to challenge the technical understanding of the person of Jesus Christ in subsequent ages.

The enduring value of this one person–two natures dogma is the beauty of its perception of the intimate union of God and humanity in the person of Jesus Christ. We may never be able to answer all the questions that arise from the claim that God became human, that God was present and acting in Jesus Christ. But our conviction that it in fact happened arises from our experience of Jesus Christ. And we learn from it that the incarnation

occurred because God wills to enter our world and become one
of us, one with us. This reveals the depths of God's love and the
depths of God's willingness to undergo suffering and death to
save us, thanks to God's love and Jesus' willingness to open himself to God's presence and will. Jesus Christ must be the key for
the Christian understanding of God's relation to the world and
God's action within it. In this way Christology, our understanding of Jesus Christ, ought to be the key to Christian theology.

The difficulty is that the continued adherence to the attributes of divinity assumed in Greek philosophy and taken over
in Christian theology—the attributes of impassibility and immutability in particular—make it difficult to articulate clearly
what our Christian faith implies. Both the dogma of the Trinity
and the one person–two natures dogma concerning Jesus Christ
appear to try to articulate the idea of a suffering God, who out
of compassion enters into our world and suffers to save us. But
the technical and orthodox interpretations of these doctrines actually deny that idea. The idea lives in Christian piety but is not
actually affirmed in technical theology. Many theologians today
believe that our technical or formal theology of God ought to
be revised in order to reflect what we experience in and through
Jesus Christ. Later in the book, I suggest some critical revisions
that may bring our technical understanding of God more closely
in line with our Christian experience of God in and through
Jesus Christ.

Chapter 3

From the Middle Ages to Modernity

Among several ideas that continually recur in the history of Christian thought, there is one that we rarely hear today: that our existence—indeed, the existence of all things—is actually participation in the being or life of God. This idea has profound implications, including the realization that all things are related in God. And this idea, in turn, anticipates and resonates very strongly with the amazing truth revealed by quantum theory: because the universe began in a quantum state, all things maintain a fundamental "entanglement" or relatedness. Perhaps the theological idea even reveals the ultimate cause of what quantum theory has discovered. Both Christian faith and contemporary science reveal, in very different ways, a wholeness in the universe, a fundamental relatedness, that begs for our attention. I pursue such reflections in relation to contemporary science later in the book. For the present, I call attention to how some major theologians from the Middle Ages to the modern era expressed this idea of existence as participation in the divine Being.

Anselm and Existence as Participation in the Divine Being

Anselm of Canterbury (1033–1109) is an important figure in the history of Christian thought largely because he revived Western theological reflection and rescued it from mere appeals to authority. He was convinced that Christians should seek to understand what they believe in faith and be able to give reasons for what they believe. He is a great representative of what has been called the Augustinian synthesis[1] of early medieval theology. There is much of interest in Anselm's theology, but here I focus on his intriguing analysis showing that all things exist by participating in the divine Being.

This analysis occurs in Anselm's discussion of the divine attributes. As is typical of Anselm's thought, he applies logical analysis or dialectical argumentation to prove the truth of what Christian faith believes about the divine nature. He proves first that the divine nature must be what it is through itself and not through another.[2] If it were what it is through another, then it would be dependent on that other and could not be what Christians believe God to be, namely, the supreme, absolute Being, the Creator, the source of all things. Therefore, whatever the divine nature is, it must be through itself alone. Once he establishes this general truth, Anselm turns to a consideration of the divine attributes in order to uncover the implications of God's autonomy.

Anselm points out that when we say someone is good or wise or just, we are implying that to one degree or another that person *participates* in that quality. In other words, speaking of someone as exhibiting that quality also implies a *quantity* or magnitude; that is, to one degree or another, that person exhibits goodness or wisdom or justness in her or his character. To speak in this way does not tell us what human nature is but describes the greatness of a person's character. But when we say that God is good or wise or just, we are not saying that God participates in that quality or virtue, and we are not implying a *quantity* at all; rather, we are actually describing what the divine nature *is*. Anselm's reasoning here is quite logical and can be stated in a syllogism: if a being is good only by participating in goodness, and if the

---

[1] See Jaroslav Pelikan, *The Christian Tradition*, vol. 3: *The Growth of Medieval Theology (600–1300)* (Chicago: University of Chicago Press, 1978), 9–105. See also Etienne Gilson, *Reason and Revelation in the Middle Ages* (New York: Charles Scribner's Sons, 1938), 24. Gilson writes: "Anselm was so fully convinced of the validity of Augustine's method that its most perfect definitions are to be looked for in the writings of Anselm rather than in those of Augustine."

[2] Anselm, *Monologion*, 3, 6.

divine nature is what it is through itself and not through another, then the divine nature must be goodness itself. To call God good can only mean that God *is* goodness. When we add the ideas that God does not owe God's existence to anything other than God, that God is infinite, and that God is perfect, it then follows that God's very nature is the infinite fullness of all perfections, that is, all good qualities or virtues.[3]

This analysis, while it may seem rather abstruse to us today, is interesting because in one stroke it does three things: it establishes or proves the existence of God; it shows that God is the foundation and source of all value; and it expresses the conviction that all creatures exist by participating in the being (or life) of God. These are closely related implications, and I will briefly explain each of them in turn. First, Anselm's analysis establishes God's existence in a classical Augustinian way: without the prior existence of God as the supreme actuality of all good attributes or qualities (which philosophers sometimes call perfections), there could be no lesser manifestations of any good quality or perfection, because all limited or finite examples of goodness or any other perfection can occur only by participation to one degree or another in that quality. In other words, God, as the infinite fullness of all perfections, must exist in order for anything else to exist.

Second, this analysis shows that as the infinite fullness of all perfections God is the ultimate source of all value. There can be no goodness, beauty, or virtue of any kind in this world that does not owe its existence ultimately to the infinitely perfect nature of God. This implication is very beautiful, for it is saying that God's infinite and perfect being enables all finite manifestations of virtue or beauty to be. God's infinite beauty and goodness, in short, gives life to all the beauty and goodness in the world.

And third, in a very closely related way, this implies that everything in the universe, every creature, exists by participating in God's being or life itself. God's creative power brings all things into existence by giving them a share in the divine being or life. The universe lives out of God. To be sure, this is not pantheism, because the universe is not God; it is limited in its

---

[3] Ibid., 16.

perfections, it is composed of multitudinous finite beings, and it is dependent and cannot exist without God. But the limited beings of the universe exist by participating in the infinite being of God; the creatures of the universe live by participating in the Creator's own life.

Thomas Aquinas and Secondary Causes

Much the same ideas emanate in different ways from the theology of Thomas Aquinas (1225–74), whom many regard as the greatest mind of the High Middle Ages. He lived in a period in which the rediscovery of Aristotle's philosophy, mediated to the West through Arabic-Islamic translations and commentaries, was causing much intellectual ferment and excitement.[4] He was an innovator in using Aristotle's philosophy, suitably revised, to articulate the claims of the Christian faith. In his own time he was both influential and controversial, branded by some as too conservative and by others as too radical.[5] I cannot possibly do justice to the extent and complexity of his theology here. I simply summarize how he articulates the important idea I am tracing through the history of Christian thought; that is, that all created beings exist by participation in the being of God, which is one of the central ideas of Thomas's theology.

God, Thomas held, is the unrestricted act of being; God's essence is to be (Latin: *esse*).[6] All other beings exist by participating in God's being: as he says, "all beings apart from God are not their own being, but are beings by participation [in the being of God]."[7] This idea reappears in his theology in several ways. One of them is in his summation of the various arguments proving God's existence, the famous "five ways." The fourth argument

---

[4] See David Knowles, *The Evolution of Medieval Thought* (New York: Vintage Books, 1962), 185–205. Jewish philosophical theologies, especially that of Moses ben Maimonides (1135–1204), also had a great influence on medieval Christian theologians.

[5] Ibid., 221–34, 269–77, 292–300.

[6] Thomas Aquinas, *Summa Theologica*, Ia, Q. 3, a. 4.

[7] Ibid., Ia, Q. 44, a. 1. English Dominican Province translation (New York: Benzinger Brothers, 1947). See also Ia, Q. 104, a. 1.

Thomas summarizes[8] is a version of the Augustinian analysis we discussed in Anselm, which sees the infinite being of God as the cause of all limited perfections in the world, and among these Thomas includes being. Another way this idea appears is his argument that God is present in all things as their cause.[9] If God is a causal presence in all things, then all things exist only because of their dependence on God. All finite beings, in short, exist by participation in the infinite being of God. Since God's being is God's life,[10] we can say that all creatures exist by participating in the life of their Creator; all things exist by participating in God's own life.

One of the most important applications of this idea in Thomas's theology is his argument that secondary causes—that is, the causal agencies in the created universe—have true causal power and so participate to a limited degree in the creative, causal power of God, the First Cause. God is, of course, the ultimate creative power, but Thomas believed that God, in God's goodness, intended finite, created agencies to share in that power.[11] Thomas does not mean that the finite created agencies in the universe are autonomous and independent causes, operating apart from God. Although his argument is not without its difficulties, Thomas intends to say that created secondary causes are agents of God's action. God intends to allow creatures to participate in "the perfection of causality."[12] God is present and acting in all things "as an agent is present to that upon which it acts."[13] But the secondary cause is not a mere passive instrument through which God acts, like a hammer a carpenter uses to drive a nail. Thomas intends to say that the secondary cause causes by its own power; yet it can do so only because God permits it to participate in the ultimate creative power that is God's own.

In this way Thomas wants to affirm that God's action is hidden within the operations of nature, as, for example, in this statement:

---

[8] See ibid., Ia, Q. 2, a. 3.

[9] Ibid., Ia, Q. 8, a. 1.

[10] See ibid., Ia, Q. 18, a. 3 and 4.

[11] Ibid., Ia, Q. 22, a. 3; see also Ia, Q. 103, a. 6.

[12] Ibid., Ia, Q. 103, a. 6 and ad 2.

[13] Ibid., Ia, Q. 8, a. 1.

It follows that God works intimately in all things. For this reason in Holy Scripture the operations of nature are attributed to God as operating in nature, according to *Job* 10:11: "Thou hast clothed me with skin and flesh; Thou hast put me together with bones and sinews."[14]

This argument picks up one of the implications of Jesus' view of divine action that we saw in Chapter 1: the hiddenness of God's action in and through the ordinary events and processes of nature. Although the way Thomas argues for this idea is problematic, I do not want to enter into the technical details here. I simply want to point out that Thomas, too, affirms the hiddenness of divine action in the universe as well as the participation of all things in the being or life of God.

Nicholas of Cusa and the Coincidence of Opposites

Nicholas of Cusa (1401–64) is unusual in the history of Christian theology in that he used mathematics and geometry as his analytical tools instead of some form of Aristotelianism or Platonism. He longed for unity in the Christian Church and for unity in theology and philosophy, but he observed only disputes between reason and mysticism in the approach to God, and disputes between the various Aristotelian schools of theology and philosophy and their Augustinian (neo-Platonic) opponents. Nicholas was willing to try a different approach, a logic that he hoped could unite everything.

One of Nicholas's starting points was to focus on the infinity of God. This may reflect the enduring influence of John Duns Scotus (1266–1308), who stressed that the proper object of theology is the study of *infinite* being (God).[15] There is also a

---

[14] Ibid., Ia. Q. 105, a. 5.

[15] See Frederick Copleston, *A History of Philosophy*, vol. 2: *Mediaeval Philosophy: Augustine to Scotus* (London: Burns Oates and Washbourne, 1950), 476–551; Jaroslav Pelikan, *The Christian Tradition*, vol. 4: *Reformation of Church and Dogma (1300–1700)* (Chicago: University of Chicago Press, 1984), 62–63; Etienne Gilson, *History of*

connection to Anselm's definition of God as "that than which nothing greater can be thought,"[16] which virtually all theologians agreed on and which Nicholas took to express the absolutely infinite being of God. Interestingly, he also took inspiration from an ancient fragment of Anaxagoras (ca. 500–428 BCE), which Aristotle had recorded but dismissed: "everything is in everything."[17] When Nicholas combined this idea with close attention to the infinity of God, the result led him to a fascinating understanding of God's relation to the universe.

Theologies such as that of Thomas Aquinas depend on the way of analogy, holding that there is some proportion between creatures and God. But Nicholas argues that if we take the idea of God's infinity seriously, then we must recognize that there can be no proportion between the finite and the infinite. Precisely because the infinite infinitely exceeds the finite, it is totally out of proportion with the created world—and as such the infinite is unknown.[18] The infinite being of God so far transcends the limited capabilities of our minds that the only thing we can say we know about God is what God is not. This is our necessary confession of our ignorance. But, Nicholas believes, by reflecting on the implications of infinity, we can educate our ignorance or make our ignorance "learned." The mind, in other words, can approximate to some limited grasp of the truth but can never finally grasp it. He compares this to inscribing a polygon inside a circle: we can keep adding sides, so that the polygon comes closer and closer to the circumference, but it can never fully coincide with the circle.[19] This position is virtually identical with the view—widely held today regarding scientific knowledge—that progress in knowledge is an asymptotic approach to the truth, always getting closer and closer but never finally reaching it.

Christian Philosophy in the Middle Ages (London: Sheed and Ward, 1955), 455–64.

[16] Anselm, *Proslogion*, 2.

[17] See Aristotle, *Metaphysics*, III, 5, 1009a, 27. For how this fragment of Anaxagoras inspired Nicholas, see Gilson, *History of Christian Philosophy in the Middle Ages*, 540.

[18] See Nicholas of Cusa, *De Docta Ignorantia (On Learned Ignorance)*, I, 1.

[19] Ibid., I, 3.

So, despite our finitude, we can grow in our "learned ignorance" by reflecting on infinite being. Etienne Gilson gives a
brilliant summation of Nicholas's analysis:

> The infinite is a maximum; as an absolute maximum, it is
> one (since nothing can be either added to, or subtracted from
> it); since it is unity, it is entity (because unity and being are
> convertible); if the absolute maximum is one, it is all; if it
> is all, all things are in it and all things are by it; it is wholly
> uncontracted (restricted to the form of any particular being).
> For the same reason, since it is all, nothing else can oppose
> the infinite; it has therefore no contrary; in consequence,
> this maximum is also a minimum. In short, the infinite is the
> absolute and perfect coincidence of contraries.[20]

God, then, is "the coincidence of opposites." Nicholas argues
that precisely as the absolute maximum God is also the absolute
minimum, because both are "superlatives" that coincide in the
absolutely infinite being of God.[21] Therefore one may understand
that "God is the enfolding *(complicatio)* of all things, even of
contradictories."[22]

In order to throw some light on how this might be, Nicholas
makes extensive use of mathematical and geometrical analysis.[23]
For example, if one considers a circle, it initially seems that the
curved line defining a circle's circumference and the straight line
defining its diameter are opposites. But if we make the circle
larger and larger by extending its diameter, we recognize that
the degree of curvature of the circumference gets smaller and
smaller. If we mentally extend the diameter to infinity, the degree

---

[20] Gilson, *History of Christian Philosophy in the Middle Ages*, 536,
explicating the brief and dense statement in *De Docta Ignorantia*, I, 2.

[21] See *De Docta Ignorantia*, I, 4. If one mentally removes quantity
(large and small) from the maximally large and maximally small, it is
easier to see how they coincide in absolute infinity: infinity encompasses
them both.

[22] Ibid., I, 22. Translation by Hugh Lawrence Bond, in *Nicholas of
Cusa: Selected Spiritual Writings*, The Classics of Western Spirituality
Series (Mahwah, NJ: Paulist Press, 1997), 118.

[23] See ibid., I, 13–23.

of curvature of the circumference decreases to zero and the circumference of the circle is now coincident with its diameter. In a similar way, Nicholas argues, God as infinite being is the coincidence of opposites. He carefully states that such examples are only "symbols," as he calls them, because the mathematical infinite and the absolutely infinite being are not the same; but he believes that these "symbols" can serve as an important aid to a philosophical theology of learned ignorance.[24]

Nicholas developed a truly beautiful theology of God's relation to the world. He says: "Therefore, God is the enfolding *(complicans)* of all things in that all things are in Him; and He is the unfolding *(explicans)* of all things in that He is in all things."[25] God includes all things and is present in all things. God is the infinite wholeness of being. Although those unsympathetic to Nicholas's thought might want to accuse him of pantheism, they would be wrong because Nicholas is quite clear that the universe of finite beings is not identical with God and can never exhaust the infinite being of God. It is, however, a view that will later be called pan*en*theism, the conviction that all things are in God and God is in all things.[26] Nicholas argued that the universe is the "contracted maximum" *(maximum contractum)*, which exists by emanation *(emanatio)* from God, who is the absolute maximum.[27] A *contraction* in Nicholas's terminology is a restriction to a particular form. Nicholas holds that every finite being is a contraction of all other things, or the universe, so that the universe is contracted in each and every finite thing. As a whole, the universe is the contracted maximum. Since God is

---

[24] See ibid., I, 12.

[25] Ibid., II, 3: "Deus ergo est omnia complicans, in hoc quod omnia in eo; est omnia explicans, in hoc quia ipse in omnibus." Translation by Jasper Hopkins, *Nicholas of Cusa on Learned Ignorance: A Translation and an Appraisal of* De Docta Ignorantia (Minneapolis: The Arthur J. Banning Press, 1981), 94.

[26] See John Macquarrie, *In Search of Deity: An Essay in Dialectical Theism*, The Gifford Lectures, 1983 (New York: Crossroad, 1984), 109. Panentheism is becoming a widely held view among theologians, though it was defended mainly by process theology for many years before becoming more widely accepted.

[27] *De Docta Ignorantia*, II, 4.

in the universe and the universe is in God, and since the universe is the contraction of the infinite being that is God, and since the universe is contracted in each finite thing, then God is in each thing and each thing is in God.[28] In this way "everything is in everything."

Nicholas takes an idea that initially sounds suspect or nonsensical, and interprets it in such a way that it becomes a magnificent statement of God's universal presence and of the participation of all things in God's being or life. All things unfold from God; God's infinite being is the source of each and every thing in the universe. And although the universe of finite beings cannot exhaust the infinite being of God, God nevertheless dwells in all things and enfolds all things into God's own life. There is a stress on wholeness here and on the intimate interrelation of God and the universe that we often find missing in how people think of the God-world relationship. And while it is possible to think of the universe alone and never raise the question of how and why this magnificent universe exists at all, Nicholas's vision of the universe unfolding from the infinite being of God and God enfolding its enormous plenitude of creatures into God's own life gives us a much richer sense of the beauty and value of our universe and of the all-embracing love of God.

Nicholas exhibits this sense of catholicity, this sense of the whole centered in Christ, because he goes on to apply his metaphysical reasoning to a "learned ignorance" of the incarnation. What I mean is that Nicholas will end up saying that the union of the divine and the human in the person of Jesus Christ is utterly beyond our comprehension. Yet he suggests that his reasoning allows us to conceive of the possibility of such a union, which makes our ignorance of the incarnation "educated." He points out that the universe exists only as a plurality of "contracted" finite beings and that no individual thing can embody all the perfections of all things in the universe, not even those of its own kind. But on the other hand, human beings are in a sense the universe in microcosm, since they enfold in themselves matter, organic life, sensitive animal life, and rationality and

---

[28] Ibid., II, 5. The similarity of Nicholas's view on this point to that of Alfred North Whitehead in *Process and Reality* is remarkable.

spiritual life—all the dimensions of the universe.[29] In this way a human being is a unique contraction of the entire universe in a concrete entity. The universe is the "concrete maximum," that is, all finite things. God is the "absolute maximum," that is, infinite being. We are able to conceive of a perfect human being, who would be a maximal contraction of the universe in a concrete entity; and if that perfect human nature was united to the divine nature, it would be at the same time *the concrete and absolute maximum*, the perfection and salvation of the universe. We cannot comprehend this union, but we find it in Jesus Christ. And because of our experience of Jesus Christ, even in our ignorance we see in him the coincidence of Creator and creature, divinity and humanity, infinity and finitude.[30]

In this way Nicholas of Cusa continues the emphasis of early Christian thought on the cosmic significance of Jesus Christ. He understands Jesus Christ as the perfection and salvation of the universe and presents us with a profoundly holistic understanding of the God-world relationship, which comes to its salvific climax in the incarnation. Even though we must confess our ignorance of the infinite God and of the mystery of the incarnation, we gain a glimpse of these truths and realities in our attempts to understand. In "educated ignorance" we come to appreciate the beauty of God's relation to the world and the beauty of God's infinite saving love manifest in the Incarnation.

Luther and the "Crucified and Hidden God"

The major Reformation theologians tended to reject metaphysical discussions of God and focus instead on a more "biblical" description of God as almighty or sovereign power, righteous or holy will, and gracious and reconciling love.[31] However, because of their belief in predestination and the immutability of the

---

[29] See ibid., III, 3.

[30] Ibid., III, 2–6.

[31] For a brief characterization of the central themes of Reformation theology, see Langdon Gilkey, "God," in *Christian Theology: An Introduction to Its Traditions and Tasks*, 2nd ed., ed. Peter C. Hodgson and Robert H. King (Philadelphia: Fortress Press, 1985), 95–96.

divine will and its decrees, they believed that divine love would
not result in salvation for all humans. Indeed, most Reformers stress that all humans are unworthy of salvation, and that
God's love and mercy are demonstrated in the fact that despite
human sinfulness God from all eternity elected some for grace
and redemption while others are predestined for condemnation.

The Reformers did not invent the idea of predestination. This
idea can be traced back through all the major theologians of
the Middle Ages to Augustine in his interpretations of some of
Paul's statements. Philosophically, it is a logical implication of
accepting both the immutability and the impassibility of God.
If God cannot change, then God must know (and will) from all
eternity who will be saved and who will be condemned. This
divine knowledge (and willing) cannot be based on anything
humans do, or it would mean that God can be affected by
something other than God, contradicting God's impassibility.
Therefore, God in eternity foresees and knows what humans will
do, and God's eternal and unchanging will predestines some for
salvation (and others for condemnation). Although this idea was
present in Christian theology from the time of Augustine, in the
Reformers it took on a prominence it really did not have through
the Middle Ages. Because of the centrality of this idea in their
thought, the result is a portrait of God as a harsh, if just, judge in
an adversarial relationship to the human world. It is difficult to
find in Reformation theology a conception of a *universe* in union
with God, centered in Christ. The universe seems torn between
those predestined for salvation and blessedness and those predestined for eternal condemnation; God seems remote, wrathful,
and unapproachable; and the natural world is largely forgotten
in the preoccupation with the drama of sin and salvation.

Despite this, I wish to summarize briefly an idea that was
central to the theology of Martin Luther (1484–1546), because
it picks up the theme of the hiddenness of God and introduces
the idea of divine suffering. This idea is usually called Luther's
theology of the cross.[32] It is rooted, as many of Luther's ideas

---

[32] See Walther von Loewenich, *Luther's Theology of the Cross*, 5th
ed., trans. Herbert J. A. Bouman (Minneapolis: Augsburg, 1982); and
Alister E. McGrath, *Luther's Theology of the Cross: Martin Luther's
Theological Breakthrough* (Oxford: Basil Blackwell, 1985).

are, in his reflections on statements in scripture and his personal experiences. One of the scriptural statements is Hebrews 11:1, which Luther paraphrased as "faith has to do with things not seen."[33] Another important passage is Isaiah 45:15 ("Truly, you are a God who hides himself"). He was also deeply influenced by Exodus 33:23, where in response to Moses's request to see God's glory (v. 18), God tells Moses that humans cannot see the face of God and live (v. 20), but that God will allow Moses to see God's back (v. 23). To Luther, this hiddenness of God, our ability to see only God's back, immediately relates to the cross of Jesus Christ and suffering. God is *revealed as hidden* in the suffering and cross of Jesus Christ. That is, while in faith we can discern God in the suffering and crucified One, God is there as unseen. We see only God's "back": humiliation, agony, ignominy. The very act that reveals God to faith also hides God from view. God is revealed in what is opposite to God.

The suffering and crucified Jesus Christ certainly does not seem to our senses to be God. What we see is a human being dying a horrible, ignominious death. How can the infinite, immutable, and impassible God be present in and united to this limited, changing, suffering human? Only when faith accepts what God has done are we allowed to discern God's revelation in the crucified Christ. But, even then, what we *see* in this suffering and dying human is the *opposite* of God; we know in faith that God is absolute, that God cannot suffer or die, but in the crucified Christ we see revealed God's suffering, God's dying. God is revealed in God's opposite: weakness, suffering, humiliation. For Luther, this is not merely a pious metaphor. He accepts the dogma of Chalcedon and the idea of the "communication of properties," the idea that in the union of Jesus Christ's person, the properties of the divine and human natures actually apply to each other. Luther took this to mean that in the oneness of Christ's person it is truly God suffering and dying.[34] God reveals Godself in God's opposite.

---

[33] Martin Luther, *On the Bondage of the Will (De Servo Arbitrio)*, in *Luther and Erasmus: Free Will and Salvation*, trans. and ed. E. Gordon Rupp and Philip S. Watson, Library of Christian Classics, vol. 17 (Philadelphia: Westminster, 1969), 138.

[34] See Pelikan, *The Christian Tradition*, 4:132–33.

If one were to extend this idea, it really does affirm the theme of God's hiddenness in the world, God's presence and action in Christ and in the creatures of the world. It also may owe a debt of inspiration to Nicholas of Cusa's conception of God as the coincidence of opposites, although I have not found any scholar who notes such influence on Luther. But in any case I think this idea of Luther's is quite insightful, even though I believe he pushed it too far in his dispute with Erasmus.[35]

Let me conclude by saying that I believe the fundamental religious insight of the Reformation to be its insistence that God is *infinitely* merciful. If the focus had been on tracing out the implications of God's infinite mercy instead of on predestination, the view of God and the world emanating from Reformation theology might have been quite different. But in an era marked by divisions, antagonisms, and heated controversies, we should not be surprised that it is difficult to find theologies of wholeness and harmony.

Friedrich Schleiermacher and Religious Experience

The beginning of the scientific revolution was occurring during the Reformation period with the development of the heliocentric theory by Polish astronomer Nicholas Copernicus (1473–1543) and its subsequent defense by Galileo (1564–1642) and development by Johannes Kepler (1571–1630). But there were no significant theological responses to the emerging sciences because theologians in the late sixteenth and seventeenth centuries were preoccupied with the Reformation controversies and with questions of church order and discipline. In the eighteenth century the few theological responses to the new sciences were mainly defensive, and theologians were more directly concerned with attacks on religion emanating from Enlightenment thinkers such as David Hume (1711–76). It is not until the very early nineteenth century that we find the first creative theological response to science, and to the Enlightenment critique of religion as well.

---

[35] See, for example, Luther, *On the Bondage of the Will*, 138.

Friedrich Schleiermacher (1768–1834) was a German Protestant theologian whose work is traditionally regarded as the beginning of modern theology. His response to the Enlightenment critique of religion has been very influential in theology, and he also adopted an innovative attitude toward empirical science. He was subject to much criticism in his own time, and his theology was briefly eclipsed by speculative theologies based on the work of his colleague at the University of Berlin, Georg W. F. Hegel (1770–1831). But in the end, Schleiermacher's theology has had a more enduring influence on Protestant theology in the late nineteenth and early twentieth centuries and, indeed, on the character of Christian theology in general up to the present.

In order to understand Schleiermacher's innovative insights and analyses, it is important to understand both Enlightenment critiques of religious faith, such as that of David Hume, and the influential defense of religious faith by Immanuel Kant (1724–1804). Schleiermacher was acquainted with both and found them both to have incorrect understandings of the basis of religious faith. David Hume, the great Scottish philosopher, wanted to establish philosophy on an empirical basis and developed a theory of knowledge that in essence assumed that sense experience was the ultimate basis of our knowledge regarding matters of fact. His book *An Enquiry concerning Human Understanding*[36] contains a skeptical account of the idea of causality, which seriously weakens all claims for the existence of God as the cause of the universe.[37] It also contains an attack on belief in miracles and an attack on scripture as presenting divinely revealed truth. These were in effect all the reasons Christianity put forward for why

---

[36] This book was originally published in 1748 and went through several editions in Hume's lifetime. A very useful edition is that edited by Charles W. Hendel, The Library of Liberal Arts (Indianapolis: Bobbs-Merrill, 1955), which reprints the edition of 1777, containing Hume's final corrections, with notes identifying all alterations of the previous editions.

[37] See also David Hume, *Dialogues concerning Natural Religion* (originally published in 1779), the posthumously published criticism of all arguments for the existence of God, especially those from (apparent) design in nature.

people ought to believe what the church taught.[38] In sum, Hume argues that there is no basis in human experience, no empirical basis of any kind, for religious belief. Hume ends in what we would today call an agnostic skepticism.[39]

Immanuel Kant, the great philosopher of the eighteenth century, had read Hume and was deeply influenced by him in some respects but wanted to defend religion from Hume's skepticism.[40] In essence Kant argued that while Hume was correct in saying that there is no empirical basis for religion in sense experience, Hume had failed to recognize a second, distinct kind of experience in which religion finds its empirical ground: a sense or feeling of moral obligation. The feeling of moral obligation, common to all humans, is not a sense experience, however much our sense experience and particular cultures may influence the specific moral codes that humans develop. Rather, this sense of moral obligation arises as a feeling within us. This gives rise to a different kind of reasoning and knowledge than what we know through sense experience. Sense experience raises the question What can I know? and gives rise to *pure reason* dealing with matters of fact; science is the product of such reasoning. Our feeling of moral obligation, on the other hand, raises the question What ought I do? and this gives rise to *practical reason,* reasoning about the practice of our lives (ethics), and arrives at a universal law of moral obligation: we ought to act in such a way that everyone could apply the principle of our moral action. This, in turn, leads us to ask What may I hope for? or what we may reasonably assume to be true in order to understand how and why this sense of moral obligation is within us. And this, Kant argues, reveals that it is reasonable to assume that we have free

---

[38] An additional reason was the authority of the church as a divinely instituted institution, but by Hume's time of the Enlightenment, appeals to authority of human institutions were considered so weak that Hume did not bother to attack this one.

[39] The word *agnostic* was coined in the nineteenth century by Thomas Henry Huxley, the biologist and defender of Darwin, to describe his own religious stance: he was not an atheist but simply did not know whether God exists or not.

[40] See Immanuel Kant, *Critique of Pure Reason*, 2nd ed. (1787).

will, that there is an afterlife, and that God exists.[41] We cannot *prove* the truth of any of these assumptions or postulates, but we are reasonable in *believing* them to be true. Here, at last, is where religious faith finds its experiential or empirical ground.

In short, Kant holds that the empirical ground of religion is in our moral experience. Since most humans are not philosophers and cannot reason their way to the universal law of moral obligation, religion exists to instruct humans in morality and in its necessary assumptions. By pointing out that our experience cannot be completely reduced to sense experience, and by distinguishing practical reason from pure reason, ethics from facts, Kant overcomes Hume's skeptical critique of religion and grounds faith in the existence of God and immortality in moral experience.[42] Religion is not competing with science to describe matters of fact; rather, religion concerns itself with morality, ethics, how human conduct ought to be guided. In this way there can be no conflict between science and religion; science deals with matters of fact, while religion deals with ethics.[43]

Schleiermacher had a personal background in German Pietist Christianity, which emphasized an immediate personal experience of God, a personal feeling of God's saving work in Jesus Christ. It was, in a sense, the religious counterpart to the Romantic movement in secular culture, with which Schleiermacher was familiar. Both reacted against the uninspiring mechanical view of the universe emanating from Newtonian science and the dry and equally uninspiring rationalism of Enlightenment philosophers. But Pietism was mostly indifferent to formal theology, and Romanticism

---

[41] See Kant, *Critique of Pure Reason*, 2nd ed., trans. Norman Kemp Smith (New York: St. Martin's Press, 1965), 629–44. See also Immanuel Kant, *Critique of Practical Reason* (1788).

[42] For a discussion of how Christian theologians used the "moral defense" of Christian faith, whether in a form dependent on Kant or otherwise, see Jaroslav Pelikan, *The Christian Tradition: The Development of Doctrine*, vol. 5: *Christian Doctrine and Modern Culture (since 1700)* (Chicago: University of Chicago Press, 1989), 174–90.

[43] Stephen Jay Gould, the Harvard paleontologist and evolutionary theorist, late in his life came to a very similar view in apparent unawareness of Kant's argument. See Stephen Jay Gould, *Rocks of Ages: Science and Religion in the Fullness of Life* (New York: Ballantine Books, 1999).

looked askance at traditional religion. Schleiermacher was also very familiar with Kant's philosophy and the natural theology that based itself on science, and he was well aware of attacks on religion such as Hume's. He believed that Hume, Kant, and the arguments of natural theology had all missed the actual experiential ground of religion and said so quite clearly in his book *On Religion: Speeches to Its Cultured Despisers* (1799). His understanding of religion also exhibits a profound theology of wholeness, as is evident in this statement:

> In order to make quite clear to you what is the original and characteristic possession of religion, it resigns at once, all claims on anything that belongs either to science or morality. . . .
>
> The contemplation of the pious is the immediate consciousness of the universal existence of all finite things, in and through the Infinite, and of all temporal things in and through the Eternal. Religion is to seek this and find it in all that lives and moves, in all growth and change, in all doing and suffering. It is to have life and to know life in immediate feeling, only as such an existence in the Infinite and Eternal. . . . Wherefore it is a life in the infinite nature of the Whole, in the One and in the All, in God, having and possessing all things in God, and God in all. . . . In itself it is an affection, a revelation of the Infinite in the finite, God being seen in it and it in God.[44]

Acquainted as he was with the natural theology based on science and having studied Kant's "moral" defense of Christian faith, Schleiermacher held that neither correctly understood the basis of religious faith. Religion is not based in sense experience or the sense of moral obligation. Instead, it is based on a third type of experience, one unique to religious consciousness: an "affection," an immediate "feeling," a "sense and taste for the Infinite."[45] This affection or feeling *(Gefuhl)* is an experience

---

[44] Friedrich Schleiermacher, *On Religion: Speeches to Its Cultured Despisers*, trans. John Oman (from the 3rd German edition) (New York: Harper Torchbooks, 1958), 35, 36.
[45] Ibid., 39.

quite distinct from sense experience or the feeling of moral obligation; yet it is not separate from them and actually underlies them both, pervading all knowing and doing.[46] But it produces a knowing that does not compete with science and a doing not based on a rationalist ethical system. In short, religion is based in its own unique religious experience.

In his great work *The Christian Faith* Schleiermacher defined this universal religious experience as "the consciousness of being absolutely dependent, or, which is the same thing, of being in relation with God."[47] In this feeling of absolute dependence we grasp our fundamental relation to that which evokes this feeling: God is given to us not as a concept (as in Kant's philosophy), but in feeling, experientially; and God is revealed simply as that which evokes this feeling of absolute dependence. Any further content we give to the idea of God must be developed from this fundamental feeling of relation.[48] Each religion has its own unique and specific form of this universal religious feeling. Schleiermacher says the specifically Christian form is the experience of Jesus Christ as Redeemer.[49] We Christians find ourselves completely dependent on Jesus Christ for salvation, healing, and the forgiveness of our sin, and all that we know of God is deeply rooted in this experience of Jesus Christ as Savior.

Christian beliefs, doctrines, and dogmas are the interpretations and expressions of the fundamental Christian religious experience.[50] They are derived by using the ordinary canons of reasoning in reflection on the experience. This position has two important consequences. First, it means that revelation is not a matter of propositions or verbal statements. Rather, its truth lies in the originating religious experience; revelation is experiential, not propositional. This does not mean that the subsequent doctrines and dogmas are insignificant. They express the community's tested interpretations of the fundamental religious

---

[46] See Friedrich Schleiermacher, *The Christian Faith*, 2 vols., trans. H. R. MacKintosh and J. S. Stewart (from the 2nd German edition) (New York: Harper Torchbooks, 1963), §3.4, pp. 8–11.

[47] Ibid., §4, p. 12; see pp. 12–18.

[48] See ibid., §4.4, p. 17.

[49] See ibid., §§11–14, pp. 52–76.

[50] See ibid., §§15–19, pp. 76–93; see also §13 postscript, pp. 66–68.

experience. Yet the doctrines and dogmas are not in themselves the revelation, the experience is. Second, since the beliefs and doctrines are interpretations of the foundational religious experience of God, they are and always will be historically and culturally conditioned, influenced by the time and place in which they are produced. This means, Schleiermacher held, that Christian theologians have the obligation in every time and place to work out interpretations of Christian doctrine that reflect the living and continuing experience of the Christian community, and to do so in a way compatible with the current state of knowledge.[51] Of course, Christian theology must be faithful to and in continuity with its tradition, but it cannot simply repeat formulas from the past. It must risk new formulations in order to reflect how Christian religious experience understands itself in the present.

For Schleiermacher, then, religion and theology are obviously different from science because they arise from and reflect on a different kind of experience than science studies. Yet the interpretation of Christian religion can be harmonized with and enriched by what science tells us about reality, so long as science does not illegitimately claim to be the exhaustive source of all truth. In his discussion of the doctrine of creation Schleiermacher tried to do exactly this. He makes the following statement:

It has always been acknowledged by the strictest dogmaticians that divine preservation, as the absolute dependence of all events and changes on God, and natural causation, as the complete determination of all events by the universal nexus, are one and the same thing simply from different points of view, the one being neither separated from the other nor limited by it.[52]

This is, frankly, an amazing statement. It is saying that if we look at the universe with the eyes of science, we see a universal system

---

[51] See the excellent essay by Brian Gerrish, "Friedrich Schleiermacher (1768–1834)," in B. A. Gerrish, *Continuing the Reformation: Essays on Modern Religious Thought*, 147–77 (Chicago: University of Chicago Press, 1993), 158. See also Claude Welch, *Protestant Thought in the Nineteenth Century: Volume 1, 1799–1870* (New Haven, CT: Yale University Press, 1972), 72.

[52] Schleiermacher, *The Christian Faith*, §46.2, p. 174.

in which all events and causes are completely natural. But if we look at the universe through the eyes of faith, we see that everything is absolutely dependent on God. The same universe—yet both ways of seeing it are correct. This can be true only if God's creative and providential action is hidden within the natural, not opposed to it. This also helps us to understand how it can be that science need not appeal to God to explain anything in nature. All things are related within the "universal nexus," the natural system of the universe, and therefore naturalistic explanation is sufficient for scientific purposes. Religious experience reveals to us that all things are related in their dependence on God. These two truths are not in opposition to one another, but it requires a shift in viewpoint to see them both and a willingness to integrate one's viewpoint and expand one's mind to assert them both, to accept that no one way of knowing exhausts all truth.

Schleiermacher in the early nineteenth century pointed the way toward interpreting our religious faith in harmony with the current state of knowledge about the universe. And he did so while affirming a theology of wholeness, seeing all things related to each other and in dependence on God, the finite in the Infinite, and the Infinite in the finite. In this, I would argue, he was faithfully expressing a very ancient theme of Christian thought: being aware of the cosmic whole centered in Christ. It is truly an obligation of Christian theology to articulate an understanding of Christian faith in harmony with the current state of knowledge, and to this task I now turn my attention.

Chapter 4

What We Can Learn from Contemporary Physics and Cosmology

As I said in Chapter 1, science is neither the source of the Christian doctrine of God nor the ultimate criterion by which we evaluate and judge our understanding of God. But an idea of God that is not at least in conversation with what we know of reality through the sciences will remain unconnected to how our culture understands the universe. In the previous chapter we have seen that Schleiermacher believed it an obligation of Christian theology to work out new formulations or interpretations of Christian faith in relation to the best knowledge available at the time. For us, that means we must be open to interpreting our understanding of God in relation to what we know of the universe through the sciences. Science is widely regarded as the surest way to knowledge of the truth. Christian theology today, I am firmly convinced, must work out its interpretations of God and God's relation to the universe in conversation with the sciences or it runs the risk of being regarded as irrelevant to our understanding of reality.

The developments in twentieth- and twenty-first-century physics and cosmology are fascinating in themselves and also, I believe, have important implications for our understanding of God's relation to the universe. I need not enter into any detailed description of the development of physics and cosmology since the early twentieth century, but I do summarize some of the major discoveries and theories of contemporary physics and cosmology so as to discuss their possible implications for theology.

Relativity Theory

Albert Einstein (1879–1955), the greatest mind in physics since Newton, developed two theories of relativity, the special theory published in 1905 and the general theory published in 1915.[1] Each of these theories was revolutionary, and each has very important implications for the understanding of reality.

Relatedness and Energy

One of the surprising implications of the special theory of relativity is that time and space are not absolute and independent realities, but are relative to the observer and interconnected. The key to understanding this is that both time and space are defined by measurement; the speed of light is involved because all measurement depends on light reflected from objects to our eyes (or some other electromagnetic signal striking some detector, because all electromagnetic signals travel at the speed of light). Time and space, therefore, will be measured differently by observers in different frames of reference. An observer in a moving frame of reference will see events occurring at different places and times than an observer in a stationary frame of reference observing the same events. And, amazingly, both sets of observations are correct, given the different frames of reference. The mathematics of the theory implies this, and experiments have supported this conclusion.

The theory of special relativity also reveals to us the interconnectedness of matter and energy. The one equation virtually everyone has heard of is $E = mc^2$ (energy equals mass times the

----

[1] There are many introductions to Einstein's theories of relativity available. For a relatively brief and simple explanation, see Nathan Spielberg and Bryon D. Anderson, *Seven Ideas That Shook the Universe* (New York: John Wiley and Sons, 1987), 163–83. The classic scientific biography of Einstein is Abraham Pais, *Subtle Is the Lord: The Science and the Life of Albert Einstein* (New York: Oxford University Press, 1982).

speed of light—186,000 miles per second—squared. This equation, emanating from the special theory of relativity, tells us that energy and matter are convertible, that matter is fundamentally energy. Material objects lock up an incredible amount of energy, as the explosion of bombs demonstrates in a very horrific way.

The special theory of relativity, then, reveals to us the fundamental interconnectedness or relatedness of time and space, observer and observed, matter and energy. As we will see, this fundamental interrelatedness of all things is revealed by science in other ways as well.

The Expanding Universe

Einstein's general theory of relativity eventually led to the recognition that our universe is expanding. American astronomer Edwin P. Hubble (1889–1953), observing the light from distant nebulae, saw that the absorption lines of certain elements (hydrogen and helium) were shifted toward the red end of the light spectrum. This implies that these nebulae, later discovered to be other galaxies, are moving away from us (the familiar Doppler effect applied to light). This led Belgian Roman Catholic priest and cosmologist Georges Lemaitre (1894–1966) to work with Einstein's original field equations from the general theory of relativity to find a solution for a variable radius of the universe, and in 1927 he published a paper laying out the mathematics of an expanding universe. In 1929 Hubble announced his further discovery, soon known as Hubble's law, that the other galaxies of the universe are moving away from us at velocities proportional to their distances. Lemaitre took this as empirical evidence of his mathematical theory, and in 1931 he published a complete theory of the origin of the universe.

Lemaitre reasoned that if the universe is expanding, then one could mentally reverse its expansion, and if one went back all the way to the beginning, then all the matter of the universe must have been contained in an extremely dense state. He proposed that this would have exploded in a super-radioactive disintegration and begun the expansion of the universe. While his model had numerous problems—and Lemaitre himself recognized that it would need to be revised as more was learned about the atom—he was the first to propose that the universe was expanding because of a physical event. He was also the first to try to bring together cosmology, the science of the very large, and physics, the science of the very small. Lemaitre's work is really the beginning of the theory of the origin of the universe that eventually came to be called the Big Bang theory.[2]

Hubble's work included the development of a way to estimate the age of the universe; Hubble's law involves a quantity called Hubble's constant,[3] which is crucial to determining the age of the universe. Between improvements in the measurements of the distances of other galaxies from us and adjustments to Hubble's constant, over which there has been much controversy,[4] estimates of the age of the universe have continually changed over the years. Currently, our universe is estimated to be roughly 13.8 billion years old.

George Gamow (1904–68) produced a revision of the Big Bang theory that had its own problems, but he and his colleagues in 1949 predicted from the theory that there should be some residual heat remaining from the originating explosion, detectable as microwave radio radiation.[5] At the time, however, there was no way to detect such radiation, and Gamow's prediction was forgotten. Later, Princeton physicist Robert Dicke (1916–97), who favored the oscillating universe theory, independently came to the idea of a cosmic fireball as the midpoint between cycles of cosmic collapse and rebound into expansion. He also came to the idea that there ought to be background radiation left over

---

[2] The nickname Big Bang was initially used as a derogatory put-down of George Gamow's version of the theory by the astrophysicist Fred Hoyle (1915–2001), who held to his own "steady-state" theory, later shown to be wrong. The nickname stuck. See Dennis Overbye, *Lonely Hearts of the Cosmos: The Scientific Quest for the Secret of the Universe* (New York: HarperCollins, 1992), 39; and Timothy Ferris, *Coming of Age in the Milky Way* (New York: William Morrow, 1988), 211.

[3] Hubble's law is stated as $v = Hr$, where v is the velocity of the galaxy, r is its distance, and H is the proportionality constant called Hubble's constant.

[4] For the adjustments to Hubble's constant up to 1992, see Overbye, *Lonely Hearts of the Cosmos*, 45–53, 57–59, 161–73, 263–84, 405–9, 415–16.

[5] See George Gamow, *The Creation of the Universe*, rev. ed. (New York: Bantam Books, 1965).

from the Big Bang and had his assistants try to devise a way to detect it. Meanwhile, two Bell Laboratory researchers, Arno Penzias (1933–) and Robert Wilson (1936–), had been trying for a year to get rid of an anomalous signal in a microwave horn Bell had built for satellite communication experiments. In 1965, a scientist acquainted with Dicke's search and Penzias and Wilson's work suggested that Penzias contact Dicke. Dicke realized that Penzias and Wilson had discovered what Dicke was searching for: the cosmic background radiation. Penzias and Wilson received the Nobel Prize in 1978 for their discovery. This discovery was strong empirical evidence for the Big Bang theory of the universe's expansion.

In subsequent years there have been many refinements of the theory, and there is no question that we live in an expanding universe. We need not pursue most of the refinements. However, two discoveries show that we still have much to learn about the universe. First, astronomical observations have discovered gravitational effects of some matter that neither emits nor reflects light and consequently cannot be directly observed. The gravitational effects are quite significant and are caused by some sort of *dark matter*, as astronomers and physicists call it. We still have no idea what this matter is. It may be "normal" matter that for some reason is not directly observable, or some exotic kind of matter that we as yet do not understand. More recently it has been discovered that the rate of expansion of the universe is not steady but is accelerating, which must mean that there is some force counteracting gravity causing the acceleration. This force is called *dark energy*. While astrophysicists are offering suggestions as to what it might be, no one yet knows what it actually is. The most recent estimate I have seen by cosmologists is that the universe is composed of roughly 5 percent "normal" matter, 24 percent "dark matter," and 71 percent "dark energy."[6] Roughly 95 percent of the universe is currently a major mystery to science.

The discovery of the cosmic background radiation was a great triumph for the Big Bang theory of the expanding universe. There is still a possibility that the idea of an oscillating universe (with

---

[6] This information is available in several places online by using the search terms "dark matter" and "NASA."

several or many phases of expansion, contraction, and renewed expansion) could be correct, but since each collapse would wipe out all evidence of previous expansions, it is hard to know how evidence for that hypothesis could be found. In any case, no one doubts that we live in an expanding universe. The most widely accepted view is that our universe originated in a cosmic *singularity*. Singularities are an implication of Einstein's general theory of relativity and result mathematically when an equation requires division by zero. The result is an infinity, a totally undefined and undefinable situation. Einstein's equations indicate that if enough matter-energy were accumulated in one place, the result would be a point so dense that particles, space, and time would simply disappear, collapsed in on themselves, so to speak, into an unknowable condition of infinite energy. In this condition the laws of physics completely break down. The singularity marks the boundary between what is potentially knowable by physics and what is ultimately unknowable. In short, the singularity itself cannot be explained by physics. If it can ever produce the hoped-for super-symmetry theory uniting all four major forces (electromagnetism, the weak and strong nuclear forces, and gravity), physics could get back to 10^{-43} seconds after the Big Bang (the so-called Planck time), but it could go no farther. If the universe originated in a singularity, as the Big Bang theory implies, then the origin of the universe is ultimately unknowable by physics.

Needless to say, many physicists are unhappy about this, since they operate under the ideal of complete explanation. And so alternative theories of the origin of the universe have been suggested. But before considering them, we must discuss quantum theory.

Quantum Theory

Quantum theory originated in 1900 with a paper by the German physicist Max Planck offering a solution to the "black-body radiation" problem.[7] The radiant heat energy emanating from a

---

[7] For a good brief summary of quantum theory, see P.C.W. Davies and J. R. Brown, *The Ghost in the Atom: A Discussion of the Mysteries of Quantum Physics* (Cambridge: Cambridge University Press, 1986;

hot body does not match the expectations from classical physics. Planck argued that the only way to solve this problem was to assume that electromagnetic energy is emitted in discrete bundles or packets he called *quanta,* not in a smooth, continuously variable spectrum. It is as if change from a dollar bill can be given only in nickels—no pennies. So energy is "quantized." Another of Einstein's famous 1905 papers, the one on the photoelectric effect, was central in the next development. Einstein showed that the photoelectric effect could be understood only by thinking of light as composed of discrete particles called photons.[8] But there was also sound observational evidence for the older wave theory of light. Light seemed to act sometimes as if it were composed of particles and sometimes as if it were waves of pure energy. Since both had observational support (through the famous slit experiments), it seemed that light manifests both wave-like and particle-like behavior and properties. Further research showed that this wave-particle duality extends to all subatomic particles. This means that classical Newtonian physics, while it works well enough in the macro world of ordinary daily experience, fails to describe the actual behavior of the quantum world. Reality at its most fundamental level operates differently.

Austrian physicist Erwin Schrödinger (1887–1961) and German physicist Werner Heisenberg (1901–76) independently developed quantum mechanics to deal with the wave-particle duality of elementary particles.[9] English physicist Paul Dirac (1902–84) later developed better equations that are used to this day. Quantum mechanics allows observed quantum events to be predicted statistically. It analyzes the behavior of elementary particles as "wave functions" for a mixture of possibilities, a

---

Canto edition, 1993), 1–39. The remainder of their book consists of interviews with leading physicists on quantum theory. See also John C. Polkinghorne, *The Quantum World* (London: Longman, 1984); idem, "The Quantum World," in *Physics, Philosophy, and Theology: A Common Quest for Understanding*, ed. Robert John Russell, William R. Stoeger, SJ, and George V. Coyne, SJ (Vatican City State: Vatican Observatory, 1988), 333–42.

[8] See Spielberg and Anderson, *Seven Ideas That Shook the Universe*, 194–98.

[9] See ibid., 207–22.

"superposition of states," and this allows for the calculation of the probabilities of a particle manifesting a particular state. The exact behavior of the particle cannot be predicted, but the probability of outcomes can be. This is similar to the way in which insurance companies can make very accurate statistical predictions about the mortality rates of different groups and ages of people, even though no one can predict when any given individual will die. The wave function for an atomic electron defines a charge "cloud" of possible positions at various distances from the nucleus.[10]

In reflection on this Heisenberg formulated his famous "uncertainty principle" concerning the indeterminacies of the quantum world. Most basically the uncertainty principle states that we cannot simultaneously determine both the momentum and position of an electron; the more accurately we know the one, the less accurately we know the other. Heisenberg initially thought this is because we affect the state and behavior of the electron by the act of measurement. But eventually it became clear that there is indeterminacy even in undisturbed systems, such as in the radioactive decay of an atom. Indeterminacy characterizes the entire quantum world. Not all physicists agree on how this fact should be interpreted. Einstein, for example, thought that there might be hidden variables of which we are unaware, making us unable to grasp the fundamental deterministic order of the universe.[11] But most physicists adopt the view of Heisenberg in his later writings that indeterminacy is an actual feature of the universe; the future is not determined but is to one degree or another flexible, open to different possibilities. There is, in short, some potential for unpredictable novelty in the universe, an openness to possibility. Physics no longer affirms the "hard" determinism of the Newtonian world view.

Niels Bohr (1885–1962), the great Danish physicist, held that indeterminacy is intrinsic to reality.[12] He believed that the wave-like and particle-like properties of quantum phenomena are complementary aspects of those phenomena and their behavior.

---

[10] See ibid., 212.

[11] See Ian G. Barbour, *Religion and Science: Historical and Contemporary Issues* (San Francisco: HarperSanFrancisco, 1997), 171.

[12] See Davies and Brown, *The Ghost in the Atom*, 11–12.

He emphasized the *wholeness* of quantum systems; that is, one must always look at the whole situation, not just its isolated elements, to understand the quantum world. The parts have no meaning except in relation to the whole. This became even clearer as physics discovered more and more subatomic particles, such as the quarks that compose protons and neutrons. Ian Barbour has summarized this well:

> The various "elementary particles" composed of quarks seem to be temporary manifestations of shifting patterns of waves that combine at one point, dissolve again, and recombine elsewhere. A particle begins to look more like a local outcropping of a continuous substratum of vibratory energy. . . . A bound electron in an atom has to be considered as a state of the whole atom rather than as a separate entity. . . .
>
> Interpenetrating fields and integrated totalities replace self-contained, externally related particles as fundamental images of nature. The being of any entity is constituted by its relationships and its participation in more inclusive patterns.[13]

This holistic view of reality is supported by what is known as quantum entanglement. Various quantum phenomena must be regarded as a state of the whole system, not merely a property of some isolated element of the system.[14] Properties such as spin, polarization, momentum, and position are correlated in pairs of particles so that any quantum state must be described for the quantum system as a whole; in fact, the quantum state cannot be described independently for each particle. And this is true even if the particles are subsequently separated by a long distance. Einstein, with his colleagues Boris Podolsky and Nathan Rosen, devised a thought-experiment (known as the EPR experiment, after their initials) trying to show that this was not possible. But in later years actual experiments (the John Bell and Alain Aspect experiments) have shown that quantum entanglement appears to be a fact. There is an unexpected persistence of relationship

---

[13] Barbour, *Religion and Science*, 174, 175.
[14] For good examples of this, see ibid.

among the parts of a quantum system, no matter how far apart they may be separated.

Quantum Cosmology

The standard cosmological view is that the universe began its expansion from a singularity, in which all the matter and energy of the universe was compacted into a point no larger than the diameter of a proton. If this is true, then the universe began in a quantum state. Before the expansion of the universe began, there was no difference between the macro world (the universe) and the micro world (quantum reality); they must have been identical. Understanding the origin of the universe, then, would necessarily seem to involve quantum theory.

Some physicists have found the idea that the universe began from a singularity to be distasteful, since at the singularity the laws of physics break down. Since the singularity cannot be explained by physics, it would simply have to be accepted, a given, the unexplainable beginning point of explanation. To some physicists this offends the ideal of complete explanation under which physics operates. And so there are theories of the origin of the universe that seek to avoid the singularity.

The most interesting of these explains the origin of the universe as the result of a quantum fluctuation in the "false vacuum."[15] In Newtonian science a vacuum was the empty space between material objects or particles. Quantum theory, however, has radically changed the understanding of supposedly empty space. The quantum vacuum, a well-established fact, is not empty at all. It is an energy field, all around us actually, that can give rise to "virtual particles." These can suddenly pop into existence out of the quantum vacuum and disappear back into it without violating the law of conservation of energy. One of the implications of the uncertainty principle is that vacuum fluctuations can produce virtual particles in opposed pairs (an electron and a positron, for example). These pairs of virtual particles can come into existence for a brief time, borrowing energy from the vacuum, and then canceling each other out and releasing the energy back into the vacuum. In this way they do not violate

---

[15] See Ferris, *Coming of Age in the Milky Way*, 351–62; Overbye, *Lonely Hearts of the Cosmos*, 247–60.

the law of conservation of energy. Theoretically, there is no limit on the potential energy value of the quantum vacuum. There is also no upper limit on the masses or lifetimes of the particles that can appear out of the vacuum. It is also possible that given certain conditions, virtual particles might be "cut off" from returning to the vacuum and remain in existence in the universe.

These interesting properties of the quantum vacuum make it possible to think of the universe as coming into existence from a fluctuation in the quantum vacuum rather than from a singularity. The key to this theory is thinking of the universe as actually having a net energy value of zero. The amount of "positive" energy in the universe, of course, is unimaginably enormous. But physicists argue that gravity must be considered as "negative" energy, because enormous amounts of "positive" energy must be expended to counter it. If the rate of universal expansion is near or at "flatness" (due to the mass density of the universe causing the expansion to be perched halfway between gravitational collapse and endless expansion), this could indicate that the universe has a net energy sum of zero. And this permits thinking of the universe as an unimaginably massive virtual particle that arose from the quantum vacuum and which does not violate the law of conservation of energy.[16] While the probability of this actually happening is extremely low, it is not impossible.

There are other quantum cosmological theories, such as the Hartle-Hawking theory, named after James Hartle and Stephen Hawking.[17] But all such theories have numerous problems.[18] One

---

[16] This was first proposed by Edward Tryon, "Is the Universe a Vacuum Fluctuation?" *Nature* 246 (December 14, 1973): 396–97.

[17] See Stephen Hawking, *A Brief History of Time* (New York: Bantam Books, 1988); and C. J. Isham, "Creation of the Universe as a Quantum Process," in Russell, Stoeger, and Coyne, *Physics, Philosophy, and Theology*, 375–408.

[18] See C. J. Isham, "Quantum Theories of the Creation of the Universe," in *Quantum Cosmology and the Laws of Nature: Scientific Perspectives on Divine Action*, 2nd ed., ed. Robert John Russell, Nancey Murphy, and C. J. Isham (Vatican City State: Vatican Observatory Publications; Berkeley, CA: The Center for Theology and the Natural Sciences, 1996), 51–89.

of the problems is that such theories are highly speculative, and because they deal with the origin of the universe, it is exceedingly difficult even to know how one might find the empirical evidence needed to test them. The most difficult problem is that there is yet no successful theory of quantum gravity. Most physicists and cosmologists, therefore, hold that the universe began from a singularity.

Another difficulty for understanding the origin of the universe is that if any one of a number of physical constants were even slightly different from what they are, the universe as we know it could never have been. The values of the physical constants, which are in a sense arbitrary because they could have been otherwise, appear to be "fine-tuned" or "designed" to produce a universe such as ours, one in which life and intelligent life can emerge. The values of the strong and weak nuclear forces, gravity, and the expansion rate of the universe at its origin all had to be exactly what they are in order to produce a universe that is capable of harboring the complexity and life we find in our universe. And there are many other physical constants that appear to be "fine-tuned" in this way.[19] To avoid any implication of "design" by some supernatural force, several physicists and cosmologists have embraced a "many worlds" or "multiverse" theory: that there are an infinite number of universes, and that all possible values of the physical constants are actualized in one or another of them. It would then be no surprise that we have come about in the one in which life is possible and there would be no need to explain why the physical constants have the values they do in our universe. Since communication of any kind between these universes seems impossible, it is hard to know how any empirical evidence could be found to support these speculative fancies. They seem to be designed to avoid having to deal with the mystery of the origin of our universe. These speculations also seem to confuse merely *possible* universes with the actual universe. The mere fact that we can conceive of many or an infinite number of *possible* universes

---

[19] For a discussion of many such "fine-tunings," see Holmes Rolston III, *Science and Religion: A Critical Survey* (New York: Random House, 1987), 67–72.

does not give us any grounds for supposing that there *is* more than the one actual universe we know.

Implications for Theology

In conclusion to this chapter I consider three major topics and pursue their implications for an understanding of God and God's relation to the universe. The first of these topics is energy. Energy seems to be the most pervasive and fundamental concept employed by physics. Einstein has taught us that matter and energy are convertible, that all things are made up of energy. Quantum theory reveals that we are immersed in a sea of energy, surrounded by an energy field of unimaginable power, with virtual particles winking into and out of existence all around us. Photons, wave-particles of pure energy, are constantly streaming throughout the universe, interacting with all things and bathing us in light. Even the "empty" space surrounding material objects seethes with invisible particles of energy. It is interesting that energy is so pervasive a presence in the universe, and so fundamental a concept in physics, and yet no one seems able to improve on the very old definition of energy as "the ability to do work."

None of the theories of the origin of the universe even tries to explain where the energy constituting the universe comes from. In the standard Big Bang theory the singularity itself, which contains the entire energy of the universe, cannot be explained; it must simply be assumed. And in the quantum fluctuation theory no one even tries to explain why or how the quantum vacuum comes to be; it is simply presumed. Alexander Vilenkin (1949–), a cosmologist who developed a quantum fluctuation theory, has called his theory a naturalistic "creation out of nothing," but this is disingenuous, because the quantum vacuum is not nothing: it is, to repeat, an energy field of unimaginable power. My point is that none of the current cosmological theories can explain the energy that *is* our universe. Give physicists and cosmologists the energy, either in the form of a singularity or the quantum vacuum, and they can explain everything. But they cannot explain the energy itself. They must simply assume it.

It is interesting to me that the classical arguments seeking to prove the existence of God arrive at a very similar position. As any philosopher will tell you, the classical arguments for the existence of God—the cosmological and teleological arguments—are not actual proofs in the strict sense of the word. Philosophers have found flaws or leaps or gaps in each of them that render them failures as strict proofs. But in a sense they are arriving at much the same point as the current cosmological theories of the origin of the universe. I mean that these classical arguments are saying, in effect, give us God and the whole world becomes intelligible. The reasoning in the arguments goes in the other direction, starting with the universe, but it concludes that one must assume the existence of God in order to explain the universe of our experience. For example, one of Thomas Aquinas's "Five Ways" is the argument from the existence of contingent beings, each of which owes its existence to something else, concluding to the necessity of assuming a *necessary* being that does not owe its existence to another and that is the ultimate cause of all contingent beings.[20] In effect the classical arguments are saying that without God we cannot find answers to our questions of origin and cause; the only way to make sense of the universe is to assume the fact of God as its cause. No one can explain God, but give us God and we can explain everything. In a very similar way, physics says, give us energy and we can explain everything.

Surely this shows us that both in physics and in theology the human intellect runs into its ultimate limit, where we must assume when we cannot explain or prove. But what interests me is the possibility that what perhaps in some fundamental sense God and the energy constituting our universe are deeply *related*. Perhaps it is possible that the energy constituting our universe is properly interpreted *theologically* as a participation or sharing in the divine life. Christian theology has held over the centuries that all finite beings exist by participating in the infinite being of God. Perhaps today, in light of contemporary science, we may understand that this means that the energy constituting our universe truly is the universe living by sharing in the very life of God. Perhaps the energy constituting the universe is rightly understood as a gift given from God without reservation and endowed with autonomy, so that just as parents give life to their children and allow them to make whatever they will of themselves, so God

---

[20] See Thomas Aquinas, *Summa Theologica*, Ia, Q. 2, a. 3.

endows the universe with a share in the divine life but allows it to be free and able to make of itself something other than God. I pursue this idea in a later chapter.

The second topic I wish to consider here is the role that possibility plays in the current scientific understanding of reality. In quantum theory, reality at its most basic level is understood in terms of possibility. The quantum wave function describing a quantum system is understood as a "superposition of states," which is a probabilistic description of all the possible states the system might manifest. Phenomena at the quantum level can be predicted only statistically, in terms of probabilities, or the relative likelihood of certain possibilities being actualized. Classical causality disappears at the quantum level, and with it classical determinism as well. The indeterminacy of the quantum world may be indicating that there is some degree of freedom, or, if one prefers, *flexibility* present in nature, some capacity for novelty at the heart of reality. As the evolution of our cosmos seems to make clear, nature is capable of actualizing novel possibilities. This does not mean that there are not deterministic structures and processes in nature. There obviously are. Order requires some degree of determinacy, and the achievements of novelty can be preserved only in the context of a background of order. But the history of the universe in many ways seems to be a vast exploration of possibility. And we will soon see that biology and evolution reveal the same story. Possibility and the actualization of novel possibilities seem essential to reality, and it is hard to understand the unfolding of the universe and of the life forms on our planet as anything other than a wide-ranging exploration of possibilities.

Possibility is fascinating, and the point I would make here is that possibility is not self-explanatory. Where do possibilities come from? Must we simply say, as we do for energy, that possibilities just *are*? Must we simply assume them without being able to explain where they come from and how they function? Possibilities by definition are not *actual*, even though they are *real*. They are real in the sense that we can think of possibilities and interact mentally with them, but they are not actual in the sense that they are not *agents*, nor are they *actual* things. We cannot hold a possibility in our hands or take it on a walk. Possibilities must be actualized in and by some actual agent of the universe to become actualized. How then, if they are not actual things, can they interact with actualities? These are not scientific questions but philosophical ones. Yet the importance of possibility to the scientific account of nature really begs for some philosophical understanding of how possibilities function.

Possibilities are also important to religion. For example, Jesus' proclamation of the kingdom of God is really the presentation to the world of a possibility, not an actual situation. The kingdom of God is a counter-factual vision of what the world could be like if all people placed themselves under God's rule, a vision of how beautiful the world could be if ruled by compassion, mercy, healing, and love. Jesus holds that possibility in front of people, actualizes it in his own actions, and asks all his hearers to give themselves over to it. We can see here quite clearly the power that possibilities possess; they can motivate life commitments, hopes, and actions. The kingdom of God is in our midst to the extent that people show compassion, mercy, and love, and as they forgive and heal one another. But in its fullness it remains a possibility, an ideal luring our commitment and action. And so an understanding of the nature of possibility and how possibilities can interact with the actual agents of the universe is as important to the theological understanding of God and God's interaction with the universe as it is to the scientific understanding of the universe. If we are to mediate between the vastly different under-standings of possibility in science and in religion, it is important to have an acceptable philosophical analysis of possibility that can be open to both science and religion, respecting and accom-modating both. I pursue this in a later chapter as well.

Finally, the third topic I want to consider briefly is the very important truth taught to us by contemporary physics and cos-mology: the interconnectedness of things in the universe. Any philosophy or theology that seeks to learn from contemporary science must have this at the forefront of its concern. Relativity theory, as I summarized above, shows the relatedness or inter-connectedness of space and time, of energy and matter, of the observed to the observer. Quantum theory reveals that reality at its most fundamental level consists of integrated wholes, with in-dividual particles woven together in a unified system and gaining their identity from the whole in which they participate. Quantum entanglement tells us of the persistence of relationship, even if particles of a quantum system are separated by great distances. And since the universe apparently began in a quantum state, it is possible that everything in the universe retains a fundamental relationship to everything else (a surprising scientific confirmation, as it were, of Nicholas of Cusa's philosophical and theological understanding of the universe in the fifteenth century). Relativity theory, quantum theory, and contemporary cosmology all point to interrelatedness as a fundamental feature of our universe. This has powerful implications for understanding God's relation to the universe. Christian theology, of course, has always held that all things are creatures and are related in God as their Creator. However, it did not always grasp all the implications of this relationship and in its focus on the world's dependence on God, it often lost sight of what the world might mean to God. I pursue these implications in a later chapter as well.

But before focusing on the understanding of God, I summarize in the next chapter the important contributions to our understanding of life made by developments in the field of biology.

Chapter 5

What We Can Learn from Biological Evolution

The story of the development of the modern theory of evolution is fascinating. It took the combination of Darwin's theory of evolution by natural selection and Mendel's theory of genetics, as well as many subsequent developments, and the story is not yet complete. Despite decades of research we still do not know how life actually originated on our planet.[1] But there is no doubt that life has been evolving for a very long time. Theology cannot afford to ignore what the evolution of life tells us.

Darwin's Discovery

Charles Darwin (1809–82) is usually regarded as the discoverer of the theory of evolution by natural selection, though Alfred Russel Wallace (1823–1913) is technically considered its co-discoverer. I cannot here rehearse the story of Darwin's discovery,[2] but I do highlight a few aspects of his ideas, especially

---

[1] The best summary of this research I have seen is Michael Marshall, "The Secret of How Life on Earth Began," bbc.com/earth (October 31, 2016).

[2] There are a multitude of books on Darwin. Two excellent biographies both trace the development of his ideas. See Adrian Desmond and James Moore, *Darwin* (New York: W. W. Norton, 1991); and the two-volume biography by Janet Browne, *Charles Darwin: Voyaging* (Princeton, NJ: Princeton University Press, 1995) and *Charles Darwin: The Power of Place* (Princeton, NJ: Princeton University Press, 2002).

his struggle with religious belief that I believe to be important for theology to consider.

Darwin presented his theory of evolution in *On the Origin of Species by Means of Natural Selection.*[3] He had only one sentence on human beings in the first edition, but everyone realized that the theory implied that humans are part of the natural world and evolved from some "lower" form of primate. Much of the initial opposition to Darwin's theory was motivated by outrage at how his theory "demeaned" humanity by linking it to the "lower" animal world. It took people some time to accept that we are animals and subject to the same natural processes that govern the natural world. The view that we are a special creation of God, separate from animals and "above" nature, was still quite common in Darwin's day. His later book on human evolution did nothing to reassure those with traditional views.[4]

Darwin did not intend to attack religion with his theory. He came from a family that held Unitarian beliefs, though when he was young his family frequently attended Anglican services, as did his wife and children in later years. Darwin himself never really had firmly orthodox Christian beliefs, even of the Unitarian version, but he did not seek to disabuse others of their beliefs. His wife, Emma, for example, was firmly Christian in her beliefs, and Darwin never tried to dissuade her. He was also open to the beliefs of his fellow scientists. His leading supporter in the United States was Asa Gray (1810–88), the Harvard botanist, who was a strongly committed Christian. Gray believed that evolution was compatible with religious faith, indeed, that one could interpret evolution as God's means of creation. He wrote to Darwin asking if Darwin believed his theory of evolution to be atheistic. Darwin's response is quite instructive:

> With respect to the theological view of the question. This is always painful to me. I am bewildered. I had no intention to write atheistically. But I own that I cannot see as plainly

---

[3] Charles Darwin, *On the Origin of Species by Means of Natural Selection* (London: John Murray, 1859). See Charles Darwin, *On the Origin of Species*, facsimile of the 1st ed. (New York: Atheneum, 1967).

[4] See Charles Darwin, *The Descent of Man, and Selection in Relation to Sex*, 2 vols. (London: John Murray, 1871).

as others do, and as I should wish to do, evidence of design and beneficence on all sides of us. There seems to me too much misery in the world. . . . On the other hand, I cannot anyhow be contented to view this wonderful universe, and especially the nature of man, and to conclude that everything is the result of brute force. I am inclined to look at everything as resulting from designed laws, with the details, whether good or bad, left to the working out of what we may call chance. Not that this notion *at all* satisfies me. I feel most deeply that the whole subject is too profound for the human intellect. A dog might as well speculate on the mind of Newton. Let each man hope and believe what he can. Certainly I agree with you that my views are not at all necessarily atheistical.[5]

Darwin vacillated on religious questions most of his life. He often said that he was inclined to believe in some sort of designed laws, but his vague willingness to believe was seriously weakened by suffering, both of humans and especially of animals. He thought human suffering could at least be understood as having some benefit in ennobling a person's character; but what possible benefit is there in animal suffering? Suffering can be more easily understood as the byproduct of an imperfect and unthinking natural force, namely, natural selection.[6] Darwin assumed the traditional idea of God as all-powerful and all-good and as controlling all things that happen in the universe. When he could not reconcile his actual experience of the world with that idea, he found he could not believe in God. He had theistic leanings of a sort, but he was also plagued with serious enough doubts that in the end he used Thomas Huxley's newly coined word *agnostic* to describe his views.[7]

---

[5] Francis Darwin, ed., *The Life and Letters of Charles Darwin*, 2 vols. (New York: Appleton, 1891), 2:105 (to Gray, May 22, 1860).

[6] See Charles Darwin, *The Autobiography of Charles Darwin, 1809–1882*, with original omissions restored, ed. Nora Barlow (New York: W. W. Norton, 1958; 1969 Norton paperback edition), 90.

[7] See Darwin, *Autobiography*, 94. Darwin wrote this in 1876. Huxley coined the word *agnostic* to describe his own position on the existence of God.

Darwin's own religious difficulties mirror in some ways the challenges his theory presented to religion. First, his theory undercuts the classical argument from design in nature that had been the mainstay of natural theology for centuries. This argument, as it was developed in the early modern period with support from the emerging empirical sciences, held that the adaptation of animals to their environments and the complexity and delicacy of such organs as eyes could not be explained except by reference to a supreme intelligence that had designed everything to work as it does. Such phenomena could not arise by chance and seemed so similar to the products of human design that one could rightly conclude the existence of a Supreme Intelligence that had designed the systems of nature. In its classical form this argument assumed that organisms had not changed much since creation, and it tended to downplay suffering. William Paley, for example, in seeking to prove God's goodness from this argument, writes: "It is a happy world after all. The air, the earth, the water teem with delighted existence. In a spring moon, or a summer evening, on whichever side I turn my eyes, myriads of happy beings crowd upon my view."[8] Paley seems to be contemplating his garden after a good dinner, brandy and cigar in hand, content with the world. He is not taking seriously the ambiguity of nature in its frequent harshness.

Darwin, on the other hand, had seen nature in the raw, so to speak. He did, especially in his younger days, have aesthetic experiences of the beauty of nature, but he could also write: "What a book a devil's chaplain might write on the clumsy, wasteful, blundering, low, and horribly cruel works of nature!"[9] Darwin had a much deeper sense of the ambiguities of nature than Paley did, a more profound grasp of animal suffering. His theory of natural selection destroyed the classic form of the argument from design by providing a completely naturalistic explanation of how animals become adapted to their environments and how they acquire complex and delicate organs. This same explanation gives

---

[8] William Paley, *Natural Theology: Selections*, ed. Frederick Ferre (Indianapolis: Bobbs-Merrill, 1963), 54. Originally published in 1802.

[9] Charles Darwin, *More Letters of Charles Darwin*, ed. Francis Darwin and A. C. Seward, 2 vols. (London: John Murray, 1903), 1:94 (to J. D. Hooker, July 13, 1856).

us a more understandable, if not comforting, explanation for suffering: if evolution is being driven by an unfeeling, uncaring natural force (natural selection), then one can expect suffering as its natural byproduct. Suffering is only an intractable problem if one assumes that an all-powerful and all-good God controls what happens in evolution and in history. While this does not in itself call into question the existence of God, it certainly challenges the traditional *idea* of God, as well as the traditional understanding of the doctrines of creation and providence.

Darwin's theory presented several other challenges to Christian belief as well.[10] As the immediate reaction to his theory shows, people saw it as challenging the uniqueness and place of humans in the world and certainly as challenging the traditional Christian world view. Christians for centuries had seen the universe as fixed, static, hierarchically ordered (with humans at the top, of course), relatively young, and centered on humans—in short, a universe made for humans. While many aspects of this world view had been challenged earlier by the developments in the scientific understanding of reality, evolution destroyed it completely. It revealed a universe immersed in change, unimaginably old, and certainly not centered on us. In place of God's providential governance, it posited an uncaring, unthinking, unfeeling natural force and mere chance as controlling the conditions of life and even what forms of organisms emerge and survive. Most important, it placed humans firmly *within* the world of nature, not above it, and it understood our origin as caused by a natural process of evolution from "lower" animals, not by some direct divine creative act. Tradition held that we are radically different from the animals, possessing an immortal soul destined for eternal life with God. Tradition denied that animals have immortal souls and held that their mortal souls died with their bodies. By placing us in the animal world, evolution called into question the whole idea of an immortal soul and eternal life and shrouded the meaning and destiny of human life in ambiguity.

Two other challenges were just as devastating. If evolution is true and is revealing our actual origin, then the creation stories

---

[10] For an excellent discussion of several of these, see Ian Barbour, *Religion and Science: Historical and Contemporary Issues* (San Francisco: HarperSanFrancisco, 1997), 57–63.

in Genesis cannot be literally true, and for many Christians this called into question several doctrines associated with scripture, namely, the beliefs that scripture is divinely revealed and therefore is both divinely inspired and inerrant. How can scripture be inerrant and a source of divinely revealed truth if it is wrong about the origin of the earth, the animals, and humans? And what happens to the doctrine of original sin if the story of Adam and Eve in Genesis 3 is not historically true? And what, then, of the doctrine of redemption or salvation? The challenge to scripture was not just to the literal interpretation of the Bible, but to this entire network of doctrines. This is then connected to another challenge: the basis of ethics. Christianity (and Judaism) had taught that the basis of ethics was in the divinely revealed will of God, enshrined in the Ten Commandments.[11] But if humans have evolved just as other animals, then perhaps what we call ethics is nothing more than the development of social codes necessary for humans to get along and succeed. This seems much more likely than believing that God spoke to us from the top of a mountain and revealed the codes for our conduct directly from heaven. In effect, Darwin's theory of evolution by natural selection challenged the entire traditional Christian world view, forcing theologians to rethink and reinterpret the entire understanding of God and God's relation to the universe. We are still engaged in this rethinking today.

The Roman Catholic Response to Evolution

The old adage that Rome moves slowly certainly applied to the Roman Catholic Church's response to evolution. The first official step was taken in Pope Pius XII's 1943 encyclical letter *Divino Afflante Spiritu*, which freed Catholic biblical scholarship from biblical literalism. The church had from the beginning employed other modes of understanding scripture, but this encyclical letter made clear that Roman Catholic exegetes were under no obligation to interpret the creation narratives in Genesis as factual revelations of how the earth and its life had actually originated. Pius XII followed this in 1950 with his encyclical

---

[11] See Exodus 20; Deuteronomy 5.

letter *Humani Generis,* in which he specifically addressed the theory of evolution. While his language makes clear that Pius did not especially care for the theory of evolution, and perhaps even hoped it might someday be proven wrong, he nevertheless stated that Catholics were free to accept the theory as accounting for the origin of the human body so long as they continued to believe that God creates the soul and infuses it in each individual. The clear intent is to say that even if human beings arise by a natural process, God is still to be understood as the Creator of each person and that the scientific explanation of human origins is not an exhaustive explanation.

On October 22, 1996, Pope John Paul II, who had a personal interest in the dialogue between science and religion, addressed the topic of evolution in the *Message to the Pontifical Academy of Sciences concerning the Relationship between Revelation and the Theories of Evolution.* In this message John Paul II acknowledged that developments since Pius's time have provided much evidence for the theory of evolution, even if there was still some debate about its exact mechanism. He reaffirmed Pius XII's position, saying that "if the human body takes its origin from pre-existent living matter, the spiritual soul is immediately created by God" (section 5). If we step back from this specific language, its meaning is quite clear: science is not an exhaustive explanation of humans, and God as Creator is involved in the creation of each one of us.

The official teaching does not go beyond this; it does not offer an explanation of how this is possible or how it occurs. This is wise because our religious conviction about God as Creator is not tied to any specific theory of creation. Our faith leaves room for a variety of ways of expressing or explicating what we believe, and it leaves room as well for the development of scientific knowledge. But by implication the church's teaching is saying that despite the scientific account of natural processes, God is somehow involved in the creation of all things (not just humans, though the church's teaching tends to focus on humanity). There are, in other words, dimensions of reality and human existence that science alone cannot illuminate. Theology can propose more specific theories of how this is possible, how God can act within or alongside the natural processes of evolution.

But the important point theologically is to preserve the church's insistence on God's creative involvement in the universe.

DNA and the Relation of All Forms of Life

With the rediscovery of the genetic theory of Gregor Mendel (1822–84), and with many further developments, the so-called modern synthesis of the theory of evolution finally emerged just before the outbreak of World War II.[12] Mendel was an Augustinian monk in the Abbey of St. Thomas in Brno, in what is today the Czech Republic.[13] His experiments with pea plants in the monastery's garden and his careful observations and analysis enabled him to establish the basic rules of heredity, sometimes called the laws of Mendelian inheritance. This work was complete by 1866, but he published the results in possibly the most obscure scientific journal in all of Europe, little more than the newsletter of a local scientific club. The work was therefore unknown until its rediscovery in the early twentieth century. Mendel's work explained the source of the variations among individuals of the same species, the one thing Darwin was never able to explain. It took several decades to work out the understanding of how genetics and natural selection each had a role in the evolution of life. But finally uniting the theory of genetics with Darwin's theory of natural selection enabled biologists to craft a more complete theory of the mechanisms of evolution.

The discovery of the structure of DNA in 1953 by Francis Crick (1916–2004) and James D. Watson (1928–) at Cambridge University enabled a much deeper understanding of how reproductive genetics works. With help from the work of Rosalind

---

[12] For an exhaustive history of this development by one of its leading architects, see Ernst Mayr, *The Growth of Biological Thought: Diversity, Evolution, and Inheritance* (Cambridge, MA: Harvard University Press, 1982). See also Peter J. Bowler, *Evolution: The History of an Idea*, 3rd ed. (Berkeley and Los Angeles: University of California Press, 2003), chap. 9.

[13] For a very readable biography of Mendel, including a simple explanation of his genetic theory, see Robin Marantz Henig, *The Monk in the Garden: The Lost and Found Genius of Gregor Mendel, the Father of Genetics* (Boston: Houghton Mifflin, 2000).

Franklin (1920–58) and Erwin Chargaff (1905–2002), Crick and Watson were able to discover the famous double helical structure of the DNA molecule. This structure is the key to how DNA works as a blueprint even though it is metabolically inactive in the cell. The sequence of bases along the DNA strands encodes information that allows the genes to control the developmental process of the organism. In groups of three ("triplets"), the sequence of bases along each strand corresponds to the twenty amino acids out of which the protein chains composing all organisms are built. The DNA is, in short, coded information on how to go about building the organism by stringing together the amino acids to create the linear protein chains.

The genes of all known organisms are constituted by DNA that varies only in the length of its strands and the sequence of the four base pairs. Every living thing has this same structure in its cells, controlling its growth and development. This is extremely strong evidence for the view that Darwin suggested more than a century and a half ago; that is, that all living organisms have evolved from common ancestors and that, ultimately, all living forms can be traced back to some first simple form of life.[14] So far as we can tell, all living things have a common origin. Every living thing is a cousin to some degree of all other living things.

The Origin of Life
and Complexity Theory

As I mentioned at the beginning of this chapter, we still do not know exactly how life originated on our planet. One intriguing suggestion is that under certain conditions chemical systems can self-organize in ways that may have led to life. In 1977 Ilya Prigogene (1917–2003) won the Nobel Prize for his researches into non-equilibrium thermodynamic systems,[15] which can

---

[14] See Darwin, *On the Origin of Species*, facsimile of the 1st edition, 488.

[15] See Ilya Prigogene, *From Being to Becoming: Time and Complexity in the Physical Sciences* (New York: W. H. Freeman, 1980); and Ilya Prigogene and Isabelle Stengers, *Order out of Chaos: Man's New Dialogue with Nature* (New York: Bantam Books, 1984).

achieve new states of order far from equilibrium and maintain them for significant amounts of time so long as energy continues to flow into them. The amazing thing about such systems is that they *self-organize*. Prigogene showed that many inanimate self-organizing systems can move from a disordered state to emergent ordered states. He argued that this development appears to be governed by new laws of complexity. His research contributes to understanding the origin of life from inanimate systems, because all living things are open non-equilibrium thermodynamic systems, and presumably, one of the first steps in the emergence of living things would have been the formation of such self-organizing systems (metabolic networks) in the organic chemistry of the early earth.

Stuart Kauffman has for many years pursued the understanding of self-organization and the development of complexity theory, applying this not only to evolution and origin-of-life questions, but extending his reflections into philosophical considerations on human life and the meaning of existence.[16] Kauffman modeled hypothetical metabolic networks on a computer in terms of a network of lightbulbs connected by electrical circuits, each bulb receiving inputs from two other bulbs.[17] The inspiration for this model came from the discovery by Francois Jacob and Jacques Monod in the mid-1960s that genes, to put it very simply, can switch each other on and off.[18] It seemed to Kauffman that we might learn something about the interactions of molecules forming a metabolic network, the interactions of genes within a cell, and the interactions of cells in forming an organism by modeling these interactions in terms of lightbulbs switching each other on and off. The analysis of such networks

---

[16] Kauffman's work is difficult for the nonspecialist but well worth the effort to understand. His books are the following: *The Origins of Order: Self-Organization and Selection in Evolution* (New York: Oxford University Press, 1993); *At Home in the Universe: The Search for the Laws of Self-Organization and Complexity* (New York: Oxford University Press, 1995); *Investigations* (New York: Oxford University Press, 2000); *Reinventing the Sacred: A New View of Science, Reason, and Religion* (New York: Basic Books, 2008); and *Humanity in a Creative Universe* (New York: Oxford University Press, 2016).

[17] See Kauffman, *At Home in the Universe*, 74–92.

[18] For the technical details of this discovery, see ibid., 95–97.

employs the mathematics of dynamic systems. Kauffman used the rules of Boolean algebra to assign the behavior of each lightbulb depending on the nature of the inputs it receives. For a network of one thousand bulbs, with each bulb having two possible states (on or off), the number of possible configurations of the system (or patterns of bulbs on and off) is $2^{1,000}$. This range of possible states the system might exhibit is called *state space*. If the system is allowed to run with continued input of energy, it will eventually begin to follow and repeat a sequence of states. Working with networks of various sizes, Kauffman discovered that even very large systems, with huge ranges of possible states, quickly settle down to a repeating cycle of relatively few states and thus achieve a dynamically stable order. This stable cycle of exhibited states is governed by the mathematical object called an *attractor*.

An attractor is a "region" in state space that draws the dynamics of the system toward it.[19] This attraction occurs because the state space is "folded" (or structured) in such a way that starting from a variety of initial conditions, the system is inevitably drawn toward the region of the attractor. An example that may help is to think of a ping-pong ball and the surface of an ocean.[20] No matter where the ball is released (under water or above it), the ball will move toward the surface of the ocean. The ocean surface is the attractor, and the ball will inevitably end up there. But its actual behavior on the surface is unpredictable and complex because it will depend on currents, waves, wind, and so on. A dynamic system may have more than one attractor; in such cases, starting from different initial conditions the system, or parts of it, may be drawn toward different attractors. The set of points in state space evolving toward a given attractor is

---

[19] See James P. Crutchfield, J. Doyne Farmer, Norman H. Packard, and Robert S. Shaw, "Chaos," in *Chaos and Complexity: Scientific Perspectives on Divine Action*, ed. Robert John Russell, Nancey Murphy, and Arthur R. Peacocke, 35–48 (Vatican City State: Vatican Observatory; Berkeley, CA: The Center for Theology and the Natural Sciences, 1995), 39. See also Jack Cohen and Ian Stewart, *The Collapse of Chaos: Discovering Simplicity in a Complex World* (New York: Penguin Books, 1995), 204–7.

[20] For this example, see Cohen and Stewart, *The Collapse of Chaos*, 206.

called a "basin of attraction."[21] A good image for this is to think
of how a mountain range may have many lakes; the lakes can
be thought of as attractors, and each drains a certain region of
the landscape; the drainage patterns leading to each lake are the
basins of attraction.[22] Depending on exactly where the drops of
rain fall on the mountain peaks, they will be drawn toward one
or another of the lakes. Yet the exact path the drops of water
will take cannot be predicted.

An important part of Kauffman's theorizing is the argument
that the interaction between self-organization and natural selection drives successful networks (or species) to the "edge of
chaos": a "point" very near the "phase transition" between order
and chaos.[23] In other words, the successful network (or species)
has enough order to maintain stability and survive, but is flexible
enough to deal with novelty and change (mutations, changes in
environment, and so on). If it is too ordered, it becomes inflex-
ible and cannot respond well to change, but if it slips over the
"edge" into chaos, it will not survive. Dynamic living systems,
Kauffman argues, do best at the edge of chaos, where order is
not deadening and novelty does not become chaotic.

The mathematical concepts of attractors and basins of attraction are usually employed in the analysis of dynamic systems
to show how very complex kinds of order and very complex
effects evolve from simple causes. This is the important field of
chaos theory, which has been shown to apply to many phenomena in nature, including the weather. Kauffman is showing the
reverse: how very complex situations and causes can give rise
to remarkably simple kinds of order and effects. He has been
developing a theory of complexity and a theory of emergence.
He holds that natural selection is not the cause of the order we

---

[21] Crutchfield et al., "Chaos," 39.

[22] See Kauffman, *At Home in the Universe*, 78.

[23] See ibid., 86–92, where this argument is introduced. He expands
on this argument throughout the rest of the book. See also Brian Good-
win, *How the Leopard Changed Its Spots: The Evolution of Complexity*
(New York: Charles Scribner's Sons, 1994), 181–87; Richard Solé and
Brian Goodwin, *Signs of Life: How Complexity Pervades Biology* (New
York: Basic Books, 2000).

see in the living world and that it cannot explain the origin of life. He does not deny that natural selection is involved in evolution. Instead, Kauffman's "heretical" proposal in contemporary biology is that natural selection operates on the spontaneous order that arises quite naturally in complex dynamic systems. If we ask how life originated, the standard answer we hear from Darwinian orthodoxy is that it arose by chance. And if we ask how it evolved, the standard answer is by natural selection operating on chance mutations of the genetic basis of life. Kauffman does not think the marvelous web of life arose by chance. And he thinks that life is not the passive reflector of selective environmental factors. Instead, he sees life as actively involved in its own emergence, self-organizing and creative in its response to the environment. It is the dynamic self-organizing order of living systems that generates the patterns upon which natural selection operates. Life is an emergent property of dynamic self-organizing systems, and it is a holistic phenomenon, a characteristic of the self-organizing and self-reproducing system itself.

There is much more that could be said about evolution and debates over its mechanism(s), but we have seen enough for my purposes here. There is, however, something to be gained from a brief examination of the history of life on our planet.

The History of Life and Mass Extinctions

We do not know exactly when life emerged, but the evidence seems to show that it emerged as soon as it could. The planet is estimated to be 4.5 billion years old, and for quite some time it was too hot (because of meteor impacts and radioactive decay) for life to emerge—or so most scientists believe. The oldest sedimentary rocks, the 3.75-billion-year-old Isua series of west Greenland, record the cooling and stabilization of the earth's crust and the presence of liquid water. These rocks apparently contain the earliest evidence of life. They contain the enhanced ratio of the carbon isotope ^{12}C that is the chemical signature of organic life. In late August 2016, it was announced that scientists believe they have also found stromatolites—layers of sediment trapped and bound by colonies of bacteria and blue-green algae—in these Greenland rocks.[24] If this proves to be correct (there is some debate about it), then these are the oldest actual fossils of living organisms. There are definite fossils of living organisms, both stromatolites and actual cells, that have been found in Australia and Africa in the oldest known sedimentary rocks that have not been metamorphosed, dating to about 3.5 billion years old. All these earliest known organisms are simple single-celled forms, prokaryotes. Prokaryotic cells have no organelles: no nucleus, no paired chromosomes, no mitochondria, and no chloroplasts.

As far as we can tell from the fossil record, life remained at this simplest possible level for the astounding period of 1.6 billion years, or nearly 40 percent of the entire history of life on this planet. The earliest evidence we have for eukaryotic cells—complex cells with nuclei, chromosomes, mitochondria, and chloroplasts—dates from approximately 2.15 billion years ago.[25] This type of cell probably evolved from colonies of prokaryotic cells, since mitochondria and chloroplasts (both of which retain their own DNA) look very much like prokaryotic organisms that were incorporated inside other cells in a symbiotic relationship, as the biologist Lynn Margulis (1938–2011) argued.[26] They produce energy for the cell in return for a sheltered environment. But having achieved a new level of complexity, life may have remained at this level for another amazing period of time: approximately 1.45 billion years. Although there have been recent claims that multicellular organisms have been found dating back to more than two billion years ago, these claims are still controversial. The earliest solid evidence for multicellular organisms dates from approximately seven hundred million to six hundred million years ago. Unless the recent claims for two-

---

[24] For a report of this discovery, see Nicholas Wade, "World's Oldest Fossils Found in Greenland," *New York Times* (August 31, 2016).

[25] See Kauffman, *At Home in the Universe*, 158.

[26] See Lynn Margulis, *Origin of Eukaryotic Cells* (New Haven, CT: Yale University Press, 1970); see also, idem, *Symbiosis in Cell Evolution*, 2nd ed. (New York: W. H. Freeman, 1992), and Lynn Margulis and Dorian Sagan, *Microcosmos: Four Billion Years of Microbial Evolution*, reprint ed. (Berkeley and Los Angeles: University of California Press, 1997).

billion-year-old multicellular fossils hold up, it seems that for approximately five-sixths of the history of life on this planet, all forms of life were single-celled creatures, or colonial organisms. The emergence of true multicellular organisms and the incredible evolution of their diverse forms has occurred in only the last one-sixth of that history. Life was slow to develop beyond single-celled organisms, and it is assumed that environmental factors, such as low oxygen levels in the atmosphere, are at least partially the reason for this. But once the step to multicellular life was taken, life has since resembled a gigantic exploration of possible forms. The fossils of the so-called Cambrian explosion (for the geological period in which it occurred) reveal an incredible variety of organic forms, and new forms of multicellular life have continued to evolve ever since.

There is one last feature of evolutionary history that deserves our attention: the mass extinctions that have punctuated life's history. There have been six major mass extinctions, including the one we are currently witnessing. This last seems due entirely to the deleterious effects of human beings on the ecosystems of the world through overpopulation; habitat destruction; depletion of forests and other resources; and pollution of the air, water, and land. But prior to human existence there were five other mass extinctions due to various natural causes. The most famous of them occurred at the end of the Cretaceous period, approximately sixty-five million years ago, when the dinosaurs went extinct due (most probably) to the effects of a large meteor striking the planet. By far the worst of them was the "Great Dying" at the end of the Permian period, approximately 245 million years ago. It has been estimated that up to 96 percent of all species living at that time went extinct.[27] Mass extinctions disrupt the planet's ecosystems for perhaps as long as ten million years and are one of the major causes of rapid evolutionary change or diversification, which occurs to "fill in" the spaces (ecological niches) of

---

[27] See David M. Raup, *Extinction: Bad Genes or Bad Luck?* (New York: W. W. Norton, 1991), 72–74. Raup emphasizes that his estimate is an upper limit and may be too high. For the most thorough study of this extinction event, see Douglas H. Erwin, *Extinction: How Life on Earth Nearly Ended 250 Million Years Ago*, updated ed. (Princeton, NJ: Princeton University Press, 2015).

the species, genera, families, and orders that went extinct. Mass extinctions, ironically, always result in speciation events.[28]

Mass extinctions, especially when caused by random events such as the impact of large meteors, seem to indicate that evolutionary history is at least to some extent contingent.[29] Stephen J. Gould (1941–2002) was fond of arguing that the forms of life that survive and those that are enabled to emerge due to extinction events seem to be as much a matter of luck or chance as of natural selection and adaptive fitness. No organism can adapt to a meteor impact or a massive volcanic eruption. It is not always adaptive fitness that determines which forms of life or which individuals will survive. Niles Eldredge, a paleontologist, gives a good example to illustrate this point. When a baleen whale in feeding mode cruises through a cloud of krill, the krill that survive do not do so because they are somehow better adapted, but because they were lucky.[30] Evolution is not always a matter of older, less well-adapted forms giving way to newer, better adapted forms. Evolution simply works with what survives, and sometimes this seems to be a matter of luck. But not all paleontologists agree that the history of life is as contingent as Gould believed. Simon Conway Morris (1951–), for example, has been pursuing the phenomenon of evolutionary convergence as indicating that evolution has a kind of directionality to it.[31] If this is the case, then contingency is not the basic story of evolution, even though no one would deny that it plays a role in the

---

[28] See Niles Eldredge, *Reinventing Darwin: The Great Debate at the High Table of Evolutionary Theory* (New York: John Wiley and Sons, 1995), 152–61.

[29] Stephen J. Gould advanced this argument in his book *Wonderful Life: The Burgess Shale and the Nature of History* (New York: W. W. Norton, 1989); see esp. 277–323.

[30] See Eldredge, *Reinventing Darwin*, 36–37.

[31] See Simon Conway Morris, *Life's Solution: Inevitable Humans in a Lonely Universe* (New York: Cambridge University Press, 2003); idem, "Evolution and Convergence: Some Wider Considerations," in *The Deep Structure of Biology: Is Convergence Sufficiently Ubiquitous to Give a Directional Signal?*, ed. Simon Conway Morris, 46–67 (West Conshohocken, PA: Templeton Press, 2008); idem, *The Runes of Evolution: How the Universe Became Self-Aware* (West Conshohocken, PA: Templeton Press, 2015).

specifics, in details. Evolution may not be as contingent as Gould so passionately believed, but it may instead favor certain solutions to the problems of existence, as Conway Morris believes. The debates over how to understand the ultimate implications of evolution go on, but for my purposes we have seen enough.

Implications for Theology

Although evolution challenges the traditional idea of God in many ways, it can actually tell us a great deal of interest to our view of God and how God acts in relation to the world. One thing it shows us quite clearly is the dynamism of the world: it is always changing and developing. This is true even of the physical planet on which we live, with continental drift, volcanic activity, earthquakes, uplift, erosion and deposition, and so on. But it is even more obvious in the living world, in the history of life, and in the story of each individual's life. The living world is a dynamic world of interaction between various organisms and the interaction of all organisms with the physical environment. The back-and-forth influences in the living world at all levels of complexity are truly astounding when one studies them. Even the dynamic interactions within a single cell are amazingly complex and beautiful. When this first began to be understood, it appeared to challenge the traditional static view of creation common in Christian thought. But it actually enables us to recapture the very ancient Judeo-Christian view of God's dynamic interaction with creation.

The ancient Judeo-Christian understanding of salvation history—God's dealings with the world—takes the form of a story. And stories narrate dynamic interactions. In brief, the salvation history story, which forms the basic structure of the Hebrew and Christian scriptures, goes as follows: God creates a perfect world and places humans in it with one simple command; humans, thinking they can be the center of their world and in total control of their lives, sin and break that command; God reaches out in covenant after covenant seeking to heal humans and revealing how to live in harmony with God; but humans continue in their sinful ways; God promises to send a Redeemer; God finally becomes incarnate in the person of Jesus Christ, suffers and dies for the salvation of humans, and is raised from the dead; and one day Christ will return to bring to completion all of God's healing purposes in history and restore the whole of creation. One could argue that evolution enables us to recapture this original understanding of God's dynamic interaction with the universe that had been lost in Christian theology due to the use of a metaphysics that assumed a static world. I show in later chapters how this religious vision of God's action can be reconciled with the naturalistic story of evolution as one usually hears it. But for now I simply state that the dynamic view of God's interaction with the world is potentially compatible or resonant with the dynamic understanding of reality revealed to us by the discovery of evolution.

Contemporary biology also teaches us the same truth taught by contemporary physics: the interrelatedness or interconnectedness of all things. Many biologists today take a holistic approach to the understanding of life. Biologists also recognize that life is ordered in a hierarchical way, with higher levels of order and complexity emerging from lower levels. We grow more aware of the interconnectedness and mutual influence of the various levels of order in the biological world with advancing biological research. Most of all, the science of ecology, which has become so extremely important in our time, teaches us that every organism can exist and flourish only in a complex web of relationships to other organisms and to the physical systems of the earth. It is wondrous to recognize that we cannot think, or feel, or live without the oxygen provided for us by the plants we so often take for granted. We rely on other organisms and on the physical systems of the earth for this and all the other ways in which our lives are sustained. It is very beautiful to recognize our kinship with every living thing, all of us descendants of the first form in which the spark of life was ignited so long ago. The biological world is astoundingly pluralistic, and often at odds with itself, but it constitutes a single family, each individual organism related to all others, and all of us dependent on the earth and the sun.

Theology cannot afford to ignore this profound truth. Even though the Christian tradition from the beginning recognized that all things are related in God as Creator, it assumed that there was some profound gulf between humans and all other creatures. The Genesis story of human creation directly by God was assumed to mean that we are not part of nature and that we are ontologically different from the rest of life. This assumption was crystalized in the belief that we alone have immortal souls, whereas the rest of the animals have only mortal souls. We can no longer sustain such a view, assuming that there is some absolute gulf, some ontological difference of status, separating us from all other creatures. There is a wholeness to life that we must respect, and we must respect that we are part of the natural system. Humans certainly have some unique capabilities, but we are not above nature. Evolution has shown that we are undoubtedly part of the natural system. Perhaps this will enable us to recognize the inherent value of all living things. And perhaps if we can begin to understand how God acts in hidden ways within the natural world, we will gain new insights into how God acts among us. I address these issues in a later chapter.

This hiddenness of God's action is an important topic. We have seen that the Christian theological tradition has implied or explicitly stated that God's action in the world is hidden, occurring (in most cases) through natural processes and the agents of the world. The ambiguity of evolution and of life, with all its suffering and tragic events, requires that we find some persuasive way of understanding how God might act in evolution without totally controlling it. We can no longer hold that God controls every event occurring in nature, as the tradition so often assumed. So how is it that God acts in hidden ways but does not control every event? I suggest in a later chapter that the key to understanding this may be in an examination of the role of possibility in evolution and in our experience of life.

The role of possibility in the scientific understanding of reality is very important. As we saw in the discussion of contemporary physics, quantum theory reveals that possibility is essential to reality and that our universe is a wide-ranging exploration of possibility. The same conclusion emerges even more strongly and obviously from contemporary biology. Whether we look at the world of DNA coding for protein formation, or how networks of genes and cells form organisms or the complex interactions within ecosystems, or the emergence and radiation of novel forms of life and other large-scale patterns in evolutionary history, what strikes us over and over is the enormous range of possibilities being explored by living things. As in physics, this seems to imply a kind of indeterminacy in the living world. I mean that while there is clearly an ordered and deterministic basis for life, at all levels we find flexible systems capable of adopting novel forms and capable of responding to novelty and change impinging on them. While built on a basis of lower-level deterministic processes and structures, life seems to be able to utilize this basis and background of deterministic order to arrive at new forms of organization with an amazing degree of flexibility to them. There is, if this is not too strong a word for it, a great deal of *freedom* manifested by life in its exploration of possibility within the context of order. The determinism we find in such complex systems is "soft," not "hard," and mingled with some degree of freedom to explore the range of possibilities. The "hard" (or absolute) determinism of classical Newtonian science is as inappropriate to the understanding of the biological world as it is to the understanding of the quantum world.

We have seen that the complexity theory developed by Stuart Kauffman analyzes the dynamics of such complex systems in terms of the mathematical concept of attractors pulling the dynamics of the system through the range of possible states open to that system along basins of attraction. This is an attempt to find an underlying order or determinism in the emergence and behavior of such complex systems. I call attention to three features of this theory. The first is that while the idea of the attractors is a deterministic idea, which leads us to think that some external factor (or the mathematics itself) inevitably causes certain results, we should note that this sort of determinism is *internal* to the system. Kauffman continually speaks of it as *self*-organization. Philosophically, this seems to imply that in such systems we are dealing with agents *determining themselves* in a collective system. I suggest that this understanding of complex dynamic systems is not incompatible with the idea that such systems have and display some degree of freedom in their behavior. It is analogous, it seems to me, with how human society self-organizes: we allow ourselves to be influenced by our fellows and most often act for our collective common good, but we do so freely because we give ourselves over to certain ideals or values shared among us. Our freedom is influenced and formed and constrained, but not obliterated, by the common ideals and values that attract us. If this analogy has any worth in this context—and Kauffman does apply his theory to economic systems[32]—then it is possible that the underlying determinism of living systems is a "soft" kind of determinism, self-determinism, which implies some degree of freedom within the agents of the system. The very flexibility of the systems implies the presence of some freedom, however constrained that freedom might be by the underlying order.

Second, Kauffman's intriguing theory leads one to ask about the attractors and basins of attraction. Exactly what are they in the real world? The abstract generalization that they are mathematical objects in state space due to the "folding" of state space does not tell us what they are concretely in the functioning of actual living systems. Perhaps a first step toward understanding what they are can be taken by translating the mathematical abstraction into a metaphysical one. State space is the set of all possible states that might be displayed by a dynamic system. Since we are dealing with possibilities, it seems clear that the basin of attraction and the attractor form a set of linked or interrelated possibilities. The very terms *attractor* and *basins of attraction* lead us to think of them as attractive in some manner, that is, as exerting some kind of attractive force. But since possibilities are by definition not *actual*, and since we usually reserve the power of agency to actualities, what kind of attractive force can a mere possibility exert? In human experience possibilities attract us because for one reason or another we find them of interest or value to us. If we can generalize from our experience to form a metaphysical abstraction, we would have to say that basins of attraction and attractors are an interrelated set of possibilities experienced in terms of value or interest. This, in turn, would require us to affirm that the agents in a dynamic system must somehow be capable of experiencing value and responding to it by actualizing those possibilities that have attracted them the most. Once again, this implies a "soft" self-determinism and some (constrained) degree of freedom.

I pursue this line of thought in a later chapter, but my present point is that "soft" determinism and freedom are not incompatible ideas. If we examine our own lives, it is clear that looking at our choices with hindsight, we can see that the course of our

---

[32] See Kauffman, *At Home in the Universe*, chap. 12; idem, *Investigations*, chap. 9; idem, *Reinventing the Sacred*, chap. 11.

actions is determined; that is, because I chose this possibility, it led to me choosing this one with these results, and so on. But in each case I freely chose that possibility; there were other options open to me. Hindsight displays determinism, the effective linkages between various chosen possibilities, and it may also display the constraints affecting our choices. But there are always other possibilities that we did not choose, and this displays the freedom in which we made our choices.

The third feature of complexity theory I call attention to is that it clearly indicates that abstract possibility has a structure. I have already mentioned that the language of attractors and basins of attraction can be understood to be referring to an interrelated or linked set of possibilities. But possibilities, while real in the sense that we interact with them and can grasp them mentally, are by definition not actual things. How can mere possibilities have a structure? And if they have a structure, which the mathematics of dynamic systems clearly reveals, then what is the cause of that structure? Structure reveals order, and some ordering agency seems required to understand this. Since we usually reserve agency to actual things, and possibilities in themselves are not actual, to what ordering agency might we appeal to explain how possibilities gain a structure? I pursue this question in the next chapter.

Finally, I want to return to the topic of animal suffering, which affected Darwin so deeply. I believe that theology must recognize that biology raises the traditional problem of evil to a new and more powerful level. As traditionally discussed, the problem of *natural evil* has been concerned exclusively with human suffering and death. The term is probably not a happy one but was used to distinguish the topic from *moral evil,* all of which can be traced to the exercise of human free will. Natural evil refers to the bad things that happen due to no human action, such as natural disasters, disease, and death. But ecology and the history of life on earth demand that we recognize a much broader problem of evil, as they demand that we recognize our interconnectedness and kinship with all living things. If we accept these truths, then it is not just *human* suffering and death that matter; we must face up squarely to the enormity of the suffering, pain, misery, and death that the entire history of life, complete with its mass extinctions, represents. Any attempt to speak of God as the source of this universe and as active within it must deal with the ambiguities of nature. John F. Haught has argued that in calling this to our attention, Darwin gave Christian theology a gift in helping us to recover the ancient Christian theme of the self-emptying and humility of God.[33] I agree, and to the discussion of God I now turn.

---

[33] John F. Haught, *God after Darwin: A Theology of Evolution*, 2nd ed. (Boulder, CO: Westview Press, 2008), 49–60.

Chapter 6

The God of Possibility and Empowerment

In this chapter I begin formulating an interpretation of God and God's relation to the world that respects the Judeo-Christian tradition and also takes account of what contemporary science tells us about the universe. Because of widespread agnosticism and atheism, one might expect this chapter to begin with some attempt to prove the existence of God, an attempt to persuade skeptics and atheists. But for several reasons such an exercise is not necessary. For believers, no proof is necessary; the existence of God is an axiomatic truth, self-evident because of religious experience. The encounter with God in religious (revelatory) experience carries with it a certainty regarding the reality of the God whom we experience and who evokes our response of faith; that is, we know we have encountered something quite real even if God remains a mystery and unknown. The experience needs no proof beyond itself. For religious consciousness, the question is not whether or not God exists, but rather what the proper understanding or interpretation of this mysterious Being is. We want to know God's *character*, or what God is like.

For agnostics or atheists, no proof can establish the existence of God beyond question. The classical arguments for the existence of God, originating with the ancient Greek philosophers and revised by Christian theologians, sought to prove God's existence in a formal way. But since the time of Kant in the eighteenth century most philosophers and theologians have acknowledged that there are flaws or leaps of thought that render these so-called proofs failures as proofs in a technical sense.

At best these arguments, and arguments such as Kant's moral defense of faith, are reasonable hypotheses attempting to show that to believe in God's existence is not irrational or unreasonable. The "new atheists"[1] do not even engage such arguments; they simply attack religion as irrational without even studying how thoughtful believers seek to show the reasonableness of faith. The best we can do is to offer a coherent exposition of faith in God in relation to what science has taught us about the universe and its processes, and suggest that it offers a more adequate interpretation of our experience and our universe than the simple assertion that all is the result of blind chance. Even this will not persuade people who are "religiously" committed to atheism. And so it is fruitless to seek to prove God's existence. It is unnecessary for believers and will be rejected in any case by those committed to atheism.

The Doctrine of Creation out of Nothing

The heart of the Christian doctrine of creation is the teaching known as *creatio ex nihilo*, the position that God creates the universe out of nothing. Even though early Christian theologians acknowledged that this teaching cannot be found directly stated in scripture,[2] they nevertheless saw this as the biblical view, implicit in scripture, that needed to be upheld over against the Platonic idea of the co-eternity of God and matter. To accept this idea of the co-eternity of God and matter, Christian theologians held, would compromise God's absoluteness as Creator

---

[1] See, e.g., Richard Dawkins, *The God Delusion* (Boston: Houghton Mifflin, 2008); Christopher Hitchens, *God Is not Great: How Religion Poisons Everything* (London: Atlantic Books, 2008); Sam Harris, *The End of Faith: Religion, Terror, and the Future of Reason* (New York: W. W. Norton, 2004); and Daniel Dennett, *Breaking the Spell: Religion as a Natural Phenomenon* (New York: Viking, 2006). For an excellent critical analysis of these "new atheists," see John F. Haught, *God and the New Atheism: A Critical Response to Dawkins, Harris, and Hitchens* (Louisville, KY: Westminster John Knox Press, 2008).

[2] See Jaroslav Pelikan, *The Christian Tradition: A History of the Development of Doctrine*, vol. 1: *The Emergence of the Catholic Tradition (100–600)* (Chicago: University of Chicago Press, 1971), 36.

and would also compromise the basic and essential doctrine of monotheism. There can be nothing co-eternal with God as Creator. To say that matter is co-eternal with God would lead either to pantheism (identifying God and matter), which compromises God's transcendence and the absolute difference between the Creator and the creature, or it would lead to a dualism of God and matter that compromises God's absolute freedom, power, and will. Neither of these options seemed compatible with the God revealed in scripture.

And so against the mythological polytheism of Greco-Roman religions and the philosophical teaching of the co-eternity of God and matter, Christian theology taught absolute monotheism and creation out of nothing. The same Christian doctrines were important in combating internal Christian heresies, such as those of Marcion (d. ca. 160) and Gnosticism. Marcion taught that the God of the Old Testament was an evil creator God different from the good redeemer God revealed by Jesus. He, along with the Gnostics, devalued the material world (since it was the creation of an evil God).[3] In response to such views, orthodox Christianity taught that there is only one God, who created the world from nothing, and that the Creator is the Redeemer. These teachings are fundamental to the whole of Christian theology. The doctrine of creation out of nothing insists on the absolute difference between Creator and creature, but it also insists on the fundamental goodness of the physical world as the creation of God.

It is important to ask at this point if the doctrine of creation out of nothing necessarily implies that there was an absolute temporal beginning to the universe. At first glance it might seem that it does. But Thomas Aquinas in the thirteenth century showed that the Christian doctrine of creation is compatible with a universe that might be eternal, without a first moment in time. Thomas held that by reason alone we can demonstrate neither that the universe had a beginning nor that it is eternal.[4] This was a hotly debated question in Thomas's day,[5] and because the

---

[3] See ibid., 1:71–97.

[4] See Thomas Aquinas, *Summa Theologica*, Ia, Q. 46, a. 1.

[5] See Cyril Vollert, Lottie H. Kendzierski, and Paul M. Byrne, trans. and eds., *St. Thomas Aquinas, Siger of Brabant, St. Bonaventure: On*

arguments proving the existence of God were based on reason alone, Thomas crafted his arguments so that they worked even if one thought of the universe as eternal. In these arguments Thomas is thinking of causality in a hierarchical sense, not a linear one.[6] Examples may help to understand the difference. If I ask you what the cause of your existence is, you might be tempted to point to your parents, your grandparents, and so on in a linear and temporal chain of causes. But your existence is also dependent on the proper functioning of your body at every instant, on the oxygen that you need to keep your brain and body running, on the plants that provide that oxygen, and ultimately on the sun that pays the entropy debt for all living things. This is a hierarchical set of causes operative at each moment and upon which your existence depends. So, in a similar way, even if the created world is eternal (that is, never had a first moment), God is still its Creator in the sense that in each and every moment the contingent world is dependent on God as its First Cause, the necessary being. God has causal, creative influence at the base of each moment, not temporally prior to a first moment.[7]

Thomas showed, then, that the doctrine of creation out of nothing stresses the dependence of the universe on God as its sole ultimate cause but does not necessarily imply that the universe must have an absolute first moment. It is also true that Thomas believed revelation taught us that the universe *did* have a temporal beginning.[8] But I would argue that he, along with the entire tradition, read this into the scriptural texts that express faith in creation. Contemporary biblical scholarship does not find any

---

the Eternity of the World, Medieval Philosophical Texts in Translation, 16 (Milwaukee: Marquette University Press, 1964).

[6] See F. C. Copleston, *Aquinas* (Harmondsworth, England: Penguin Books, 1955), 122–24.

[7] It is this sense of hierarchical causality that Stephen Hawking overlooks when he assumes that if there is no first moment of time, then there is no need for a creator. See Stephen W. Hawking, *A Brief History of Time: From the Big Bang to Black Holes* (New York: Bantam Books, 1988), 140–41.

[8] See Thomas Aquinas, *Summa Theologica*, Ia, Q. 45, a. 1 and 2; Q. 46, a. 2 and 3.

clear affirmation of an absolute beginning to the universe in the Genesis creation narratives or the other places in scripture where creation is mentioned.

One would think that whether or not the universe had an absolute temporal beginning is an empirical question that science might resolve. But surprisingly, as we have seen, contemporary cosmology cannot answer this question. The scientific consensus is that our universe has existed and has been evolving for some 13.8 billion years. But we do not know whether the origin of our universe is *absolute* (that is, preceded by literally nothing in the philosophical sense), or whether that origin evolved out of some preceding state of some other universe or a preexisting quantum vacuum seething with energy. And the multiverse theory postulates an infinity of universes and the question of the origin of the multiverse does not even come up. The conclusion I draw from this is that at present scientific cosmology cannot tell us whether the universe has an absolute beginning or not. We know that our universe had a *relative* beginning some 13.8 billion years ago, but our knowledge stops at the condition making that relative beginning possible and science cannot explain that condition (the givenness of the singularity or the quantum vacuum).

The dominant theological position in the Christian tradition from the second through the nineteenth centuries has favored the view that creation out of nothing means that there was an absolute beginning to the universe, that God created out of nothing the first moment of time along with space and matter. But this dominant theological tradition, in my view, is not the only legitimate way of interpreting the Christian faith's affirmation of God as Creator, nor is it the only way of achieving the basic intent of the doctrine of *creatio ex nihilo*. Moreover, it is an idea only tenuously grounded in the biblical witness regarding God as Creator. Even though it is a long-favored tradition, in my judgment one cannot claim that the proper or orthodox understanding of the Christian faith *requires* the belief that the universe had an absolute beginning.

In fact, the majority of recent and contemporary theologians has departed from that dominant tradition and has held instead that the doctrine of *creatio ex nihilo* is really about the fundamental *relationship* between God and the universe, not about a temporal beginning.[9] Still, some theologians want to defend the dominant tradition in its assertion that there was an absolute beginning to the universe. Ted Peters, for example, has argued for retaining the notion of an absolute beginning as central to Christian theology and as better serving the dialogue between science and religion.[10] But despite Peters's arguments, I am not persuaded that either Christian faith or the conversation between religion and science is assisted by this claim. Although I believe that we may speculate—and I later develop my own speculative view—for the present I think we must leave this as an open question.

How Might We Understand God's Creative Activity?

We naturally would like to understand *how* God creates. So often the way people talk about creation makes it seem like a magical act, that God simply wills it and, poof, the universe comes into being. We must have great humility here, but we ought to be able to suggest some way of understanding how God creates that squares with our experience and with what we know of the universe through science. My own understanding has been deeply influenced by the philosophy of Alfred North Whitehead (1861–1947), the great English mathematician and

---

[9] See, e.g., the classic statement of Paul Tillich, *Systematic Theology*, 3 vols. (Chicago: University of Chicago Press, 1951/1957/1963), 1:252–54. See also Ian Barbour, *Religion and Science: Historical and Contemporary Issues* (San Francisco: HarperSanFrancisco, 1997), 201–2, 212–14; and David Kelsey, "The Doctrine of Creation from Nothing," in *Evolution and Creation*, ed. Ernan McMullin, University of Notre Dame Studies in the Philosophy of Religion 4 (Notre Dame, IN: University of Notre Dame Press, 1985), 176–96.

[10] See Ted Peters, "On Creating the Cosmos," in *Physics, Philosophy, and Theology: A Common Quest for Understanding*, ed. Robert John Russell, William R. Stoeger, SJ, and George V. Coyne, SJ, 273–96 (Vatican City State: Vatican Observatory, 1988); idem, "Cosmos as Creation," in *Cosmos as Creation: Theology and Science in Consonance*, ed. Ted Peters, 45–113 (Nashville: Abingdon Press, 1989); and idem, *God—The World's Future: Systematic Theology for a Postmodern Era* (Minneapolis: Fortress Press, 1992), 122–32.

philosopher. His philosophy is not easy to communicate in a simple way because he had a fondness for abstract thought, he developed a highly technical metaphysics, and he also developed an unusual technical vocabulary.[11] I will do my best to express the heart of his understanding of God and God's interaction with the universe in relatively simple and clear language. I focus first on God's role as Creator.

Long before the advent of chaos and complexity theories, Whitehead understood God's role as Creator to be deeply involved with possibility. In his view there could be no universe without order:

> It is not the case that there is an actual world which accidently happens to exhibit an order of nature. There is an actual world because there is an order in nature. If there were no order, there would be no world. Also since there is a world, we know there is an order.[12]

Whitehead understood order to require the organization of infinite abstract possibility. If every possibility were equally possible at each moment, we would have chaos in the philosophical sense, the complete absence of order. Order results from some sort of limitation on abstract possibility, "introducing contraries, grades, and oppositions."[13] Whitehead also committed himself to what he called the "ontological principle,"[14] the empirical demand that all explanations be referred somehow to some actual agent. Since all agencies in the universe presuppose the existence of the universe, and since the existence of the universe presupposes the

---

[11] For a more technical introduction to Whitehead's thought, see Thomas E. Hosinski, *Stubborn Fact and Creative Advance: An Introduction to the Metaphysics of Alfred North Whitehead* (Lanham, MD: Rowman and Littlefield, 1993).

[12] Alfred North Whitehead, *Religion in the Making* (New York: Macmillan, 1926), 104.

[13] Alfred North Whitehead, *Science and the Modern World* (New York: Macmillan, 1925), 256.

[14] See Alfred North Whitehead, *Process and Reality: An Essay in Cosmology*, corrected ed., ed. David Ray Griffin and Donald W. Sherburne (New York: The Free Press, 1978 [1929]), 18–19, 24, 40, 43, 244; and Hosinski, *Stubborn Fact and Creative Advance*, 20.

organization of possibilities, Whitehead found it necessary to affirm God as the actual agent of that organization. The above quotation ends with the statement, "The ordering entity is a necessary element in the metaphysical situation presented by the actual world."[15]

Whitehead called this aspect of God the "Primordial Nature" of God and defined it as the eternal and unconditioned grasping and valuation of all possibilities.[16] This is the foundational role of God as Creator because it is God's valuation of all possibilities that *organizes* them relative to God's aim and relates them to one another, thus forming the basis of order for all possible worlds. God's valuation of these possibilities organizes them by investing them with value relative to God's own aim. To put it simply, because of the way God values the possibilities, they are related in a graded order of value, from higher to lesser, and we might even say that some possibilities God abhors. This implies that the general order of the universe is an *aesthetic* order, an order of potential beauty and goodness. (Whitehead thought of goodness as a particular kind of beauty.) God's "vision" of possibility therefore constitutes the ultimate actual ground of order, value, and novelty; it is the ultimate actual source of all value and the general potentiality of the universe. This aspect of God is absolutely necessary for there to be any universe, any course of events at all.

Before pursuing this line of thought any further, I would like to point out two things. My first point relates to the Christian theological tradition. In a very different way Whitehead comes to basically the same position that the Augustinian tradition did on God as the ultimate source or cause of all value. That tradition, the reader will recall from our discussion of Anselm, held that there could be no lesser or limited instance of any "perfection," any good quality, without the prior existence of God as the infinite fullness of that perfection, since all finite instances of that quality to one degree or another participate in that perfection. Whitehead's

---

[15] Whitehead, *Religion in the Making*, 104; see also *Science and the Modern World*, 256–58.

[16] Whitehead, *Process and Reality*, 31. For other relevant texts and a more thorough discussion of the Primordial Nature of God, see Hosinski, *Stubborn Fact and Creative Advance*, 164–80.

analysis of God's valuation of all possibilities in essence implies that the agents of the universe can experience value only because possibilities come to us already invested with value that attracts or repels us to one degree or another. The finite agents of the universe react to the value already inherent in possibilities and thus participate in that value when they actualize a possibility. Although the path by which they each come to it differs greatly, the Augustinian tradition and Whitehead both affirm that God is the ultimate and infinite ground of all value.

The second point to which I want to call attention is how relevant Whitehead's understanding of God's relation to possibility is to the questions raised by chaos and complexity theory, and evolution as well. We saw in the last chapter that the mathematics used to analyze and understand dynamic systems indicates that there is a structure in possibility, the attractors and basins of attraction, that draw the dynamics of the system toward particular possible states. Stuart Kauffman argues that the simple forms of order that emerge in the development of complex systems are important for understanding how evolution works. But he does not address the issue of how mere possibilities, real but not actual things, can have a structure. And Simon Conway Morris, a paleontologist and evolutionary theorist, has argued that the phenomenon of evolutionary convergence may show that evolution favors certain "solutions," as he calls them, certain evolutionary pathways, rather than randomly wandering through the entire range of possibilities. Whitehead's way of thinking of the Primordial Nature of God as the grasping and valuation of all possibilities offers an explanation for how mere possibilities can have a structure and why certain possibilities in evolution may be more likely than others. This is God functioning as the ground of order. At the same time Whitehead's conception of the Primordial Nature of God shows that God is the ultimate source of all novel possibilities that are actualized over the course of evolution and over the course of the development of any dynamic system. Considering that Whitehead was dead long before chaos and complexity theories were developed, it is striking that his analysis of possibility and God's role in organizing it is compatible with what current research seems to be discovering.

If God is Creator in the sense of being the ultimate ground of order and the ultimate source of potentiality that makes the universe possible, how is God directly involved in the creation of each agent in the universe? The reader will recall that the official Roman Catholic teaching on evolution as related to divine creation states that while there are natural processes responsible for physical origins, God is the Creator of each individual in a direct way (through the infusion of the immortal soul in humans). Whitehead's philosophy can speak of God as Creator of every individual agent in the universe. It is important to understand at the outset that Whitehead conceives of God and the world in a dynamic relationship in which they interact in each moment. So creation is not something that happened "once upon a time" in the past; it is happening at each instant of the universe's existence, with the origin of each and every agent in the universe. It will be easiest to understand this by first speaking of human beings and then discussing how Whitehead applied this view to all agents in the universe. First, since every actual agent in the universe is an actualized possibility, one can understand that God's grasp of all possibilities includes a grasp of the potential standpoint of every possible agent in every possible universe at every possible moment of that agent's existence. In other words, God knows *as a possibility* exactly what situations we each face at each single instant of our lives. (We later discuss how God knows the *facts* of each moment of our lives.)

In each moment we inherit the energy of our existence from the physical processes of universe, but ultimately from God. At each moment God creates us by endowing us with all the possibilities open to us in the situation we face, with the drive to make something of ourselves at that moment (in other words, the drive to actualize one of the possibilities), and with freedom, our share in the divine life.[17] God creates us not by determining what we must be or do or say, or what events must occur, but rather by providing all that we need to create ourselves in that moment and leaving us free to complete our own creation. God seeks to attract us toward the best possibility as God has valuated the possibilities open to us. But each of us is free to actualize

---

[17] I am here departing from Whitehead's own view by revising his treatment of "creativity" in a way I explain below. For a technical treatment of what I have very simply summarized, see Hosinski, *Stubborn Fact and Creative Advance,* 155–80.

any of the possibilities open to that moment. God is present in each of us, empowering us and seeking to attract us toward actualizing the best possibilities. But we have freedom; we may be influenced by many things other than God's aim or will, and we may actualize even the possibilities that God values least or abhors. God has given us free will, and there is no guarantee that we will always use freedom in the best or even a good way. God creates us not by determining us but by *empowering* us, by giving us what we need to create ourselves. God does not create by controlling or determining our choices or our actions. Traditional Christian theology has long recognized this in holding that we humans each have free will. What is unique about Whitehead's view is that he ties this to creation *at each moment* and that he extends this to every agent in the universe.

We have seen that if we accept the truth revealed by evolution, we must recognize that we humans are part of nature, not somehow ontologically removed from it or above it. But this cuts both ways. If we are part of nature, then what we experience is a clue to what is present to one degree or another in all of nature. Whitehead firmly believed that we can take our own experience as telling us something about the whole of nature.[18] He extends freedom to every agent in the universe. He is not naive and recognizes that there is a great difference in the degree of freedom enjoyed by the various agents of the universe. But, influenced by what quantum theory seems to be telling us about nature at its most fundamental level, he argued that all agents in the universe have some degree of freedom, even if it is so minimal that we cannot ordinarily recognize it.[19] If we are unwilling to extend freedom this pervasively to all the agents of the universe, then we are faced with the very difficult problem of explaining how freedom can suddenly arise in a universe without it. It may also help to understand this if I mention that Whitehead does not attribute *consciousness* to all agents. Consciousness is restricted to animals; but experience, the power to feel, select, and actualize possibilities, and some degree of freedom are present in all agents, conscious or not, down to quantum events.

---

[18] See Alfred North Whitehead, *Modes of Thought* (New York: Macmillan, 1938), 156–58; idem, *Process and Reality*, 119.

[19] See Whitehead, *Process and Reality*, 254.

If all agents of the universe enjoy some degree of freedom, however minimal, then what I said above for humans is true of all agents in the universe, and this is exactly what Whitehead held. God is present in every single agent in the universe, empowering it and seeking to attract it and the universe as a whole toward actualizing the best possibilities. But all the agents of the universe enjoy some degree of (constrained) freedom; they may be influenced by many other things besides God's aim or will, precisely because God does not control which possibilities must be actualized or determine what must happen. The effects of efficient causation can constrain freedom enormously but do not totally eradicate it. And the possibilities that are in fact actualized in universal history are the result of how the agents of the universe exercise their freedom. The process of the universe's becoming, however constrained by order, is free.

There is another aspect to how God creates. In presenting to each agent all the possibilities relevant to its situation, including those that have never before been actualized, God "lures" the creative advance of the universe by the attractive force of the possibilities. The agents of the universe are not fated to the repetition of the same possibilities but can actualize new forms, develop new types of order, and can make of themselves something new in the universe. God uses novel possibilities as "lures" toward transcending what has been and reaching for what might be. It is this interaction between God as the ground of actuality and possibility and the freedom of the agents of the universe that results in a universe characterized by order but also by flexibility and creativity, so that it is constantly changing and developing in new ways while relying on the underlying basis of order and stability. God and the agents of the universe in their interaction are co-creators of the actual universe.

This view of creation goes a long way toward helping us understand the ambiguity of the world and of our experience. Life is filled with suffering, pain, and evil, as well as beauty, joy, and goodness. Terrible things happen: innocent children suffer from leukemia and other forms of cancers and terrible diseases; floods, earthquakes, hurricanes, and wildfires ravage the world; accidents, diseases, and death befall humans and other living creatures alike; and so on. Why does God permit this? Why doesn't God do something to prevent it? These common questions and protests against God are based in the unspoken and uncritically accepted idea that God can and ought to control all the events of nature. But if God creates not by determining or controlling things but by empowering the agents of the universe to create themselves, then we can expect that things will not always turn out well. If the agents of the universe are free, then it is they, in their freedom, that determine what occurs; they are co-creators of the universe.

There will be competing aims and goals among the various agents of the universe, and conflicts and oppositions will emerge. Hence, the sufferings within the world are due to how the agents of the universe exercise their freedom and pursue their own aims. Traditional Christian theology has long recognized that God gives humans free will and does not determine their choices, decisions, and actions. Consequently, the evil humans do to one another is due to them and not to God. Whitehead, recognizing that we are part of nature, argues that freedom to some extent characterizes all the agents of the universe. Anglican physicist and theologian John Polkinghorne adopts a similar view and calls this "free process," an extension of the "free will" defense of God's goodness in the face of evil.[20] God does all God can do to lead the universe in positive directions, but God cannot prevent evil and suffering without destroying the freedom with which God endows the agents of the universe. This requires that we understand God in an unusual and yet not untraditional way.

God's Restraint, Humility, and Self-Limitation

Recognizing that God does not control or determine our choices, decisions, and actions leads us to recognize God's self-restraint. If we believe that God is all-powerful, omnipotent, and also believe that God gives humans free will, then we must conclude that God freely chooses to limit God's own power so that we might be free. Traditional Christian theology has long recognized that there is a limitation on God's power, but it is a

---

[20] See John Polkinghorne, *Science and Providence: God's Interaction with the World* (Boston: Shambhala, 1989; reprint: West Conshohocken, PA: Templeton Press, 2005), chap. 5.

limitation that results from God's own choice. The all-powerful One freely chooses to restrain that power and endows humans with free will. Whitehead extended freedom to every agent in the universe, but he did not believe that freedom was a gift from God. For reasons that are a bit too complicated to enter into here, he believed that the limitation on God's power was "built into" the metaphysical system, so to speak. He believed that every agent in the universe ("actual entities" in his technical vocabulary) inherently enjoyed *creativity*, the drive to become something new for itself. In his philosophy, freedom is correlated with creativity. So in his metaphysics, freedom is inherent in the universe, a function of the creativity driving all processes of becoming; it does not come as a gift from God.[21]

In my judgment this position is incompatible with the Christian understanding of God and reality; it compromises what Christianity intends to affirm in its doctrines of monotheism and *creatio ex nihilo*. Consequently, I agree with a revision of Whitehead first suggested by the great American Protestant theologian Langdon Gilkey (1919–2004).[22] Following his teacher, Paul Tillich, Gilkey argued that we must regard creativity as the divine life itself, not as a force independent of God. Doing this allows one to retain much of Whitehead's philosophy, but enables a revision of it that makes it compatible with what Christianity affirms in its doctrines of monotheism and creation from nothing. Creativity, as in Whitehead's philosophy, is the force or power driving the processes of becoming of all agents in the universe, and it is the power or force driving the becoming of the universe as a whole. But it is the power of God's own life graciously shared with the creatures of the universe, not a force independent of God. This means that the freedom enjoyed by all agents in the universe is a gift, part of the endowment with which God creates each and every agent.

If God wishes the universe to be free, then God must limit God's own power. Therefore, the freedom with which the agents

---

[21] See Whitehead, *Process and Reality*, 7, 31, 88, 225, 349; and Hosinski, *Stubborn Fact and Creative Advance*, 207–11, 215–18, 244–46.

[22] See Landon B. Gilkey, *Reaping the Whirlwind: A Christian Interpretation of History* (New York: Seabury Press, 1976), 112–14, 248–51, 300–318.

of the universe create themselves displays God's humility. If one thinks of the incarnation of God in Jesus Christ in this context, the humility of God becomes even more obvious. Jesus did not seek to control people's behavior or force them to do God's will. He held before us an ideal toward which we might strive: the vision of the kingdom of God, marked by the beauty of mercy, compassion, healing, forgiveness, and love. He asked us to give our hearts to this possibility and modeled it for us in his own ministry of healing and forgiveness. He sought to attract us to it by his teachings and parables. But he left us free to respond as we will. If we truly believe that God was incarnate in Jesus, then in him we see what God is like: a non-coercive power who seeks to attract us to the good, but who puts himself in our hands, humble and vulnerable to our choices. This is totally compatible with the theology of God's self-emptying *(kenosis)* so powerfully expressed in the ancient Christian hymn quoted by Paul in his Letter to the Philippians (2:6–8).

Existence as Participation in the Divine Life

The Philippians passage concerning God's self-emptying implies that God chose to enter into human life in a unique way. But as I have already begun to indicate, and as Nicholas of Cusa argued so long ago, God is present in every agent in the universe, and every agent in the universe lives by participating in the divine life. I believe that the best way to understand creation is to think of it as God sharing the divine life with all agents in the universe, all creatures, not just with humans.

Long before I had read much theology, I happened to read Whitehead's book *Religion in the Making*, and one sentence in it has haunted me ever since. Whitehead writes: "The world lives by its incarnation of God in itself."[23] This sentence ought to evoke wonder in us, for it is saying that the becoming of the universe and of every creature in it really is participation in the divine life.[24] We live out of the God who dwells within us. We

---

[23] Whitehead, *Religion in the Making*, 156.

[24] This is one reason why I believe Whitehead subverted his own insight when he treated creativity as a force independent of God.

saw in Chapter 3 that throughout the Christian theological tradition this same truth has been affirmed in different ways. The
tradition has been saying for centuries that God is in all things
and that the world lives by participating in the divine life. This
conviction is rooted, I believe, in the teachings of Jesus, because
it coheres so well with the image or metaphor Jesus used to refer to God: Father. If God is Father, then all of creation is to be
understood as God's children; the life of a child, we intuitively
understand, comes from and participates in the life of the parent. Jesus' understanding of God as Father implies that we may
understand the act of creation to be God sharing the divine life
with the universe.

I do not know that there is a better metaphor or analogy to
assist our understanding of creation than a parent sharing life
with a child. A child is a life that comes from the parents' life,
but it is other than the parent. With its first cry it asserts its autonomy, its needs and wants, its freedom as other. Every parent
knows the paradox that is a child: dependent and needing care,
yet free to assert itself and pursue its own will. The wise parent
does not try to suppress or crush that freedom and will, for to
do so would damage the child in horrible ways. Instead, the wise
parent tries to guide the free self-development of the child, to
persuade the child's action toward the good. Analogously, God's
sharing of the divine life allows the universe to be other and
endows it with its limited share in the autonomy and freedom
of the divine life. As a parent seeks to guide the development of
the child, so God seeks to guide the development of the universe.
But as a parent must ultimately accept what the child chooses
to become, so God, in respecting the freedom that is the sharing
in the divine life, must accept what the agents of the universe
choose to make of themselves. But as we will see in Chapter 8,
God can heal and lead the world beyond the tragedies and evils
that may come about. This analogical understanding of God's
creative relation to the universe is coherent with the implications
of the teachings of Jesus about God as expressed in many of the
parables of the kingdom, especially the parable of the Prodigal
Son (Lk 15:11–32).

We saw in the last chapter that physics teaches us that the
universe is fundamentally energy, which can take on many forms,
including becoming matter. And we saw that theories of the

origin of the universe all assume the energy of the universe but cannot explain it. Whichever theory of the universe's origin we prefer, the ultimate philosophical conclusion is the same: science must assume the energy, must have it given, and cannot explain where that energy comes from or why it is there. I pointed out earlier that the same sort of assumption occurs in arguments seeking to prove the existence of God: we cannot explain God, but give us God and the universe becomes intelligible. I suggested then that perhaps it is possible to claim that a proper *theological* interpretation of the energy constituting the universe is that it is a sharing or participation in the life of God. I do not mean this in a pantheistic sense. The universe is not God. But just as in the incarnation God chose to share our life, perhaps the energy of the universe is God's gift of allowing us and all agents of the universe to share in God's life. The universe does not exhaust the life of God, and is not God, but as Nicholas of Cusa said, it unfolds from God and is enfolded by God. If this is the case, then creation from nothing really means creation from nothing other than God's own life. This is why I said earlier that we inherit the energy of our lives at each moment from the natural physical processes of the universe, but ultimately from God.

Not only is the *energy* a share in the divine life, but so is *what God enables us to do* with that energy. If we recall how God creates, we can see that God enables every agent in the universe to do in a limited way what God does as Creator. God creates by organizing and valuating all possibilities, placing a condition on them so that an actual course of events is made possible. God endows every agent in the universe with freedom and with all its relevant possibilities, allowing it to grasp the inherent value of the possibilities relative to its situation and its own freedom to actualize one of the possibilities. The freedom God shares with creatures includes the aim at actualizing some possibility in and for themselves. All of this allows each agent in the universe to do in a limited way what God does. Because it is provided with its relevant possibilities and its freedom and aim, every agent is enabled to select from among a group of relevant possibilities on the basis of how that agent valuates those possibilities. The possibility it chooses reflects its preference, and the actualization of that preference establishes a condition affecting future agents, limiting them and perhaps opening the way for a novel course of events. In short, every agent in the universe establishes conditions for the future world by how it reacts to the possibilities open to it, just as God's grasping and valuation of all possibilities sets conditions on the course of actual events. In this way every agent in the universe is co-creator with God of the actual universe. Its creativity, in a limited way, mirrors God's infinite creativity.

To sum this up, God's creative activity makes possible free and creative creatures that mirror God's own freedom and creativity and participate, in a limited way, even in God's own autonomy. "The world lives by its incarnation of God in itself." When one continues to reflect on Whitehead's amazing statement, we can see that it is God who holds all things together, who sustains at each moment each agent in the universe in its relationships to all others, for it is the energy of the universe that binds all things together and that energy, I believe, is God sharing the power of the divine life with the universe. Moreover, God is the source of all novel possibilities and God assists the creative advance of the world with the "lure" of novel possibilities, so that the world is not deadened by order but is creative and flexible in its ability to adopt new forms and to arrive at emergent forms of higher-level order and complexity. God creates by organizing and valuating all possibilities, thereby establishing the basic order necessary for any universe. But God also creates by endowing each agent in the universe with what it needs to create itself: its relevant possibilities, its drive to actualize some possibility, and its freedom. God creates the universe as a whole and each agent in the universe individually. And creation is at root a sharing of the divine life with all the creatures of the universe. It is the divine life that holds all things together and enables the existence and creative advance of the universe and all its agents. Truly, there is, as Ilia Delio has said, "divine incarnational energy at the heart of cosmic evolution."[25]

---

[25] Ilia Delio, *Making All Things New: Catholicity, Cosmology, Consciousness* (Maryknoll, NY: Orbis Books, 2015), xiv.

Chapter 7

How Does God Act?

In this chapter I study the question of how God acts, which is traditionally known as the doctrine of divine providence. When creation is thought of as a singular event that took place in the past, the doctrine of providence concerns God's continuing involvement with creation over the course of history. If, however, one thinks of creation occurring at each moment, then the doctrines of creation and providence actually coalesce. Discussing them separately, however, enables us to consider additional questions not yet addressed, specifically the question of how God acts in the context of the dialogue between religion and science.[1]

Criteria for a Theory of Divine Action

Before suggesting a theory of divine action, it is important to have a clear idea of the criteria such a theory ought to satisfy and by which it ought to be judged. Some theories of divine action being discussed in the current dialogue between religion and

---

[1] For an extensive discussion of providence and divine action that focuses on human experience and history and uses a revised version of Whitehead's metaphysics, see Langdon Gilkey, *Reaping the Whirlwind: A Christian Interpretation of History* (New York: The Seabury Press, 1976).

science allow science to dominate the nature of the theory.[2] In contrast, I believe that a theory of divine action ought to satisfy certain religious criteria as well as scientific ones. I first outline what I see as necessary religious criteria in a Christian context.

Religious and Theological Criteria

For Christian theology, Jesus Christ must be the key to understanding how God acts. If we take this seriously, then any successful theory of divine action ought to meet several criteria centering on Jesus Christ. I briefly state the criteria and their justification here and employ them later in the chapter.

1. Since Christian faith believes that Jesus Christ has taught us correctly about God, then *the theory ought to be compatible with the implications of Jesus' teachings about God*. This is especially the case if we believe God is incarnate in Jesus Christ.
2. Since Christian faith believes that God has acted in and through Jesus Christ, then *a theory of divine action ought to be compatible with the life and actions of Jesus Christ*.
3. Since Christian faith holds that God became incarnate in a unique way in Jesus Christ, then *a theory of divine action ought to be compatible with the dogmatic statement regarding the person of Jesus Christ* (that is, the theory ought to be compatible with a defensible interpretation of the Chalcedonian dogma). If the incarnation is a divine act, then our theory of how God acts ought to be compatible with the Christian community's understanding of that act.
4. Finally, since Christian faith believes the person of Jesus Christ to be the definitive revelation of God, and since revelation is understood to be a divine act, then *a theory of divine action ought to be compatible with the theological understanding of how revelation occurs*.

---

[2] See Russell Re Manning, "Introduction," in *Science and Religion in the Twenty-First Century*, ed. Russell Re Manning and Michael Byrne, The Boyle Lectures (London: SCM Press, 2013), xliii. He points out this asymmetry in the dialogue between religion and science.

Scientific Criteria

It is important for Christian theology to work out its interpretations of Christian faith in a way compatible with what science has learned about the universe and its processes. Therefore, our theory of divine action ought to meet two criteria in relation to science.

1. A successful theory of divine action ought to be compatible with the major, well-established scientific theories of the universe and its natural processes. This is a very general criterion that will have several specific implications. For example, it means that a theory of divine action ought not assert a form of divine action that violates the law of conservation of energy (since science has never observed a violation of this law). This, in turn, means that successful theories of divine action will be noninterventionist in nature; they will not assert that God suspends the laws of nature and intervenes directly from "outside" the universe. To forestall a potential objection, this criterion does not assume that science can make no mistakes, nor does it assume that science has achieved a complete explanation of the universe. But a theory of divine action that flies in the face of well-established scientific understanding cannot be persuasive.

2. *A successful theory of divine action ought to be able to offer some persuasive reason for why science fails to find any acts of God in its examination of the universe and its processes.* If there is a God who acts, why is it that science can find no traces of divine action? This has often been used as "proof" that religious claims about divine action are baseless. Any theory of divine action must confront this question.

The Religious Ground of the Theory and Types of Divine Action

It is somewhat controversial to claim that we know what Jesus taught about God. New Testament scholars are not in agreement about which teachings of Jesus in the Gospels originated with him and which may have been modified or added by the early Christian community. Yet there is enough of a consensus regarding the basic outlines of Jesus' teachings to draw some conclusions on this topic.

Jesus preached and enacted the kingdom of God, a rich symbol for how God is, how God acts, and how we ought to act in order to be under God's "rule." Jesus presents the kingdom of God as an ideal, a complex possibility held before his hearers as a beautiful and holy ideal for human action. In this sense it is always future, yet to be actualized. But at the same time it is present, actualized, whenever anyone does the will of God. Jesus himself actualizes it by enacting his teachings in his healings and ministry to the poor, the oppressed, and the excluded. Through his teachings and actions Jesus presents God as life-giving, compassionate, merciful, forgiving, healing, and loving to all. In his parables and his actions alike we see an understanding of God that envisions God exercising power in a self-limited, not coercive, way: (1) through the attractive and persuasive power of ideals (as in Jesus' teaching ministry itself); and (2) through the power of forgiveness, mercy, compassion, healing, redemption, and restoring to life.[3] In his parables Jesus presents God acting in hidden ways, in and through the ordinary processes of nature, in the lives of birds and the beauty of flowers, in the growth of crops. God judges the world, recognizing evil and tragedy for what they are and suffering their effects, but God can overcome them and transform them with compassionate and healing wisdom and love. God's salvific will and redemptive love are truly universal, saving all creatures, including what we humans judge to be unlovable and unredeemable.[4]

Even this compressed summary of what I discussed in Chapter 1 shows that we must distinguish between two principal

---

[3] A classic example of the latter in Jesus' teaching is the parable of the Prodigal Son (Lk 15:11–32), and, in his actions, the treatment of the woman caught in adultery (Jn 8:3–11), among many others.

[4] I realize this last statement is controversial. But I am basing it on what I believe to be the implications of Jesus' teachings as I analyzed them in Chapter 1. The profound theological reflection in Wisdom 11:23—12:1 also expresses this view.

types of divine action, which we may express in two questions: (1) How does God *influence* events? and (2) How does God *respond* to events? Because there is an ongoing dynamic interaction between God and the universe, how God responds to any event will influence future events. Thus the two questions, while distinct, are truly related. A theory of divine action must be able to distinguish between them but also relate them into a single coherent theory. I deal with how God influences events in this chapter and discuss how God responds to events in the following chapter (on salvation), where I also show the coherence of these two discussions.

Finally, we must also distinguish between God's response to any individual event and God's response to the collective that is the entire history of the universe. Jesus' teachings and life exhibit the conviction that some day God will bring the kingdom of God to completion and fulfillment. This sort of question, dealing with the ultimate fate of the universe, is related to the traditional topic of eschatology, and I will briefly address this in the Conclusion.

How God Influences Events

How God influences events is actually identical with how God creates. The doctrines of creation and providence are actually speaking of the same divine activity when one ceases thinking of creation as an event that happened only once ("upon a time") at the origin of the universe. In my judgment the revised Whiteheadian theory of divine creative action through the organization, valuation, and presentation of possibilities meets all the criteria for a theory of divine action, and does so better than any alternative theory with which I am acquainted. I will summarize this theory and its implications, address some objections to it, and discuss how it meets the criteria by which we must evaluate the theory.

What does it mean to say that God acts through the organization, valuation, and presentation of possibilities? How does this influence events in the actual world? We saw in the last chapter that Whitehead understands the Primordial Nature of God to be the unconditioned grasping and valuation of all possibilities or potentials. It is this function of God that establishes the basic order necessary for there to be any course of actual events, any universe whatsoever. The order is the outcome of God's valuation of the possibilities, relative to God's aim. This establishes not just the general metaphysical conditions and more specific conditions governing our universe,[5] but also the relevance or irrelevance of every possibility to any particular standpoint in the universe. *Every* possibility is included in God's organization and valuation of possibilities for the universe. This means that for any standpoint in the universe—which is, of course, a possibility that can be envisioned apart from any experience of the actual course of events—the relevant possibilities are graded in an order of value that reflects God's preference. There will be one possibility for that specific situation that God values most highly, with varying valuations for the other possibilities, including one God values least (or abhors).

God endows each actual agent of the universe with its relevant possibilities at the beginning of its process of becoming. The free and autonomous becoming of an actual agent in its situation is influenced by the attractiveness of the possibilities; that is, the possibilities "lure" the agent to actualize them. The actual agent has an "initial aim," part of the endowment it receives from God. This aim is the drive to become something, to actualize a possibility with its energy. This aim initially orients the agent toward the possibility God values most highly, because this aim also constitutes the agent's initial standard of value, enabling it to experience and respond to value, and this is initially in harmony with God's valuation of the possibilities open to that agent in its situation.[6] But that agent's process of becoming is influenced by

---

[5] Whitehead argues that God's Primordial Nature is responsible not just for the general metaphysical conditions, but also for more specific conditions such as the dimensional character of the actual world. See Alfred North Whitehead, *Science and the Modern World* (New York: Macmillan, 1925), 255–57; and idem, *Process and Reality: An Essay in Cosmology*, rev. ed., ed. David Ray Griffin and Donald W. Sherburne (New York: The Free Press, 1978 [1929]), 40, 46, 87–88, 108, 164, 207, 247, 257, 344–45.

[6] This is a simple summary of Whitehead's technical analysis of how each actual agent (actual entity) in the universe begins its process of becoming by receiving its aim from God. For a detailed explanation of this, see Thomas E. Hosinski, *Stubborn Fact and Creative Advance: An*

many factors in addition to God's Primordial Nature; all *past* agents to one degree or another influence the present agent in its process of becoming. These other influences may exert a higher relative weight than the influence of God's valuation of the possibilities. The becoming agent is free to alter its aim and select and actualize any of the possibilities open to it, even the one God values least (or abhors). This is its freedom, which is God's gift to all actual agents of participation in God's own life. The gift of a share in the autonomy, freedom, and creativity of the divine life means that God cannot coerce the choice of possibilities. God exercises influence by seeking to persuade through the lure of true and ultimate beauty. Thus, although God's influence on every actual agent or entity is necessary for that agent to become, it is not determinative. In the end the actual agent's own "preference" among the possibilities is the "reason" for what it becomes, for what possibility it has actualized in itself, and that preference can be influenced in a variety of ways.

The theory of divine creative action at each moment means that *with regard to observable events, God acts in the universe only through and with the cooperation of the agents of the universe.* That is, there is no *observable* act of God apart from the acts of the creatures of the universe. Every event is the act of some agent or agents in the universe (*actual entities* and *societies* in Whitehead's metaphysical terms) and God acts *internally* in the becoming of every actual agent, by making it really possible and "luring" it toward the possibility God values most highly. God does not act *externally* upon the agents of the universe as a competing agent. When an actual agent actualizes the possibility God values most highly for that situation, it can rightly be called an act of God; but it is also rightly understood to be the act of the agent itself within the universe. I repeat here that God acts as Creator by empowering the actual agents of the universe to create themselves, giving them all they need to complete their own creation. And so God and the actual agents of the universe are co-creators of the universe. This implies that God can bring about no event except through the cooperation of the actual agents of the universe.

Introduction to the Metaphysics of Alfred North Whitehead (Lanham, MD: Rowman and Littlefield, 1993), 164–76.

It should be noted that this mode of divine action is the same for all types of actual agents or entities, at all levels of complexity in the universe. However simple or complex the actual agents are, God seeks to attract their freedom toward actualizing the best possibility for their specific situations. This theory is thus able to account for divine action at all levels of complexity, from the moments of human decisions, through the moments in animals' lives, through complex dynamic systems, down to the simplest level of quantum events. It should also be noted that even for actual agents capable of consciousness, such as the majority of a human being's moments of experience, the divine action occurs at the most basic levels of the process of becoming[7] and is usually not consciously grasped. Only in extraordinary moments of religious awareness are humans conscious of the divine action upon them, and even then it is not always clear that this feeling is a grasping of *God's* influence upon that moment. We can be misled and can even mistake our own desire for the will of God. But authentic religious experience does claim to grasp the presence and influence of God upon us and upon events. Only in these truly exceptional moments of experience are we conscious of God's influence.

Finally, it is important to draw out the implications of this theory of divine action for an understanding of God's power. The theory implies that we must revise the traditional attribute of absolute divine omnipotence, or at least how that attribute was often interpreted. In creating and influencing events God exercises power by making every actual agent in the universe possible and influencing their processes of becoming toward the best possibilities; but God does not determine what any actual agent will make of itself, or be, or do (more technically, what possibility it will actualize in itself). God creates every actual agent as an autonomous and free agent (within the limits set by God's eternal valuation and organization of possibilities), so that it truly participates in the divine life and enjoys its limited share in the divine autonomy and freedom. The actual agents of the universe create themselves on this divinely given ground. God *empowers* but does not use power to force or coerce the

---

[7] For a full technical discussion of Whitehead's analysis of the process of becoming and its different levels of complexity, see ibid., 46–127.

agents' self-creation. Thus, with regard to God's influence on events, God's power is limited to luring the freedom of the actual agents involved toward the best possibilities. God cannot, solely by God's own will, make any event occur.

This limitation on God's power seems to many people to make God in effect powerless. It seems to contradict the traditional interpretation of divine omnipotence and make God seem to be less than what God ought to be. It seems to say that God has less power than even a child. After all, even very young children can impose their wills on things by throwing rocks and toys and pulling up plants and molding clay. Yet this theory of divine action says that God can do none of these things, that God's will cannot be imposed on the agents of the universe. This leads many people to object that such a portrait of God and God's power is simply not "Godlike" enough to be believed. It seems to be totally unorthodox.

In response to such objections I make several observations. First, Christian theology has long held that God is not a being or an agent in the world like the beings or agents with which we are familiar in the universe. Simply to magnify to infinity the modes of action of the agents of the universe and imagine that we have understood God is a category mistake that does not respect God's otherness. As the Prophet Isaiah has it, "My thoughts are not your thoughts, nor are your ways my ways, says the Lord" (Is 55:8). And St. Paul reports as a word of the Lord, "[My] power is made perfect in weakness" (2 Cor 12:9).[8] This very thought-provoking understanding of power seems to capture exactly how God's power takes the form of empowerment and persuasion toward the good, not force or coercion. The father in the parable of the Prodigal Son (Lk 15:11–32) illustrates this perfectly; the father empowers his younger son by giving him his inheritance but does not seek to control his decisions and actions.

Second, I submit that in its need to accept and understand the crucifixion of Jesus Christ as an event that in some sense happened to God, Christian theology has very good reason for

---

[8] The NRSV omits the bracketed "my" but reports in a note that other ancient authorities have "my" in the text, as the older RSV had translated this verse.

accepting that God is in a sense powerless in relation to the world. If nothing else had led us to question divine omnipotence, or its traditional interpretation, then surely, in light of the central christological claims of Christian faith, the crucifixion ought to give us cause to entertain the idea that God makes Godself vulnerable to the agents of the universe.

Third, the theory of divine action I am presenting and defending here does not say that God's will cannot be achieved in the universe. It says that God can accomplish what God wills only when the actual agents of the universe cooperate with God's will. God is always acting within each and every actual agent in the universe. And in those cases in which the agents of the universe actualize the possibility God values most highly, God's will is accomplished. But absent that cooperation of the agents in the universe, God does not impose God's will.

Fourth, to say that God does not act with coercive power in the universe does not make God completely powerless. As we know from our own experience, persuasion can be quite powerful in influencing our free decisions and actions. God can influence events with persuasive power through the attractive-ness of the possibilities God presents to the actual agents of the universe. We ought not underestimate the surprising effects such persuasive influence can have.

Finally, to hold that there is a limit on the divine power is not unorthodox. As I mentioned in the last chapter, the orthodox tradition has always held that God limits God's omnipotence in allowing humans free will. The theory of divine creation and action I have presented holds that God has endowed *all* of the created world, not just humans, with a limited share in God's own freedom. For too long we have supposed that only humans have such limited freedom and autonomy. God has given these gifts to the entire universe, not just us. If this reflects God's desire to have a universe of "free process," as John Polkinghorne has called it,[9] then it follows that God freely chooses to limit God's omnipotence so that the world might be free. The limitation on God's power is a *self*-limitation, a freely chosen divine act of

---

[9] See John Polkinghorne, *Science and Providence: God's Interaction with the World* (Boston: Shambhala, 1989; reprint edition, West Conshohocken, PA: Templeton Press, 2005), chap. 5.

humility and love. The decision to create a universe that shares in the creativity, freedom, and autonomy of the divine life reflects God's gracious generosity and willingness to be vulnerable. To determine what actual agents of the universe will be, to be coercive in determining what events will occur, would in effect violate God's own life by violating the creatures' participation in it; and it would violate God's own creative intention and decision to make possible a universe that lives out of and shares in God's own life. It would be God at odds with Godself.

God uses power in beautiful ways to empower and to persuade toward ultimate beauty and goodness. But God does not use power in ugly ways to force, to coerce. No one appreciates being acted on with coercive force. Why would we imagine that God would use power in distasteful and ugly ways? We can imagine that theoretically God could have chosen to organize possibilities in some other way, to have created some other kind of universe. We can imagine God to have *theoretical* absolute omnipotence. But the *actuality* of God is a self-limited power that makes possible a universe participating in God's own creativity, freedom, and autonomy. I would call to mind here what we saw in Chapter 3, that Thomas Aquinas taught that God wanted secondary causes (that is, all causes other than God) to share in the dignity of causation.[10] God, therefore, cannot intervene coercively in such a universe without compromising God's own creative intention and God's own life. To put it in terms of Christian theology, were God to intervene coercively in the universe, God would cease being the God revealed in the cross of Jesus Christ.

The Test against the Religious and Theological Criteria

Because this theory of divine action seems quite novel in comparison to the traditional affirmations of Christian theology, the test against the religious and theological criteria I set out at the beginning of this chapter will help to show that it really does cohere with the Christian tradition.

---

[10] Thomas Aquinas, *Summa Theologica*, Ia, Q. 22, a. 3.

1. This revised Whiteheadian theory of divine action is compatible with the implications of Jesus' teachings regarding how God acts. Several of Jesus' parables speak of divine action in a way that can be interpreted as the presentation of possibilities for the world's action; the parables of the Sower (Mk 4:3–9 and parallels) and of the Wheat and Darnel (Mt 13:24–30) come immediately to mind. Seed is a natural symbol of possibility and hope; the seed carries in itself the possibility of a mature plant and grain (in food crops), and when one plants seed one hopes for that desired outcome. In both of these parables the seed is "presented" or sown, and the sower awaits the earth's (or the world's) response. So to think of God as presenting the world with possibilities and having differing outcomes (as in both parables) is compatible with how Jesus spoke of divine action in at least some of his parables.

In a number of sayings and parables Jesus implies that God acts in hidden ways through natural processes. The Father feeds the birds of the air and clothes the lilies of the field (Mt 6:26, 28–29; Lk 12:24, 27), yet Jesus clearly understood that birds work for their food and that the blooming of flowers is a natural process. His point is that God provides the food for the birds through natural means and the beauty that results from the natural process of the flowers' growth and blooming is ultimately to be understood as due to God. Jesus expresses this same conviction that God's action is in and through natural processes in his statement that the Father causes the sun to shine and the rain to fall on the just and the unjust alike (Mt 5:43–45). Sunshine and rain, of course, are natural processes and necessary for growing food crops. Jesus' point is that they are ultimately God's gifts, and God does not withhold these necessary gifts from anyone. This is totally compatible or coherent with understanding that God empowers all agents in the universe, whether they do God's will or not. We should note that these statements clearly show the connection between creation and providence, since through natural processes God gives the gift of life and cares for living things.

Likewise, several of Jesus' parables speak of the kingdom of God, or God, hidden and active within the ordinary, within natural processes: the parables of the Mustard Seed (Mk 4:30–32 and parallels), the Seed Growing Secretly (Mk 4:26–29), and the

Leaven (Mt 13:33; Lk 13:20–21) all express this understanding. The parable of the Leaven, in particular, as well as the parable of the Talents (Mt 25:14–30; Lk 19:12–27) also imply that God's kingdom grows and has its influence through human cooperation (the woman who kneaded the leaven into the dough, the servants who invested their master's talents). Finally, many parables imply that God's will is presented to the world, but humans are free to actualize that will or not (as in the short parable of the Two Sons asked by their father to work in his vineyard [Mt 21:28–31]).

2. Equally important, a revised Whiteheadian theory of divine action is quite compatible with what we know of Jesus' actions and life. Jesus did not seek to change the world through coercive force. Instead, he proclaimed the kingdom of God, a rich symbol representing how God is, how God acts, and how we ought to act in order to be under God's "rule." Jesus proclaims it as a possibility and an ideal, but also as fact, as present to some degree whenever anyone does the will of God. Thus one of Jesus' principal activities, his teaching, is the presentation of the beautiful and holy possibility of what we might make of ourselves and our world if we acted in accord with God's will. And his enactment of that vision in his own ministry shows that it is also present whenever people act toward each other as God acts toward us all. While there is a clear sense that God has the initiative and will one day consummate the kingdom, there can be little doubt that in Jesus' view it is also true that humans can assist in the actualization of the kingdom through their own free decisions, cooperating with God's initiatives. The presence of the kingdom is always God's act, but it becomes present through the ordinary processes of nature and free human acts, most especially Jesus' own free actions.

Jesus' free acceptance of his arrest and execution is also relevant here, because it illustrates God's willingness to be vulnerable to the choices of the agents in the universe. I will deal with other aspects of Jesus' actions, most especially his acts of forgiveness and healing, in the next chapter.

3. I stated above that because Christian faith holds that God is present and active in Jesus Christ, a successful theory of divine action ought to be in harmony with a defensible interpretation of the Chalcedonian dogma concerning the person of Jesus Christ. While limitations of space prevent a thorough defense of this

position here, I briefly point out how a revised Whiteheadian theory of divine action is in basic accord with this dogma.

We saw in Chapter 2 that in the christological disputes leading to the Council of Chalcedon, the Alexandrian party stressed the divine initiative in the incarnation, while the Antiochene party stressed the necessity of human cooperation (Jesus' perfect obedience). It can be argued that the Chalcedonian dogma, in its compromise statement (the definition of faith), sought to preserve the truth in both these positions. This is further supported by the fact that the Third Council of Constantinople (680 CE), the last of the ecumenical councils before the major divisions within Christianity, reaffirmed Jesus' truly human nature by rejecting monothelitism, the view that Jesus Christ has only one will (that of the divine Logos or Word of God). The council affirmed that Jesus Christ has two wills, one of them truly and completely human, the other truly and completely divine. Therefore, it seems to me a legitimate interpretation of the Chalcedonian dogma to hold that the incarnation occurred only because of the divine initiative, on the one hand, and the cooperation of Jesus' human will (his obedience to the will of the Father) on the other. If the central christological claim of the Christian faith recognizes the necessity of human cooperation in the very occurrence of the incarnation, then a theory of divine action holding that observable divine actions always occur with the cooperation of the agents of the universe can claim to be in harmony with this central Christian dogma.

4. This theory of divine action is also in harmony with the contemporary theological interpretation of how revelation occurs. Revelation, of course, is understood to be a divine act, God reaching out to humans to reveal Godself to us in revelatory encounter. Contemporary theology holds that revelation always occurs through some medium, whether a person, a natural event, a historical event, or a person's own inner experience. The Exodus experience provides examples of all of these. The revelation of God's power to the Egyptians first takes the form of the ten plagues, most of which, even as recorded, are natural events. The Hebrews' final escape from the Egyptians occurs in the crossing of the Sea of Reeds, a historical event. God's will, the revelation of the Law, comes to the Israelites through Moses. And, contrary to a literalist reading of Exodus 19—20, Moses receives God's

revelation of the Law through his own inner reflections concerning how God wants people to respect God and treat each other within society. So the divine act of revelation always occurs through some medium.

This means that *there is no unmediated revelation*. God reveals, but always through something that is not God. Even in the case of Jesus, the "not God" part of this truth is maintained in the church's insistence that Jesus is truly a human being, like us in all things but sin, even as it affirms that God is incarnate in him. The theory of divine action I have presented above—that with regard to observable events, God acts only through and with the cooperation of the agents of the universe—is in harmony with this theological understanding of how revelation occurs. Just as all divine revelation is mediated, so are all of God's acts mediated (with regard to observable events in the universe).

This theory of divine action, it seems to me, finds strong support in the fact that it reflects the implications of Jesus' own teachings and actions for understanding God's action and can unify the understanding of the Christian doctrines of creation, providence, revelation, and the incarnation. But for many religious people and theologians this theory and its implications regarding God's power raise a serious question about the possibility and meaning of miracles. I believe this theory, in conjunction with the contemporary understanding of the laws of nature, can offer a persuasive analysis of miracles.

The Understanding of Miracles

The emergence of modern science in the eighteenth and nineteenth centuries created difficulties for belief in miracles. Miracles were understood to be violations or suspensions of the laws of nature, and science thought of these laws, especially as unified in Newtonian physics, as absolute and inviolable. David Hume, the eighteenth-century skeptical philosopher, based his attack on belief in the occurrence of miracles on the conviction that the laws of nature represent universal human experience. Since all reasoning and knowledge concerning things other than mathematics and logic must be based in experience, Hume argued that to believe in miracles is to subvert the principles of reason, since universal human experience testifies against the possibility of the occurrence of miracles. Belief must be proportioned to evidence, Hume argued. If the laws of nature state *universal* human experience, how can there be any experiential evidence for the occurrence of miracles?[11]

Yet the testimony of Christian religious experience, and that of other religious traditions as well, holds that miraculous events do occur. The Gospels present Jesus as one who worked miracles. Even more important, the heart of the Christian gospel proclamation includes the miracle of the resurrection of Jesus from the dead. It does not seem that the Christian tradition can easily give up the claim that miraculous events occur, despite the fact that the intellectual history of the last three centuries in the West has led even many Christian theologians to "demythologize" or spiritualize such claims, including the claim for the resurrection of Jesus.

In this matter everything depends on how one defines what a miracle is. Hume lived when Newtonian science dominated how the natural world was understood. His definition of miracles as violations of the laws of nature seemed quite reasonable at the time. It is likely that most religious thinkers in the eighteenth century would have agreed with that definition. If we grant Hume that definition, then it is very hard to find a flaw in his reasoning as to why one ought not believe that miracles occur. But the whole argument really rests on the assumption that the laws of nature are in fact inviolable.

One of the keys to understanding miracles in a new way resides in the revised understanding of the laws of nature made possible by contemporary science. Many laws of nature are not absolute, deterministic laws that allow no exceptions. Instead, some laws of nature are *statistical* in character, such as those emerging from quantum mechanics or the study of human and animal populations and their behavior. These laws predict not what *must* occur, but rather the likelihood or probability of events. For example, the Schrödinger wave function for the hydrogen atom includes a small probability—amounting to less

---

[11] See David Hume, *An Enquiry concerning Human Understanding*, ed. Charles W. Hendel; The Library of Liberal Arts (Indianapolis: Bobbs-Merrill, 1955 [reprint of the 1777 edition with Hume's final changes; originally published 1748]), Section 10 ("Of Miracles").

than one chance in a billion years—that the electron may be found a mile away from the nucleus.[12] This is incredible given the number of atoms that would be found between the nucleus and its electron; yet it is possible. With regard to such statistical laws, a miracle may be defined not as a violation of the laws of nature but as an extremely unlikely or improbable event. This may seem to be an insignificant difference in definitions, yet it makes all the difference. Metaphysically, there is an important consequence of such a definitional change, because one can never rule out the possibility of an unlikely or improbable event. So long as that event is not impossible, but is merely highly unlikely, our metaphysics would have to allow for the possibility of its occurrence.

Whitehead regarded the laws of nature as emergent within the universe rather than imposed upon it.[13] He understood them to be the outcome of the social environment, that is, the collective influence of actual agents ("actual entities") imposing certain forms of order on all agents in their processes of becoming. Because the laws are emergent within the social development of the universe, they all have the character of statistical laws and may even change over time. Although these laws can be extremely dominant because of the dominance of actual agents of a particular type (such as the "society" of electromagnetic occasions), they may not be completely dominant and there may be events that do not "obey" the laws.[14]

Since the theory of divine action I have presented above employs Whitehead's metaphysics (revised), it can affirm the possibility of miracles understood as extremely improbable events. If God acts through the presentation of possibilities and lures actual agents toward actualizing the possibility God values most highly, there is no theoretical obstacle to affirming that on occasion God can lure actual agents into actualizing an extremely improbable possibility. This must still be done through the cooperation of the actual agents involved, but in Whitehead's metaphysics miracles in this sense are not out of the realm of

---

[12] See Nathan Spielberg and Bryon D. Anderson, *Seven Ideas That Shook the Universe* (New York: John Wiley and Sons, 1987), 212.

[13] See Whitehead, *Process and Reality*, 90–92, 98, 106, 204–7.

[14] See ibid., 98, 207.

possibility.[15] I believe, for example, that the resurrection of Jesus from the dead could be understood as an extremely improbable but nevertheless possible objective historical event, not just a subjective event occurring in the hearts and minds of his disciples, as so many theologians have proposed. How exactly the resurrection occurred I cannot suggest, but I would offer the judgment that God elicited life out of an inanimate world once before and I think it is not impossible for God to have elicited life out of death in this instance, raising Jesus to new and transformed life as a promise and revelation of what awaits us all.

The Test against the Scientific Criteria

I stated above that any successful theory of divine action must meet two criteria in relation to science: (1) the general criterion that it must be compatible with the well-established scientific understanding of the universe and its processes; and (2) it must offer a persuasive reason for why science, in its examination of the universe and its processes, does not find any acts of God. In my judgment the theory of divine action through the organization, valuation, and presentation of possibilities meets both of these criteria.

Why Science Finds No Acts of God

The second criterion does not require a prolonged discussion. Science finds no acts of God because, *with regard to observable events, there are no acts of God that are not also acts of the agents of the universe.* Science, in studying the agents of the universe and the processes of their production, development, and interaction, will not find God as another agent or cause needed to gain scientific understanding. God acts *within* and through the agents of the universe, not externally upon them, in competition with them, or outside of natural processes. God's action is therefore completely hidden within the ordinary structures and processes of the universe, and a completely naturalistic understanding of the universe is sufficient for scientific explanation.

---

[15] I am reminded of Jesus' statement that for God, all things are possible (Mk 10:27; Mt 19:26).

Possibility and Information

How is the theory of divine action I have defended above compatible with the contemporary scientific understanding of the universe? In general, its compatibility rests in two facts: (1) the theory does not conflict with the scientific understanding of reality; and (2) the theory is in harmony with a central feature of the contemporary scientific understanding of reality as a large-scale exploration of possibility.

In the theory I have presented, God acts by organizing and valuating possibilities, presenting the relevant possibilities to each actual agent in the universe, endowing it with all it needs to create itself, and luring the becoming of each actual agent toward actualizing the best possibility in its situation. The peculiar feature of possibilities is that they are quite *real*, but they are not in and of themselves *actual*. This distinction (based on Whitehead's philosophical analysis of possibility) means that possibilities are real factors in our experience, "entities" that we experience and to which we must refer to explain not only our human choices and decisions, but also the development and processes of all things in the universe. But possibilities are not *actual* entities, that is, they are not *agents* enjoying experience and freedom and having the power to make things happen.

We may think of possibilities as *information* about the ways that actual agents or actual entities might be. We may also think of actual agents or actual entities as information of another sort, telling us what in fact *is*, or how energy has been formed. Possibilities, in contrast, tell us not what is, but what might be.[16] Since possibilities are real entities but not *actual* entities, we may think of possibilities as non-energetic information (or what Whitehead calls "pure potential" information), while actual entities or actual agents, precisely because they are *actual*, must be understood as *energetic* information (or actual information). If God acts through the presentation of possibilities, then one can argue that God's action is non-energetic and does not violate the law of conservation of energy. God's action does not add energy to the

---

[16] Whitehead's analysis of possibility is quite detailed and profound. For the major aspects of his technical analysis, see Whitehead, *Process and Reality*, 184–207, 256–65. For an introduction to this topic, see Hosinski, *Stubborn Fact and Creative Advance*, 99–117.

universe or require the inflow of energy from a source external to the universe. Nor would God's action require a manipulation or determination of actual or energetic information. Understanding God's action as the non-energetic presentation of pure potential information within the becoming of every actual agent is a theory that I believe resolves the knotty problem of specifying how God acts in the universe without conflicting with the contemporary scientific understanding of reality. This is especially interesting since the notion of information is gaining more and more importance in both biology and physics as a foundational concept along with the concepts of energy and matter.

This theory does not seek to exploit some perceived gap in the scientific explanation of reality, nor does it postulate such a gap in the causal chain governing events. Instead, it is a product of metaphysical reflection on the nature of possibility. Possibility is central to the contemporary scientific understanding of reality, but it is not self-explanatory. Science, for its purposes, can simply take possibility for granted—or at least it has done so to this point in its development. But there is a serious philosophical question of how possibilities can interact with actualities if they are not themselves actual and therefore have no power of agency. This very question led Whitehead to his postulation of God, not in answer to any scientific questions, but in answer to the metaphysical questions his analysis of the role of possibility in the universe evokes. The theory of God acting through the organization and presentation of possibilities actually sheds some light on the ultimate metaphysical and religious implications of the role of possibility in the universe.

Compatibility with Complexity Theory

As I discussed in Chapter 5, the complexity theory developed by Stuart Kauffman analyzes the dynamics of complex systems by using the mathematical concept of "attractors" that "pull" the dynamics of the system through the range of possible states open to that system along "basins of attraction." On the face of it, this looks like a completely deterministic analysis, implying that the mathematics itself or some external factor inevitably causes specific results. Yet the language Kauffman consistently uses leads us to note that the determinism is *internal* to the system;

Kauffman speaks of it as *self*-organization. Philosophically, this seems to imply that in such systems we are dealing with agents *determining themselves* in a collective system, and this is compatible with the idea that such systems have and display some degree of freedom. The fact that Kauffman believes his theory to apply to human economic and political systems[17] gives us reason to suspect that we are dealing with a "soft" determinism, analogous to how humans self-organize in human societies.

If this analysis of the ontological implications of Kauffman's complexity theory is correct, then we can see that the theory of divine action I have proposed is in harmony with complexity theory in several ways. It affirms, as I argued in Chapter 6, that God creates by making things possible, by presenting each actual agent with its relevant possibilities, its aim or drive to actualize some possibility, and the freedom to complete its own creation. The degree of that freedom varies with the complexity of the actual agents, but it is present minimally even in the simplest sorts of agents.[18] This theory also shows how God's influence on actual agents results in a "soft" determinism, a determinism that constrains but does not obliterate the freedom of the agent. The structure and patterns within the possibilities open to dynamic systems can be understood as due to how God organizes and valuates possibilities in God's Primordial Nature. This at least suggests how it may be that things having no actuality in themselves (mere abstract possibilities) can exhibit a structure.

In a similar way one might ask how mere possibilities can exert an attractive force if they are not actual agents having the power to make things happen. The Whiteheadian understanding of God's role in creation also suggests an answer to this question, which arises from a consideration of complexity theory. It is because of God's primordial valuation of all possibilities

---

[17] See Stuart Kauffman, *At Home in the Universe: The Search for Laws of Self-Organization and Complexity* (New York: Oxford University Press, 1995), 245–304; idem, *Investigations* (New York: Oxford University Press, 2000), 211–41; idem, *Humanity in a Creative Universe* (New York: Oxford University Press, 2016), 83–95, 265–72.

[18] In his most recent book, *Humanity in a Creative Universe*, Kauffman's thought is moving toward very similar ideas.

that they can be attractive (or repulsive). Possibilities come to the agents of the universe already invested with value as the result of God's primordial valuation of them. As God presents all relevant possibilities to actual agents in the universe, they grasp these possibilities and react to their value or worth relative to their immediate situation and their aim. The possibilities attract or repel, and the actual agents will eventually energize the possibility they find most attractive. This self-organization again exhibits determinism, but a "soft" determinism that allows for some flexibility, some modest internal freedom in the development of the system.

Divine Action and Evolution

Since the time of Asa Gray in the mid-nineteenth century, some Christian thinkers have suggested that evolution is the instrument of God's continuing creation and providence. However, serious difficulties have confronted all such suggestions. No one could offer a precise theory of exactly how God acts in biological evolution. One usually encountered rather vague suggestions that somehow God caused genetic mutations or that what appeared to be the outcome of natural selection operating on random variations was actually God's direction of the evolutionary process. Although such vague suggestions express the religious conviction that somehow God is involved in the evolutionary process, it is hard to find them persuasive in relation to evolutionary science. Such suggestions also lead to serious theological problems, at least in my estimation. If God is understood to *control* evolution, it is hard to see how this could avoid the claim that God determines the course of evolutionary history. If this were the case, then God would be responsible for all the suffering and misery involved in the history of life and its dead ends, blind alleys, and mass extinctions. Moreover, standard evolutionary theory and paleontological interpretations do not perceive any clear direction in evolution; despite an overall increase in complexity of organization and mental development, the evolution of life seems to most biologists to have no clear goal.

The theory of divine action through the organization, valuation, and presentation of possibilities is compatible with the current scientific understanding of evolution and does not involve us in scientifically and theologically questionable claims about God's action. In this theory God does not control or determine the course of evolution, yet from a metaphysical and religious perspective we can say that God has acted in luring at least some of its developments. I would be willing to affirm, for example, that God's lure toward novel possibilities was actualized in the emergence of life out of the inanimate dynamic systems of organic chemistry, in the cooperation of prokaryotic cells to form eukaryotic cells, in the development of multicellular organisms out of the community of eukaryotic cells, in the beauty of all the diverse organisms of the plant and animal phyla, and in the development of self-reflective consciousness in human beings, a consciousness capable of grasping the reality of God and the wonder and beauty of the universe and capable of grasping and responding to the ideal embodied in the symbol kingdom of God. Since God makes possible and is present to and in each actual agent of the universe, luring it toward actualizing the best possibility in its situation, we can affirm that all the beauties of evolutionary history are indeed acts of God, accomplished through and with the cooperation of the agents of the universe.

Yet to affirm this does not mean we must say that God intended each and every development in the evolution of life. For a variety of reasons the divine lures will not always be followed. The agents of the world choose for themselves, and in their freedom they may actualize any of the possibilities or potentials open to them. There is nothing in the nature of freedom that determines it will always be used for the best. Because of the exercise of freedom by the agents of the world, many things can and do happen that make suffering part of evolution's operation. There is conflict of purposes pursued by different agents exercising freedom; organisms and natural processes act upon plants and animals with coercive force; agents acting with independence, freedom, and coercive power can ignore divine persuasion and lures toward better possibilities. In short, the course of evolution is affected by the interaction of all the natural systems of the earth and how living organisms are able to react to all the influences upon them. They may occasionally actualize the possibilities God values most highly, responding to God's lures, but they may also actualize possibilities God would have preferred not actualized. God can influence only through the lure of possibilities and beauty; God cannot control or determine what in fact occurs.

This theory, with its understanding of the limitations on what God can do, takes seriously the ambiguity and contingent character of the evolutionary history of life and of the experiences of any individual life. Yet it may strike some readers as being quite vague. I cannot point to any genetic mutation or evolutionary development and prove that God lured the agents of the world to actualize that particular possibility or set of possibilities. This is true. But in response I would observe that it is not the task of theological metaphysics to identify acts of God in nature, but rather to develop a general metaphysical theory showing the possibility of divine action given what we know of the universe. This is what the modified Whiteheadian theory of divine action through the organization, valuation, and presentation of possibilities to the agents of the universe accomplishes. But the very hiddenness of divine action within each agent and the ambiguity of nature and history make it virtually impossible to identify any specific instance in which the possibility God valued most highly was actualized.

Since the theory holds that the very organization of possibilities making the universe possible is due to God's absolutely free valuation and choice, we might affirm that certain large-scale developments, such as the general increase in complexity of organization and mental abilities that occur over evolutionary history, are due to God's organization of possibilities and God's luring of organisms toward actualizing novel possibilities. Evolutionary convergence, which Simon Conway Morris sees as pervasive in evolutionary history, may ultimately be due to how God ordered possibilities. Such a view would be compatible with Stuart Kauffman's analysis of the role of attractors and basins of attraction in self-organizing complex dynamic systems. Beyond such general statements the theory cannot tell us of specific instances in which we can definitively grasp the actualization of God's will. But neither is it possible for us to do this in relation to human history, with the exception of those events and persons that religious experience has grasped as revelatory of God's action. Even in these cases we cannot prove the convictions of religious faith.

Although the theory of divine action I have presented is metaphysically general and cannot reveal to us specific acts of God, it does show the possibility, even the *necessity*, of divine action, and it offers a metaphysically precise understanding of how God acts. It is a theory that does not conflict with established evolutionary theory and a theory that one can argue is compatible with the scientific understanding of how evolution occurs. Of course, one must be persuaded by the metaphysical analysis in order to find the theory compelling. But the fact that it satisfies both the religious and the scientific criteria that ought to govern any theory of divine action says much in its favor and in favor of the metaphysical analysis that undergirds it.

Conclusion

The modified Whiteheadian theory of divine action is able to show how God's action is "top down," manifesting God's transcendence. But at the same time it shows that God's action is also "bottom up," occurring *internally* in every actual agent in the universe, manifesting God's immanence. Moreover, this single, relatively simple theory of divine action through the valuation, organization, and presentation of possibilities is able to address successfully how God creates and how God acts on every level of complexity in the universe, from quantum events, to human experience, to the universe as a whole. It requires no supplementary theories. Creation and providence occur in the same divine empowering and luring of the agents of the universe. All things exist and live by participating in the life of God. It is God's immanent presence and action in each actual agent of the universe that enable the creative advance of the universe; that is, to quote Whitehead again, "The world lives by its incarnation of God in itself."[19]

---

[19] Alfred North Whitehead, *Religion in the Making* (New York: Macmillan, 1926), 156.

Chapter 8

The God Who Heals and Saves

We have seen in the previous two chapters that God continually creates the universe at each moment. God empowers all actual agents to complete their own creation by endowing them with all possibilities open to their situation, their aim at actualizing some possibility, and the freedom to select which possibility they will actualize or energize in their own becoming. We also saw in the last chapter, when examining the religious ground for understanding divine action, that both the teachings and actions of Jesus Christ lead us to make a distinction between how God influences events and how God responds to events. In this chapter I discuss the responsive mode of divine action. In his teachings Jesus consistently presents God as responding with compassion, mercy, forgiveness, healing, transforming love, and restoring to life. And in his enactment of the kingdom of God in his ministry, this is also how Jesus responds to persons and events. We may therefore characterize the responsive mode of divine action as healing, redemption, or salvation. Since this mode of divine action must be intimately related to God's action in creation and providence, we may say that the final work of creation and providence is redemption or salvation, the fulfillment of God's universal salvific will.

In traditional Christian theology salvation is usually thought of in connection with two doctrines: soteriology (the saving work of Jesus Christ) and eschatology (the "last things," the culmination of God's dealings with history). God revealed salvation in and through the person of Jesus Christ, especially in his suffering, death, and resurrection. But people tend to think of salvation as something that will happen in the future, at a personal judgment after death or the general judgment that tradition holds will occur at the eschaton, the culmination and completion of God's purposes for the world. Thinking of salvation in process terms, however, leads to a different way of understanding it. Creation is not a singular event at the beginning of the universe, but the fundamental relation of the universe to God at every moment, and thus a continually ongoing process. In a very similar way salvation is not a singular event at "the end" of existence, personal or universal, but rather a continually ongoing process. God saves at all moments. *Salvation* is the single term describing how God responds to the universe at every moment of its existence and development, and to each actual agent as it completes its process of becoming.

God's Reception of the Universe into God's Own Experience

If we take the teachings and actions of Jesus as telling us something true about God, we must recognize that many of his parables present God as continually responding to what people have made of themselves in their actions. The father in the parable of the Prodigal Son (Lk 15:11–32), for example, responds to his son's return by embracing him and taking him back into the family. Jesus' parables about finding the Lost Coin and Lost Sheep are enacted in his own acceptance of those marginalized and shunned in his society and in his inclusive table fellowship. The conversion of the tax collector, Zacchaeus, simply because Jesus was willing to stay and dine with him is a striking example of this inclusion of the marginalized and its transformative effects (Lk 19:1–10). I could go on, but my point is that Jesus' teachings and actions reveal a continuing, ongoing receptivity in God, a dynamic interaction in which God takes the world into God's own experience and reaches out to heal, to save. Faithfulness to this aspect of revelation, I believe, requires a philosophical analysis that can coherently speak of God's receptivity.

Whitehead's philosophy of God incorporates an understanding of divine receptivity. Whitehead argued that just as all actual agents must receive into themselves the effects of other agents, so God must receive into God's own experience what the actual agents of the universe have done with their freedom and the possibilities with which God endowed them.[1] Whitehead calls this aspect of God the Consequent Nature of God, since it follows upon what the actual agents of the universe have done with their freedom. God creates all agents in the universe by endowing them with their possibilities, their aim to become something (to actualize some possibility in themselves), and their freedom. The agents of the universe then complete their processes of becoming by determining themselves. God's Consequent Nature then receives them into God's experience and integrates these "facts" of existence with the eternal vision of possible beauty and value that is God's Primordial Nature.

Whitehead holds that God receives all the agents of the universe with perfect conformity or "sympathy," which means that God feels them exactly as they themselves felt.[2] But God then integrates this perfect reception of the actual agents of the universe with God's Primordial Nature, thus transforming all actual agents and harmonizing them with one another and with God in the unity of God's ongoing experience of the world. This is God healing and saving the universe. The universe obtains ultimate unity, healing, and harmony in God. Whitehead said that the Consequent Nature of God "is the realization of the actual world in the unity of his nature, and through the transformation of his wisdom."[3] One of the results of this unique understanding of God is the recognition that God has both absolute and relative attributes. It also offers us insight into God's suffering, knowledge, judgment, and salvific love. I briefly discuss each of these topics in turn.

---

[1] For a technical discussion of this aspect of Whitehead's philosophy of God, see Thomas E. Hosinski, *Stubborn Fact and Creative Advance* (Lanham, MD: Rowman and Littlefield, 1993), 181–206.

[2] See ibid., 191, 196.

[3] Alfred North Whitehead, *Process and Reality: An Essay in Cosmology*, corrected ed., ed. David Ray Griffin and Donald W. Sherburne (New York: The Free Press, 1978 [1929]), 345.

The Divine Attributes

In the foundational aspect of God's relation to the universe (the Primordial Nature of God), God is completely unaffected by the actual course of events, because God presupposes nothing, whereas the actual course of events presupposes the Primordial Nature of God.[4] Therefore the Primordial Nature of God is infinite, complete, unconditioned, absolutely free, eternal, unchanging, and impassible. Let me briefly explain each of these attributes. Since the Primordial Nature of God grasps and valuates *all* possibilities, it is both infinite and complete. Because there can be no universe whatsoever without God's ordering and valuation of possibilities, the universe can in no way condition or influence God's organization of the possibilities; therefore, God in the Primordial Nature is unconditioned and absolutely free. Again, since the very possibility of any temporal universe depends on this fundamental organization and valuation of possibilities, the Primordial Nature of God is eternal, meaning that it transcends all temporal relation and limitation. Likewise, the Primordial Nature of God must be unchanging, since change is the measure of the difference and relationship among the actual agents of the universe over time; change, therefore, is possible only in relation to a temporal course of events. The Primordial Nature of God is metaphysically "prior" to any temporal course of events; therefore, God's eternal vision of beauty and value does not change. One can even say that the Primordial Nature of God is impassible (incapable of passion or suffering). Whitehead writes that because the Primordial Nature of God presupposes no actual world, "it is deflected neither by love, nor by hatred, for what in fact comes to pass."[5]

It is important to note that all these attributes of the Primordial Nature of God, even though they are described in relation to the uniqueness of Whitehead's metaphysics, are identical with the traditional attributes of God in Christian theology. When focusing

---

[4] This expresses a revised Whiteheadian view. Whitehead himself held that God presupposes creativity. See Whitehead, *Process and Reality*, 343–45; and Hosinski, *Stubborn Fact and Creative Advance*, 192–97.

[5] Whitehead, *Process and Reality*, 344.

on God's role as the ground of the universe, or Creator, God's attributes are the same in Whiteheadian metaphysics and in the Greek metaphysics adopted by traditional Christian theology.

Where Whitehead's philosophy of God differs radically from the tradition, however, is in the recognition that there is another, quite different aspect of God's interaction with the universe. God is not only Creator but also receives into God's experience what all the actual agents of the universe have done with their freedom and the possibilities God presented to them. In this aspect God is related directly to the actual world; indeed, God is *affected* by the actual course of events. Therefore, the Consequent Nature of God is finite, incomplete, conditioned, partially determined, everlasting, developing, and passible (capable of feeling and suffering). It is most unusual to attribute these characteristics to God, especially when their opposites have already been affirmed as divine attributes. But these "opposites" do not diminish God's perfection and must be affirmed of God for the following reasons.

In the role of Creator, God is unconditioned and absolutely free. But in God's receptivity, God must receive what the actual agents of the universe have actually made of themselves. This aspect of God's experience occurs in dependence on the actual agents of the universe, and God's Consequent Nature is therefore *conditioned* and *partially determined* by the actual agents of the universe. Though conditioned, God is yet perfect in the completeness and the sympathy with which God receives these agents exactly as they actualized themselves. Although God's Consequent Nature is partially determined by the reception of these actual agents, as God integrates them with God's eternal vision of beauty and value these agents are transformed, unified, and harmonized in the unity of God's own experience.[6] The determinative influence of the world on God is tempered and not final. It is God's transformative and healing influence on the world that is final.

---

[6] The Consequent Nature of God has two phases, as it were: God first receives the actual entities of the universe in perfect sympathy, then integrates them with God's Primordial Nature, the eternal vision of beauty and goodness. For further explanation, see Hosinski, *Stubborn Fact and Creative Advance*, 190–92.

In the role of Creator, God is complete and infinite because God grasps and valuates *all* possibilities. But in God's receptivity God is *incomplete* and *finite* because at any moment God can receive only those actual agents that have completed their becoming. As long as there is some universe and a future, there will always be more actual agents to receive. The incompleteness and finitude of this aspect of God are not due to any limitation in God, because God has an *infinite capacity* to receive actual agents. Rather, they are due to the fact that the actual universe is a limited achievement at any moment in comparison to God's infinite vision of possible beauty and value. Nor ought the finitude and incompleteness of God's Consequent Nature be interpreted as imperfections in God, as they would be in Greek metaphysical thought. God is in fact receiving *all* actual agents *available to be received* in each moment of the universe's history, and God receives each actual agent completely and perfectly, without the limitations of perspective and elimination that characterize such reception among the actual agents of the universe. The incompleteness and finitude of God's Consequent Nature merely describe the factual character of the universe that God receives and that constitutes this aspect of God's experience.

The Primordial Nature of God is eternal, meaning that it transcends all temporal relations and limitations. But the Consequent Nature of God is *everlasting*,[7] including all temporal relations. Whitehead conceives of God as a process of becoming that spans all of time, receiving all actual agents of the universe as the universe develops and retaining them all in the immediacy of God's own becoming. This gives us a paradoxical understanding of God: God is not subject to the passage of time and therefore

---

[7] See Whitehead, *Process and Reality*, 340, 345–56, 350–51. Whitehead defines *everlasting* in this way: "The property of combining creative advance with the retention of mutual immediacy is what . . . is meant by the term 'everlasting'" (*Process and Reality*, 346). This means that God, in the process of God's own becoming, continues to receive what the actual agents of the universe make of themselves (the "creative advance"), but all agents are held "alive" together ("mutual immediacy"); there is no loss into the past for God. It has struck me that this is very similar to what Jesus is reported to have said in Luke 20:38: "For to him [God] all of them are alive."

God's everlasting process of becoming is to be understood as an unending development that is everlastingly present. Yet time is *real* for God, since God experiences it in the relations of the actual agents God receives. In God's Consequent Nature, then, there is an ongoing process of development without the loss of the living immediacy and togetherness of things, unlike what is necessarily the case in the universe as things perish and disappear into the past. It is this retention of things in living immediacy, their transformation by integrating them with God's primordial vision of beauty and value, and their harmonization into the unity of God's experience that is the healing and salvation of the universe.

The Primordial Nature of God does not change. But the Consequent Nature of God, the receptive aspect of God's experience, is constantly *developing*. God experiences change in the differences among all the actual agents of the universe God receives, and God is continually developing, receiving new actual agents into God's own experience. In this sense God "changes" in each moment. But there is no temporal succession in God, whose becoming is everlastingly present. Thus Whitehead's metaphysics implies a process concept of immutability that is quite different from the traditional concept of immutability. In the traditional concept immutability means God cannot develop at all (God as "pure act," as in Thomas Aquinas's metaphysics); in the process concept God is technically immutable but continually develops in relation to the changes in the universe.

Finally, the Primordial Nature of God is impassible, since no feeling in relation to the actual course of events can affect God's eternal envisagement of possibility. But in the Consequent Nature, God is *passible*, capable of suffering, and this in two different ways. First, because God receives all temporal agents into God's experience with perfect sympathy, God experiences directly the sufferings (and joys) of all temporal creatures. These sufferings are felt by God with a completeness transcending all sympathy that we know in ourselves. Just as every actual agent in the universe lives by its participation in the power of God's own life, so God lives by participating in our sufferings and sorrows (as well as our achievements and our joys), and not just those of humans, but of all sentient creatures. God suffers *with* all the suffering creatures, not only being present to them in their suffering, but feeling their suffering directly as God's own. Thus all the suffering in the world affects God directly (as does all joy). This view is in complete harmony with what is revealed in the cross of Jesus Christ: God embraces and participates in the suffering of Jesus Christ and in so doing reveals the depth of God's salvific love for the world.

But God also must suffer in God's own right because of the difference between God's eternal vision of what beauty and goodness are *possible* in the universe and what *actually* occurs. As God integrates the completed actual agents of the world with God's Primordial Nature, God knows the difference between the beauty and goodness that might have been and the tragedies and evils that have been actualized in freedom. To use the language of the religious tradition, the symbol kingdom of God represents the vision of the beauty, goodness, holiness, and peace that God holds ever before the world as possible; the difference between that eternal vision and the tortured, "fallen," "sinful" actuality of our world must cause God to suffer enormously. God redeems and overcomes evil so that it is not final, as we shall see, but this does not eliminate the *facts* of suffering and tragedy in the world and in God's own experience.

Within Whitehead's metaphysics, for reasons I cannot fully pursue here, this understanding of God as having both absolute and relative attributes is a consistent and coherent metaphysical understanding of God. We can say that God is both infinite and finite, unconditioned and conditioned, absolutely free and partially determined, impassible and passible, and so on,[8] because we can specify which attribute applies to which aspect of God's relation to the universe. Both sets of attributes are true, and there is no contradiction between them because they refer to distinct aspects of God's interaction with the universe. God is both absolute (in God's Primordial Nature) *and* relative (in God's Consequent Nature). There is no need to try to collapse all of God's attributes into the Creator-creature relationship, as the

---

[8] See Whitehead's "antitheses" between God and the world, which reveal that God has opposite attributes depending on which aspect of God's relation to the universe is being considered (ibid., 348). See also his comments on the "union of opposites" in Alfred North Whitehead, *Adventures of Ideas* (New York: Macmillan, 1933), 245.

tradition did. Whitehead's metaphysics can show quite precisely, in a way Nicholas of Cusa could not, how it is possible for God to be the "coincidence of opposites."

The problem with the traditional attributes of God in Christian theology is not that they are wrong, but that they present a half-truth out of which the tradition tried to define all aspects of God's interaction with the universe. The half-truth was absolutized. Furthermore, the tradition united this half-truth with a deterministic understanding of the divine creative act or the divine will. The classical divine attributes express the conviction of both religious experience and philosophical reflection that God is the ultimate ground and source of the universe. But the tradition understood the divine creative act or the divine will to be *determining;* that is, in creation God makes and wills the creature to be what it is. This absolutizing of the half-truth with regard to the divine attributes and the deterministic understanding of the divine knowledge and will creates several difficulties within Christian theology, including the tragic doctrine of predestination we see in Augustine, Luther, and Calvin. How can humans be truly free and God be just if from all eternity the unchanging decree of God has predestined some for salvation and many more for eternal condemnation? And how can the immutable, and impassible God become incarnate in a human being and undergo suffering and death? And, as in Thomas Aquinas, how can God's knowledge, through which God creates, be eternal, immutable, and necessary without imposing necessity on what is created, absolutely determining the course of universal history, and eliminating all real freedom and contingency in the world? These positions do not seem compatible with Jesus' portrait of God as the empowering, merciful, compassionate, and forgiving Father who reaches out to save the lost. And they do not seem compatible with the image of a God who would willingly undergo suffering and death to save us.

These problems and incoherencies can be resolved by the recognition that God's role as Creator is *distinct* from God's reception of the agents of the universe into God's own experience, and the recognition that God creates by empowering creatures to create themselves, not by determining them. If God has both absolute *and* relative attributes, then we need not try to derive all understanding of God's relation to the universe from God's foundational role as Creator. And Whitehead's metaphysics shows that we can articulate such an understanding of God with consistency and coherence. Moreover, Whitehead actually appeals to the teachings of Jesus as evidence for this unusual understanding of God,[9] which grounds this interpretation in the originating revelation of the Christian tradition.

The Complementarity of God and the World

Whitehead's cosmological vision conceives of God and the universe in a dynamic relationship of complementarity. Although God and the actual agents of the universe all illustrate the same ontological principles, they are "opposites," complementing each other, each incorporating and completing each other. God is the infinite and eternal ground of possibility, order, value, and novelty that is necessary for there to be any actual course of events, any universe, at all. This aspect of God makes the universe possible, but, we should note, is an eternal vision of merely *possible* beauty and value. The actual agents of the universe, finite, temporal, and passing, incorporate this aspect of God in receiving their aims, their creativity and freedom, and their possibilities.

In turn, these agents of the universe give God something God cannot otherwise acquire: *actualized* beauty and value. It is only through the agency of the temporal actual agents of the universe that the possibilities of God's eternal vision are gradually actualized. An analogy may help to show the importance of this. When we are hungry, we can imagine all sorts of possible foods and relish the idea of them, but until we obtain some *actual* food, our hunger is never satisfied. Analogously, God "hungers" for the actualization of the possible beauty and value envisioned in God's Primordial Nature, but only through the *actualization* of these possibilities can God's "hunger" be satisfied. This is what the world gives to God: *actualized* beauty and value. The

---

[9] See Whitehead, *Process and Reality*, 342–43, 346, 350–51. For an interpretation of these passages, see Hosinski, *Stubborn Fact and Creative Advance*, 185–87, 197–98.

growing actualization of God's eternal vision, the kingdom of God, is dependent on how temporal actual agents exercise their freedom. Generations of Christians were taught that the world can add nothing to God, can give nothing to God, that God could be perfectly happy without a world. And yet God was said to love the world. The beloved *always* adds something to the one who loves, *always* gives the one who loves something precious and irreplaceable. For God, this is the world's *actualization* of God's vision of possible beauty and value.

But the temporal agents of the universe lack permanence. They constantly "perish," swiftly completing their processes of becoming and disappearing into the past. Some beauties and values endure through the "societies" these agents create in their relationships,[10] but eventually these societies decay and their achievements vanish into the past. The problem of death faced by human beings is merely our particular experience of a larger cosmic truth: above a certain level of complexity, all things perish, and their accomplishments do not long endure. Moreover, the competing aims of the actual agents and societies of the universe produce discord, lack of harmony, suffering, evil, tragedy, and disunity. Here, in the other aspect of God's relation to the universe, God provides what the passing world cannot otherwise achieve: permanence, harmony, unity, healing, and peace. God receives into God's everlasting becoming every actual agent in the universe, and through the integration of these with God's eternal vision in the unity of God's experience, the universe obtains unity, harmony, and healing in the unity and harmony of God's own experience.[11] This is God saving the world as God takes it into the immediacy, unity, and peace of God's own life.

This cosmological vision is neither monist nor dualist, but pluralist, in which the whole is understood as a complementarity of opposites and God is understood as a coincidence of opposites

---

[10] For a discussion of Whitehead's notion of "societies," see Hosinski, *Stubborn Fact and Creative Advance,* 128–51.

[11] See Whitehead, *Process and Reality,* 345–51; and Hosinski, *Stubborn Fact and Creative Advance,* 197–203.

that both makes possible and saves the passing actual agents of the universe.[12] Every actual agent is related to all other actual agents. Whitehead writes, "No two actualities can be torn apart; each is all in all."[13] While this is true of all actual agents, it is God as "all in all" (1 Cor 15:28) that ultimately unifies and saves the universe. "The concept of God is the way in which we understand this incredible fact—that what cannot be, yet is."[14] Whitehead's cosmological vision can be described as a pan*en*theism, a vision of God as the all-inclusive reality. This is not pantheism, because God is at once transcendent to and inclusive of the universe and, as in the thought of Nicholas of Cusa, the universe can never exhaust the infinite being of God.

It should also be clear that God's reception and salvation of the universe constitutes the ultimate wholeness of things, the gathering together of all things in mutual immediacy with God in God's everlasting life. Our consciousness of this wholeness, made possible by what is revealed in Jesus Christ, is our grasp of the catholicity of the cosmos, the unity and community of all things in God. God holds all things together in God's creative energy, God's life shared with the world. But God holds all things together in an ultimate way by receiving all the world's agents into God's own experience, transforming, healing, and harmonizing them, and keeping them all alive together in the peace of God's own life.

---

[12] It is for this reason that Wolfhart Pannenberg's characterization of Whitehead's understanding of God and the world as "dualistic" is, in my judgment, erroneous. See Wolfhart Pannenberg, *Systematic Theology*, 2 vols., trans. Geoffrey W. Bromiley (Grand Rapids, MI: Eerdmans, 1991/1994), 2:15.

[13] Whitehead, *Process and Reality*, 348. This conclusion is the result of Whitehead's "principle of relativity" (see ibid., 22, 148, and throughout). It is important to note, however, that with regard to the actual agents of the universe, this statement of the presence of all actual agents in each actual agent is possible only by recognizing that there are degrees of relevance and even negligible relevance (see Whitehead, ibid., 41 [on "negative prehensions"] and 50 [on negligible relevance]).

[14] Ibid., 350.

Divine Knowledge
and Divine Judgment

Although I cannot here enter into the complexities of White-head's theory of consciousness and knowledge, it is enough to say that in Whitehead's view consciousness is the most primitive form of judgment and knowledge in that it judges what is fact and what is merely possible in the experience of the conscious subject.[15] In an analogous way we can speak of God's knowledge as resulting from the integration of the actual agents of the universe with God's eternal vision of possibility. In God's Consequent Nature, God is "conscious" of the difference between the facts of the actual course of events God receives into God's experience and the merely possible vision of what might have been that constitutes God's Primordial Nature. The foundational ontological meaning of divine judgment is the cognitive judgment in which God knows the agents of the universe for what they have in fact made of themselves.

In this metaphysical theory, then, God's knowledge occurs in dependence on the actual agents of the universe. God cannot know from all eternity what any actual agent will be, since knowledge requires experience of the facticity of that actual agent; until actual agents complete their processes of becoming, they do not yet exist as facts and cannot be known in this technical sense. This implies that the future is truly open, unknown even by God, because it does not yet exist as fact and therefore cannot be experienced. In light of this understanding of actuality and temporality, the classical understanding of the divine attribute of omniscience must be regarded as an error. God cannot know from all eternity what any actual agent will in fact be;

---

[15] See ibid., 266–75; and Hosinski, *Stubborn Fact and Creative Advance*, 110–27. There is a strong parallel here to the cognitional theory of Bernard Lonergan (see Bernard J. F. Lonergan, *Collected Works of Bernard Lonergan*, vol. 3: *Insight: A Study of Human Understanding*, 5th ed., rev. and augmented (Toronto: University of Toronto Press, 1992 [1957]).

God can know an actual agent only once it has completed its process of becoming.[16]

The view that God's knowledge is relative and dependent on the actual agents of the universe does not compromise God's perfection. Because God receives all actual agents of the universe into God's experience, God's reception of them is perfect, and God's knowledge of the universe is perfect; God knows all that it is possible to know. Does this mean that God's knowledge is limited entirely to the past? In the technical sense of knowledge I have been discussing, God's knowledge is restricted to the past. But there is a sense in which God "knows" the future, and knows it infinitely better than we do. If we reflect on how we "know" the future, we make judgments of probability based on our past experience and our awareness of possibilities. We do not know the future as fact, but we can make some judgments regarding the likelihood of many events. God's knowledge of the future must be analogous to ours, but infinitely better. Since God has a complete grasp of all possibilities in God's Primordial Nature, and a complete and perfect knowledge of all past facts in God's Consequent Nature, God clearly has judgments of probability regarding future events infinitely superior to ours. This also displays God's perfection in comparison to any awareness of the future that can be achieved in the temporal world.

I said above that the foundational ontological meaning of divine judgment is the cognitive judgment in which God knows the actual agents of the universe for what they have in fact made of themselves in freedom. But there is another aspect to divine judgment: the saving judgment in which God heals and transforms the actual agents of the universe in the unity and harmony of God's own life. God's ongoing judgment on the world is not just knowledge of the world but salvation of the world. The Christian tradition has continually stressed divine judgment as the final punishment of evil and reward of righteousness. Yet Jesus'

---

[16] Thomas Aquinas held that since eternity encompasses all of time, God could know "before" creation all future contingents as facts and create them out of that eternal, unchanging knowledge. See Thomas Aquinas, *Summa Theologica*, Ia, Q. 14, a. 13; also, Ia, Q. 10, a. 2 ad 4. But if time has any significance, the future is not actual until it happens; the future is real, but can be "known" only as possible, not as fact.

teaching about God, implied in his parables, presents God not as one who punishes but as one who forgives, redeems, restores to life, and transforms tragedies to divine victories. The parables of the Prodigal Son (Lk 15:11–32) and the Wheat and Darnel (Mt 13:24–30), among many others, portray God in this way. Jesus himself enacts this understanding of God in his own forgiveness of sinners and his healing ministry. And the fundamental Christian proclamation concerning the death and resurrection of Jesus Christ expresses the same understanding of God as one who is not defeated by sin and evil, but whose love transforms such tragedies into surprising divine victories. Our understanding of divine judgment must be integrated with our understanding of the central characteristics of God and with God's salvific will: mercy, compassion, forgiveness, healing of the broken, and love.

Whitehead's philosophy of God conceives of the divine judgment as salvific. He writes:

> The consequent nature of God is his judgment on the world. He saves the world as it passes into the immediacy of his own life. It is the judgment of a tenderness which loses nothing that can be saved. It is also the judgment of a wisdom which uses what in the temporal world is mere wreckage.[17]

As God integrates the actual agents of the universe into God's own life, they are transformed, harmonized, and united in the everlasting harmony and unity that is God. They are, in short, healed, redeemed, saved. This ultimate transformation and salvation of the universe in God in turn affects the universe because it affects the relevant possibilities toward which God seeks to attract the universe in order to overcome the tragedies and evils that have occurred in the world.

Near the end of *Process and Reality* Whitehead states that God's salvation and transformation of the world in the unity of God's experience "passes back into the temporal world, and qualifies this world so that each temporal actuality includes it as an immediate fact of relevant experience. For the kingdom of

---

[17] Whitehead, *Process and Reality*, 346.

heaven is with us today."[18] This means that God's experience of the universe and salvation of it affects how God seeks to persuade the freedom of actual agents toward possibilities that can overcome and transform the evils *in history*.[19] The salvation of the universe in God in each moment is immanent in the universe through God's effort to influence the world toward healing and redemptive possibilities in history. The ultimate love saving the world flows back into the world to heal, redeem, and transform in history.

This illustrates the coherence of the two modes of divine action in the Whiteheadian theory: how God *influences* present events is not only the result of God's eternal and unchanging organization of possibilities, but also of God's transforming, salvific *response* to the changing course of actual events in the universe. The modes of divine action are distinct, because they reflect the distinct aspects of God's interaction with each actual agent and the universe as a whole at any moment, but they are intimately related in the unity of God's dynamic involvement with the universe at all moments. Each moment in the life of each agent is made possible by God, co-creates itself by determining what possibility it will actualize in itself, and is lovingly saved by God. God's saving love for each moment of the past is immanent in God's creative influence on each present moment, and God's creative influence on each present moment finds its transcendent fulfillment in God's responsive salvation of each moment in God's transforming, salvific love. These two modes of divine action are united in the dynamism of God's interaction with the universe.

Universal Salvation

I discussed in Chapter 1 my belief that the teachings of Jesus imply that God saves all, not just human beings, but all that

---

[18] See ibid., 350–51.

[19] For an excellent technical discussion of this point in Whiteheadian metaphysical terms, see Marjorie Hewitt Suchocki, *The End of Evil: Process Eschatology in Historical Perspective* (Albany: State University of New York Press, 1988), 115–34.

God has created. We have seen that Whitehead's metaphysical understanding of God also leads to this conclusion. Although a growing number of Christian theologians in recent years have embraced such a position, the dominant strand of thought in the Christian tradition has not favored universal salvation. In Chapter 2 we saw that in the second century Irenaeus held that God would save all of creation. And later in the Patristic period, Clement of Alexandria, Origen, Gregory Nazianzus, and Gregory of Nyssa held that God would save all humans. John Scotus Erigena in the Middle Ages supported the idea of God's salvation of all creation. Nicholas of Cusa's unusual understanding of God could also be interpreted as implying that all of creation is saved in God, "enfolded" in God's everlasting love. Although the church never taught this doctrine, it never condemned it either, which means that one may hold this view and be considered orthodox. But the dominant tradition of theological interpretation on this matter is represented by Augustine, Thomas Aquinas, Luther, and Calvin in the general conviction that only some humans will be saved and that nonhuman creation has no possibility of sharing the eternal divine life.

In my judgment, if the Christian tradition hopes to achieve greater faithfulness to the foundational revelation of God in and through Jesus Christ, it must abandon its dominant theological position and develop a doctrine of universal salvation. If it wants to continue to maintain a doctrine of predestination, it must revise it (as John Scotus Erigena did) to mean that God predestines all for salvation, not just all humans but all of creation. Any lesser claim does an injustice to the God revealed in and by Jesus Christ. In addition, if only human beings or some humans are destined for salvation, this would mean that the vast majority of the divine creative effort in the universe would finally be lost—and this seems unacceptably wasteful. The author of the Book of Wisdom correctly perceived this profound religious truth and addressed God in this way:

> For you love all things that exist . . .
> You spare all things, for they are yours, O Lord,
>   you who love the living.
> For your immortal spirit is in all things. (Wis
>   11:24a, 26—12:1)

The immortal spirit of God is in all things. The Christian tradition argued from the outset that the God who redeems is the God who creates. This in turn implies that creation finds its fulfillment in redemption, especially if we understand that everything exists or lives by participating in the divine life. Unless we wish to affirm a cosmic and everlasting frustration of God's creative gift, God's universal salvific will, and God's compassionate, salvific love, we ought to affirm a truly universal salvation—salvation of all creation.

There are three common objections to a doctrine of universal salvation. The first is expressed in a reaction based in conventional expectations of justice. It does not seem right that notorious evildoers (Adolf Hitler, Joseph Stalin, serial killers, and terrorists are favorite examples) will share "heaven" with their victims and those who have lived well and done good. But this reaction is not really different from the elder brother in the parable of the Prodigal Son (Lk 15:11–32) or those who worked a full day in the parable of the Vineyard Laborers (Mt 20:1–16). Jesus' parables directly address such conventional expectations: If salvation is God's to give, why would we object against God giving it to the undeserving? Is it not our own desire for vengeance and retribution and our own self-righteousness failing to see that the "righteous," too, receive salvation as an undeserved gift that leads us to such an un-Godlike attitude? We do not love one another the way God loves us—and that is why we all need to receive God's salvation as a gift. Moreover, if God's salvation of the universe involves a purification and transformation of all actual agents in the unity and harmony of God's own life, then this implies that in some way both the evildoers and the "righteous" are purified and transformed, that both evil and good are somehow harmonized in a tragic beauty.[20] How could the awareness of the suffering we have caused God and the overwhelming beauty of God's infinite salvific love fail to purify and transform us all so that we would freely and joyously be one in and with God?

---

[20] See Lewis S. Ford, "Divine Persuasion and the Triumph of the Good," in *Process Philosophy and Christian Thought*, ed. Delwin Brown, Ralph E. James, and Gene Reeves, 287–304 (Indianapolis: Bobbs-Merrill, 1971).

A second common objection to a doctrine of universal salvation is that if all are saved by and in God, then what we do or what happens in the universe does not really matter. Why bother to live well, why bother to work for the improvement of society, why bother trying to repair the damage we have done to the earth and its forms of life? The answer is that what we do and how we live *does* matter, and it matters ultimately. Everything we do affects God. We determine what God must experience. We determine whether or not the kingdom of God is actualized in our actions and in our world. The theory of divine action I have presented here implies that salvation in history, in the temporal world, depends on the divine initiative *and our cooperation.* The kingdom of God becomes actual in our world only to the extent that we cooperate with God's will, or place ourselves under God's "rule." The transcendent salvation of our world in God heals and saves the universe in God, but this does not by itself heal and save the ongoing course of events in universal history. Therefore, all efforts to contribute to the world in education, science, and medicine, all efforts to eliminate the many forms of exclusion, oppression, prejudice, injustice, cruelty, and hate in human society, and all efforts to work for the repair of the environment and the care of other forms of life have ultimate significance for the building of the kingdom of God on earth and for what God must experience. What we do matters because we need to live with one another and nature and we need to cherish what God has brought to life. God can heal the world in history only with our cooperation, and the world needs our best efforts.

Religiously, if we have truly recognized and experienced the infinite compassion, mercy, and love that is God, if the self-sacrificing love of Jesus Christ has truly transformed our hearts and minds, then how could we think that what we do does not matter? How could we want to act differently than God acts? Would the truly converted heart and mind not want to be compassionate, merciful, and loving to all God's creatures in return, so that we might be worthy to be called children of God? Would we not in gratitude for the love we receive from God want to make all our acts contributions to the building up of God's kingdom? If the kingdom of God grows among us only to the extent that we give our hearts and minds and energies to it, then what we do has ultimate significance and value. If God values the world so much that God saves all things, then surely our religious consciousness would have to recognize that we, too, must value our world and what we can contribute to it. Far from making our actions irrelevant, God's salvation of all creation teaches us the ultimate significance of everything we do and fail to do.

The Problem of Evil

The theory of divine action I have been discussing offers a solution to the problem of evil that has long bedeviled Christian thought. Classically, this problem does not refer to *moral* evil done by humans in their freedom, but to so-called natural evil, the tragic aspects of existence in the physical world: accidents; disease; death; and the destructive consequences of natural events such as floods, tornados, and earthquakes. The problem arises from affirming both God's goodness and God's omnipotence, the latter understood classically as meaning that God has absolute power and can literally do anything. The problem also presumes the view that God can control the events of nature and history. Thus, if God is all-good and all-powerful, why does God not act to prevent the occurrence of natural evils? Why do innocent children develop cancer? And so on. So long as none of the classical assumptions are challenged or questioned, there is no solution to this problem other than appealing to the mystery of God.

Whitehead's solution to the problem of evil is based on three related positions: that God's power is limited by the metaphysical situation and hence God cannot control what happens in the universe; that God is not the sole source of all that is; and that the creativity driving the continual becoming of the universe is independent of God, inherent in every actual agent of the universe. This results in a persuasive solution to the problem of evil.[21] However, in my revision of Whitehead's metaphysics,

---

[21] For Whitehead's analysis and solution to the problem of evil, see Alfred North Whitehead, *Religion in the Making* (New York: Macmillan, 1926), 94–99; idem, *Process and Reality*, 223, 340–41, 349–50; and idem, *Adventures of Ideas*, chap. 20. For studies of the problem of evil from a process perspective, see David Ray Griffin, *God, Power, and*

I have altered all three of these positions. I have argued above that the limitation on God's power is a *self*-limitation; that God *is* the sole source of all that is *(creatio ex nihilo)*; and that the Christian tradition cannot accept Whitehead's separation of creativity from God, but must instead regard creativity as God's own life and that consequently the creativity and freedom of every actual agent in the universe originates in God's creative sharing of the divine life. This revision conceives of God as Creator in a stronger sense than one finds in Whitehead's metaphysics. But this revision also seems to undercut his solution to the problem of evil.

If God freely limits God's own power, then it seems that God *could* choose to prevent at least the worst of natural evils, but for some unknown reason chooses not to. If God is the sole source of all that is, then God could have chosen to organize possibilities in another way, creating a different kind of universe in which sufferings and evils were not so dominant, but chose not to. And if the freedom and creativity of every actual agent is a gift from God, then God bears at least indirect responsibility for all the evils resulting from the exercise of freedom in the universe.

But once one thinks through the implications of conceiving of creation as a sharing of God's own life, the practical result is much the same as Whitehead's solution. Even though the limitation on God's power is a *self*-limitation, I have already shown that God cannot remove that limitation without destroying what God wants to create or violating the autonomy and freedom that are part of the empowering gift of God to all creatures. God's choice to create a universe that participates in the autonomy and freedom of God's own life means that God cannot control or determine events in the universe. Likewise, if creatures are to be truly free, God cannot eliminate possibilities for evil. The genuine autonomy and freedom of the universe require openness to tragic and evil possibilities as well as good, for these are linked to each other. The necessary consequence of God's free decision to create a universe that participates in God's own life is that God must put Godself, so to speak, in the hands of the world and must risk the possibilities for evil, tragedy, and suffering. But is this

---

Evil: A Process Theodicy (Philadelphia: Westminster Press, 1976); and Suchocki, *The End of Evil.*

not the very portrait of God that the revelation of God in the cross of Jesus Christ delivers to us? If the crucified Christ is the deepest revelation of God's character, then revelation teaches us that God's creative choice involves a correlative choice to share the sufferings, the evil consequences of free decisions, and all the tragedies and natural evils of our world. If God were to act in any other way, then God would compromise God's own character and cease being the God revealed in the crucified Christ.

Finally, with regard to the natural evils due to temporal finitude—the fact of death in human and animal experience, the constant perishing of all things and achievements in time—it is true that God is in a sense responsible for these natural evils, because God, as the ultimate ground of all possibility, makes a temporal course of events possible. But what could God conceivably do to eliminate natural evils from the temporal world? The possibility of a universe of temporal actual agents carries with it the conditions of finitude and decay and perishing in time. If there is to be a temporal world, it will be bound by the conditions of finitude. This is analogous to the way in which parents, by giving life to their children, are in a sense responsible for the fact that their children will inevitably suffer and die. Does it make any sense to blame parents for this? They can do nothing to change the fact that all living things suffer and die, and yet their love compels them to share the gift of life with their children. Analogously, God's love compels God to give the gift of life to the universe, despite the inevitability of suffering, tragedy, and death. But unlike human parents, God can overcome the limitations of finitude by taking all things into God's own unending life:

> "See, the home of God is among mortals.
> He will dwell with them;
> they will be his peoples,
> and God himself will be with them;
> he will wipe every tear from their eyes.
> Death will be no more;
> mourning and crying and pain will be no more,
> for the first things have passed away."
> (Rev 21:3–4)

The salvific love of God does all that can be done to heal, transform, and overcome every kind of suffering and evil. In dwelling in the universe, and the universe dwelling in God, God saves all things, heals all things, and in the end transforms all evils and tragedies into divine victory and tragic beauty.

The Uniqueness of the Work of Jesus Christ

Although there has never been a universally agreed-upon theory of the saving work of Jesus Christ, the Christian tradition has regarded the salvation accomplished in the suffering, death, and resurrection of Jesus Christ as unique, a turning point in cosmic history. Yet I have argued that God saves the universe at every moment, that one of the modes of divine action is the inclusion, healing, and transformation of every actual agent, every creature, in God's everlasting life. How, then, can I claim any uniqueness for the saving work of Jesus Christ?

Although I cannot here develop a response to this question in any detail, I briefly indicate how I believe the view of God I have presented to be compatible with the traditional claim. First, Jesus Christ is unique in that his life, teaching, suffering, death, and resurrection constitute the clearest and deepest revelation of God in both modes of divine action. In his life Jesus Christ influences the world by presenting the ideal possibility of the kingdom of God, the beautiful vision of how the world could be if all placed themselves under God's "rule." This reveals God's act of creation, empowering agents to respond to the divine lures as they create themselves. And Jesus Christ responds to the world by healing, restoring to life, and forming an inclusive community as the living embodiment of God's inclusive kingdom. This reveals God's responsive, salvific act. In his suffering and death Jesus Christ reveals the vulnerability of God, God's willingness to sacrifice God's own life, to undergo suffering and death for the sake of the kingdom and the world. God "rules" from the cross of Jesus Christ in the tragic beauty of self-sacrificing love. And in his resurrection, Jesus Christ reveals that God's salvific love can overcome and transform the evils and tragedies of the world to bring about new life and hope. Jesus Christ is God's

act, as God acts always and everywhere, but it is also a unique
act, manifest, revealed, and enacted in an unparalleled way in
the historical Jesus Christ. The work of Jesus Christ, dependent
on the voluntary cooperation of the human Jesus, makes the
transcendent character of God for the first time completely incarnate in history, a "natural fact of history," as Schleiermacher
said.[22] In this way Jesus Christ is the unique manifestation and
incarnation, the most concentrated expression, of the universal
salvific will and action of God.

Moreover, this historic Christ-event has had and continues to
have objective effects that otherwise would not have occurred.
The life, teaching, suffering, death, and resurrection of Jesus
Christ—mediated through preaching, scripture, tradition, the
lives of transformed people, the sacraments, and the ministry
of the church—have opened up a way of salvation transforming countless people's lives. The historical Jesus Christ effected
what John Cobb has called a "field of force," a power of creative
transformation and a structure of existence that continues to
transform people in the present and offer hope for the future.[23]
There is, then, in history and in God, a uniqueness and objectivity to the salvation effected in and through Jesus Christ. Even
though God always and everywhere saves all things, the Christ-
event objectively mediates both the call to the kingdom of God
and the universal forgiveness, compassion, and salvific love of
God by incarnating this reality in a unique way, in a person
and an event that enables us to grasp and to be challenged and
transformed by it as never before in history. Without the light
of the crucified and risen Christ piercing the ambiguities of nature and the horrors of our human history, would we be able to

---

[22] Friedrich Schleiermacher, *The Christian Faith*, 2 vols., trans. and
ed. H. R. MacKintosh and J. S. Stewart (New York: Harper Torchbooks,
1958; reprint of the English translation of the 3rd German edition),
2:365 (§88.4): "in this whole matter we posit, on the one side, an initial
divine activity which is supernatural, but at the same time a vital human receptivity in virtue of which alone that supernatural can become
a natural fact of history."

[23] See John B. Cobb, Jr., *Christ in a Pluralistic Age* (Philadelphia:
Westminster Press, 1975). While I differ on some of the ways Cobb
develops this idea, in my judgment it is an effective way of speaking
about the continuing salvific influence of the historical Jesus Christ.

perceive the suffering, salvific love at the heart of the universe? Without the self-sacrificing love of the crucified and risen Christ healing our wounds, transforming our hearts, and liberating us from the bonds of self-concern and self-security, could we have hope that the kingdom of God can be served in the midst of all the ambiguities of nature and the horrors of our human history?

God's saving grace comes to all in many different ways—one need not be a Christian to experience God's call and God's salvific love enabling us to live with courage and hope in the face of all of life's sufferings and evils. But in the person of Jesus Christ, God has effected both the deepest and clearest self-revelation and a unique salvific act that liberates and transforms us in history, in the world. Ultimately, this, I believe, is what the Christian tradition has meant in its claims for the uniqueness of the salvation accomplished in and through Jesus Christ.

Chapter 9

The Trinity and Christology

As we saw in Chapter 2, the doctrine of the Trinity and the christological dogma concerning the person of Jesus Christ are extremely complex and created continuing problems in the history of Christian thought. I believe that many of the problems are due to the implications and limitations of the classical Greek metaphysics in terms of which the doctrines were expressed. This metaphysics makes it difficult to articulate an understanding of God that coheres with the implications of Christian religious experience. Because of the complexity of the doctrines and the problems, I can do no more here than to suggest how the understanding of God I have been proposing might address these problems. These suggestions are nothing more than the barest indication of how a revised understanding of the Trinity and of the person of Jesus Christ might flow from a revised understanding of God employing a modified Whiteheadian metaphysics.

The Trinity

Although the doctrine of the Trinity is a statement about God, both the motive and the intent of defining it dogmatically were at heart christological. That is, the church decided that the proper understanding of Jesus Christ required this statement about God. Once the Arian controversy over the divinity of Jesus Christ was settled, the dogma of the Trinity became an object of theological speculation about God apart from God's relation to the world that made it even more incomprehensible. Were it not for the facts that the doctrine expresses the Christian religious experience of God's presence and action in Jesus Christ and the direct immanence of God in Jesus (the Son) and in the world (the Spirit), one might be tempted to say that Christian theology would be better off speaking simply of the oneness of God. The "economic Trinity," in other words, remains the classic Christian way of expressing the distinctive aspects of Christian religious experience of God's action. Yet some way must be found to interpret the meaning of this doctrine so that it does not involve us in metaphysical incoherence and confuse Christians and non-Christians alike with speculations about the inner life of God that often tend toward tri-theistic language and that are so offensive to Christianity's sibling faiths of Judaism and Islam.

There is certainly no one universally agreed-upon way of understanding and interpreting the Trinity. The resurgence of interest in trinitarian theology in the late twentieth and early twenty-first centuries has produced an amazing pluralism of viewpoints and arguments seeking to make trinitarian theology understandable and effective for contemporary times.[1] Even those theologians who work with the categories of process theology have produced an amazing pluralism of suggestions concerning

---

[1] The literature is far too extensive to list here. But the diversity of interpretations can be illustrated by this small sample: Catherine Mowry LaCugna, *God for Us: The Trinity and Christian Life* (San Francisco: Harper and Row, 1991); Jurgen Moltmann, *The Trinity and the Kingdom*, trans. Margaret Kohl (San Francisco: Harper and Row, 1981); Ted Peters, *God as Trinity: Relationship and Temporality in Divine Life* (Louisville: Westminster/John Knox Press, 1993); Joseph A. Bracken, SJ, *The Triune Symbol: Persons, Process and Community* (Lanham, MD: University Press of America, 1985); Walter Kasper, *The God of Jesus Christ*, trans. Matthew J. O'Connell (New York: Crossroad, 1984); Peter C. Hodgson, *God in History: Shapes of Freedom* (Nashville: Abingdon Press, 1989); Eberhard Jungel, *God as the Mystery of the World*, trans. Darrell L. Guder (Grand Rapids, MI: Eerdmans, 1983); Anthony J. Godzieba, "The Trinitarian Mystery of God: A 'Theological Theology,'" in *Systematic Theology: Roman Catholic Perspectives*, 2nd ed., ed. Francis Schüssler Fiorenza and John P. Galvin, 131–99 (Minneapolis: Fortress Press, 2011); Karl Rahner, *The Trinity*, trans. Joseph Donceel (New York: Crossroad, 1997 [1970]).

trinitarian theology.[2] I simply add another set of suggestions as to how some of the problems might be addressed.

One of the fundamental tenets in trinitarian theology is the claim that the *economic* Trinity, or God as Christians have experienced God's action for us, reflects the *immanent* Trinity, or the inner triune being of God. The distinctions among the Persons of the Trinity, in other words, are not merely the result of human experience and knowledge and thus restricted to how God appears to us (epistemological distinctions) but are in some sense real ontological distinctions within God. If the distinctions were merely epistemological, but not ontological, it is not clear that the christological interests of Christian theology could be adequately served by the trinitarian dogma. Because of this a metaphysical discussion of God is necessary; a merely phenomenological or existential discussion of the Trinity ("God for us") cannot do adequate justice to the ontological claims of the tradition. Moreover, the coherence of the doctrine of the Trinity requires an explicitly metaphysical discussion.

I here merely indicate one way in which the revised Whiteheadian metaphysical understanding of God I have been developing might address this issue. My suggestion is a modification of a proposal originated by Bernard J. Lee.[3] Lee's approach appeals to me because of his attempt to ground it in a study of the implications of the biblical roots of trinitarian language, specifically the Hebrew words *dabhar* ("word") and *ruach* ("spirit"). My modification will also incorporate a major revision of John Cobb's preference for a "Binity"[4] composed of God's transcendence and immanence.

In Lee's proposal and my modification of it, the Persons of the Trinity reflect the distinctions between the transcendence of God,

---

[2] See Joseph A. Bracken, SJ, and Marjorie Hewitt Suchocki, eds., *Trinity in Process: A Relational Theology of God* (New York: Continuum, 1997). The nine contributors to this volume articulate viewpoints that are amazingly diverse, even though they all employ the same general philosophical viewpoint in working out their suggestions.

[3] See Bernard J. Lee, SM, "An 'Other' Trinity," in Bracken and Suchocki, *Trinity in Process*, 191–214.

[4] See John B. Cobb, Jr., "The Relativization of the Trinity," in Bracken and Suchocki, *Trinity in Process*, 1–22.

on the one hand, and a twofold immanence of God, on the other. The first Person of the Trinity (Father, Creator) corresponds to God's transcendence. Biblically and metaphysically, the recognition of the divine transcendence focuses on God's foundational role as Creator, the absolute ground of the universe. Thus in terms of Whitehead's metaphysics, we would initially identify the first Person of the Trinity with the transcendence of God in the Primordial Nature. But my suggestion is that further reflection requires us to recognize that in Whitehead's metaphysics God is transcendent also in the Consequent Nature. As Whitehead describes the Consequent Nature of God, it is God's *private* reception, transformation, and harmonization of the universe in God's own experience, transcending the universe. This is why Whitehead found it necessary to introduce the notion of the immanence of God's Consequent Nature, or the immanence of God as a complete actual entity, in the world. Were this aspect of God not immanent in the world, we could not experience or know it. Also, Whitehead's metaphysical "principle of relativity" requires that every "private" reaction must become "public" as other actual agents experience the one in question.[5] I discussed this in Chapter 8, when I said that God's transformation and harmonization of the world in the unity of God's own life pours back into the world so as to lead the world toward healing possibilities in history, seeking to overcome the evils and tragedies of the past. As Whitehead says, "The action of [this aspect of God] is the love of God for the world. It is the particular providence for particular occasions."[6] The Consequent Nature of God not only receives all completed actual agents of the universe, but it also integrates these with God's Primordial Nature, the infinite and eternal vision of possibility, which is what produces the final healing and unity of the world in God. The Consequent Nature of God therefore incorporates the Primordial Nature and is really God as a complete actual entity. My suggestion, then, is that

---

[5] See Alfred North Whitehead, *Process and Reality: An Essay in Cosmology*, corrected edition, ed. David Ray Griffin and Donald W. Sherburne (New York: The Free Press, 1978), 29, 32, 88, 351; and Thomas E. Hosinski, *Stubborn Fact and Creative Advance* (Lanham, MD: Rowman and Littlefield, 1993), 201–3.

[6] Whitehead, *Process and Reality*, 351.

the first Person of the Trinity be understood metaphysically as referring to the transcendence of God, both Primordial and Consequent, or the transcendence of God as a complete actual entity.

The second Person of the Trinity (Son, Word, Redeemer) corresponds to the immanence of God in the universe as both Word and Redeemer. Many process theologians have identified this Person as the immanence of the Primordial Nature of God.[7] But Bernard Lee has suggested that process theologians have been led in this direction by the implications of interpreting God's Word (Hebrew: *dabhar*) by means of the Hellenistic philosophical Logos tradition (as mainstream Christian theology did). Lee argues that the Hebrew *dabhar* has rather different connotations from the Greek *Logos*, and that it really expresses a "Word of God" tailored to specific or concrete historical conditions. As such, Lee argues, in Whiteheadian metaphysics this Person corresponds to the immanence of God's Consequent Nature, not the Primordial Nature.[8] The Consequent Nature is God's response to the actual, concrete situations in the universe at every present moment and thus correlates with the biblical understanding of God's Word *(dabhar)* as highly contextualized. In contrast, the eternal vision of possibility constituting God's Primordial Nature is, as we have seen, unaffected by the actual course of events in the universe and thus does not fit with the biblical connotations of God's Word *(dabhar)*.

I think Lee is correct in this analysis. I would further argue in supporting his analysis that the primary Christian religious experience of Jesus Christ is as Savior or Redeemer. In Whitehead's metaphysics, the salvific or redemptive response of God to the universe occurs in God's Consequent Nature. If the second Person of the Trinity refers to what is incarnate in Jesus Christ, then we have two biblically based theological reasons for identifying this Person with the immanence of the Consequent Nature of

---

[7] See, e.g., Dorothy Emmet, *Whitehead's Philosophy of Organism* (London: Macmillan, 1932), 252–55; John B. Cobb, Jr., *A Christian Natural Theology* (Philadelphia: Westminster Press, 1965), 225; John B. Cobb, Jr., *Christ in a Pluralistic Age* (Philadelphia: Westminster Press, 1975); David Ray Griffin, *A Process Christology* (Philadelphia: Westminster Press, 1973), 192.

[8] See Lee, "An 'Other' Trinity," 200–210.

God: Jesus' proclamation and enactment of the kingdom of God incarnates the transforming Word of God addressed to us in our historical concreteness and particularity; and Jesus' ministry of healing and forgiveness, as well as his self-sacrificing death and resurrection, incarnates and enacts the divine healing, forgiveness, suffering, and salvific love.

The third Person of the Trinity (Spirit, Sanctifier) corresponds to the immanence of God in the world in a related but distinct way from God's immanence as Word and Savior. Lee summarizes his analysis of the Spirit *(ruach)* of God passages in Hebrew scripture in this way: the Spirit of God is the creative transformer of human spirits and hearts, attuning them to the spirit of God; it effects conversion, so that the human spirit and heart can discern the divine Spirit and heart. The Spirit in this sense directly affects how humans discern value and can lead them to feel things with God's feeling and to yearn for what God yearns for.[9] This biblical understanding of the Spirit of God is remarkably correlative with the function of the Primordial Nature of God in Whitehead's metaphysics, which seeks to lure every actual agent toward the possibility God values most highly. The third Person of the Trinity, then, can be identified metaphysically as the immanence of God's Primordial Nature in the universe.

As Lee points out, however, Hebrew scripture does not present the Word *(dabhar)* and Spirit *(ruach)* of God as alternative models of divine immanence; instead, they are correlative, distinct but intimately related aspects of God's immanence in the world. Further, the Wisdom literature combines these two related forms of divine immanence and action in a third metaphor, Wisdom *(Sophia)*, which favors more the function of the Spirit but also includes the function of the Word.[10] The Jewish understanding of God, then, can speak of the one God, the Holy One of Israel, as

---

[9] See ibid., 194–95; and Bernard J. Lee, *Jesus and the Metaphors of God: The Christs of the New Testament* (New York: Paulist Press, 1993), 80–119. A brilliant study of the Spirit of God as leading the Hebrew prophets to feel God's feelings, which supports Lee's analysis, is the classic work by Abraham Heschel, *The Prophets*, 2 vols. (New York: Harper and Row, 1962).

[10] See Lee, "An 'Other' Trinity," 196–200.

transcendent, and yet as immanent and active in the world in the Spirit and Word of God, or the Wisdom of God. The Christian doctrine of the Trinity presses the affirmation of the divine immanence to a new level of intensity by personifying the modes of divine immanence and affirming the incarnation of the Word in the historical Jesus Christ. It also can affirm the oneness of God and yet distinguish the three Persons as the divine transcendence and the two modes of divine immanence. This is not the kind of modalism that the early church declared heretical, because these distinctions describe the ontologically distinct functions or activities of God always and everywhere: God is always and everywhere the infinite, transcendent, creative source of all that is; the transforming power (Spirit) that invites us to feel as God feels and to value as God values; and the Word that addresses us in the particularity of our historical situations and suffers, forgives, heals, and saves us. God is always "constituted" by these distinct aspects of God's relations to and interactions with the universe. As Karl Rahner said, the immanent Trinity *is* the economic Trinity and vice versa.[11]

What we know of God comes from our experience of God, or, if one prefers, from revelation. What revelation delivers to us is a God to whom we are related in every dimension of our experience. Theology interprets the foundational religious experience into the basic claims of our faith. It is important to note that Christian faith defines all we know about God in terms of God's relation to the universe; God is Creator, Judge, Redeemer, Sanctifier, and Consummator. What would happen to our knowledge of God if one completely removed the universe? And what would happen to God? If what God *is* must be defined entirely in relation to the universe, can God ever have been without some world?

The tradition, of course, had an answer to such questions. It argued that the economic Trinity, revealed in God's dealings with the universe, must reflect the inner trinitarian life of God; that is, it must reflect the *immanent* Trinity, the eternal triune dynamism of God's own inner life. The tradition then deceived itself that we could speculate about the inner life of God *apart*

---

[11] Karl Rahner, *The Trinity*, 45.

from the universe and it grew enchanted by such speculation. God could be without a world, the tradition held, because the mutual indwelling of the three divine Persons in the Godhead makes God eternally and completely self-sufficient. The inner triune divine nature, the relationships among the three divine Persons, is enough to make God God, so to speak. This position is also involved in the claim that God did not have to create a world but did so freely, out of pure, disinterested love *(agape)*, not out of some need in God. Most contemporary trinitarian theology suggests that the relationality of the world flows from the fact of the inner relationality of God; the inner relationships and love among the three Persons in the Trinity—so often spoken of in ways that approach conceiving of the three Persons as three distinct entities—is what gives rise to a universe in which all things are related.

But one must wonder on what basis we can justify such trinitarian speculation. If one accepts the "Rahner rule" regarding the Trinity that I mentioned above—that the immanent Trinity is the economic Trinity, and vice versa—then it seems that we have no basis for speculating about what God might be *apart* from God's relation to the universe. If the immanent Trinity *is* the economic Trinity, then the immanent Trinity cannot be understood simply as God's "internal relations" within Godself but must always imply God's relations to a world, not merely possible relations, but *actual* ones. The fundamental identity of the economic Trinity and the immanent Trinity implies, it seems to me, that God is always in relation to some universe. We actually have no basis, even in the notion of the immanent Trinity, for a speculative discussion of what God might be *apart* from a universe. I agree completely with Bernard Lee when he says: "The tradition has been fascinated by speculation about who God is without us, but the only God we know is the God who is with us. An empirical commitment leaves us with God-with-us as the only context for our knowledge of God."[12]

As we saw in Chapter 2, the Christian tradition wanted to maintain the doctrine of monotheism despite its speech regarding the three Persons of the Trinity and its insistence that these three

---

[12] Lee, "An 'Other' Trinity," 209.

Persons are ontologically distinct within the Godhead. It tried to safeguard the oneness of God by asserting the classic claim regarding the mutual indwelling or coinherence *(perichoresis)* of the three Persons and the unity of the divine "operations" (so that the other two Persons are involved in the work of any one of these Persons). Even though this gets quite technical, I want to show that these claims can be expressed in Whiteheadian metaphysics. These claims can be expressed as reflecting the relations between the transcendence of God and the two modes of divine immanence in the oneness of God.

In Whitehead's metaphysics God is a single actual entity. That one actual entity is at the same time both transcendent and immanent in both the Primordial and Consequent Natures. We are able to make distinctions between the various ways God is transcendent and immanent, but because of God's unity, these distinct aspects of God's interaction with the world are all related to each other. The "oneness" of the divine transcendence that causes us to identify it as the first Person of the Trinity is a direct consequence of the *unity* of God as a single actual entity. While the transcendence of the Primordial and Consequent Natures of God are different or distinct sorts of transcendence—the one due to the metaphysical priority of God as ground of the universe, and the other due to the inherently "private" nature of God's experience of the world—they are not separable in the *actuality* of God. Only if the Primordial and Consequent Natures of God are treated as if they are actually separate would the unity of God's transcendence be compromised. But this would be to elevate a distinction of reason to a separation in fact, and this would violate Whitehead's own understanding of actual entities as wholes that are actually undivided.[13] Thus the two aspects of the divine transcendence are in fact one "Person."

But since the divine transcendence includes the Consequent Nature, this implies that the two modes of the divine immanence are really present in the divine transcendence: to use the traditional names, the Spirit and the Son coinhere with the Father. The Spirit is the immanence of the Primordial Nature of God in the world and the Son is the immanence of the Consequent

---

[13] See Whitehead, *Process and Reality*, 227, 344.

Nature of God in the world. The divine transcendence (the Father) includes the Consequent Nature, which integrates how the Primordial Nature (the Spirit) influences the world, how the temporal agents or actual entities of the world responded, and how God in God's Consequent Nature responds to the world's actions (the Son). In this way both the Spirit and the Son are present in the Father.

Likewise, both the Spirit and the Father are present in the Son, because the immanence of the Consequent Nature as concrete Word and Savior or Redeemer must include the immanence of the Primordial Nature (the Spirit) and the transcendence of the Consequent Nature (the Father). The concrete Word addressed to us in the specificity of our historical situations is based in the immanence of the divine valuation of the possibilities open to the present; and the presence of the second Person of the Trinity in the world as Savior is based in the transcendence of the Consequent Nature, which is the divine reception, healing, and transformation of the universe.

Finally, both the Father and the Son are present in the Spirit because the immanence of the Primordial Nature of God (the Spirit) is based in the transcendence of the Primordial Nature (the Father) and seeks to lead the world's development in accord with the redemptive action and goals of God's Consequent Nature (the Son). Thus the Persons of the Trinity coinhere, and each is involved in the "work" of any one of the Persons.

We are not speaking of three different agencies, but of three distinct aspects of the agency of the one God, whose ontologically different relations and interactions with the universe require us to distinguish between the divine transcendence and the two modes of divine immanence in the universe. The distinctions are ontologically *real*, referring to different modes of the complexity of God's relations to the universe. But God is a single actual entity, a single agency, and these distinct modes of divine action and presence in the universe are indivisibly one in God. Such a view, I believe, is in harmony with the intent of the Christian tradition's doctrine of the Trinity, without tending toward tritheism.

Joseph A. Bracken, SJ, has been working out a very different trinitarian theology employing his revision of Whitehead's metaphysics of God.[14] Briefly, Bracken conceives of the oneness of God as a *society*, in Whitehead's technical sense of that term, which Bracken reinterprets as a "system" or "field" of divine activity in which the three Persons of the Trinity interact in unity. I have the greatest respect for Bracken's work. But I believe that conceiving of the unity of God as a "field" (analogous to the concept of a physical "field," such as the electromagnetic field) tends to make the unity of God too abstract. Correlatively, the stress on the concrete individuality of the three Persons (which Bracken actually calls "entities" and "agents in their own right"), tends too close to tritheism for my taste. I am not accusing Bracken of tritheism; he does try to speak of the activity of the Persons as a "unified corporate reality in which all three divine persons in different ways are fully engaged."[15] In his view this is enough to maintain the unity of God. However, I find Bracken's way of speaking about the Persons to be too misleading in seeming to treat them as individual "entities" who share a unitive divine "field" in common. To me, this seems to make the three Persons the concrete actuality of God, while the unity of God seems to be generalized and quite abstract. But I also find most contemporary discussions of the Trinity in its inner relationality (the immanent Trinity) to trend toward tritheism in their manner of speech, so Bracken is surely not alone in this respect. Trinitarian theology over the past forty years at least has stressed God's relationality, but too often, in my opinion, the three Persons are spoken of as

---

[14] In addition to Bracken, *The Triune Symbol*, see idem, *The Divine Matrix: Creativity as the Link between East and West* (Maryknoll, NY: Orbis Books, 1995); idem, *The One in the Many: A Contemporary Reconstruction of the God-World Relation* (Grand Rapids, MI: Eerdmans, 2001); idem, *Christianity and Process Thought: Spirituality for a Changing World* (Philadelphia: Templeton Foundation Press, 2006); idem, *God: Three Who Are One* (Collegeville, MN: Liturgical Press, 2008); idem, *Subjectivity, Objectivity, and Intersubjectivity: A New Paradigm for Religion and Science* (West Conshohocken, PA: Templeton Foundation Press, 2009); idem, *Does God Roll Dice? Divine Providence for a World in the Making* (Collegeville, MN: Liturgical Press, 2012); idem, *The World in Trinity: Open-Ended Systems in Science and Religion* (Minneapolis: Fortress Press, 2014).

[15] Bracken, *The World in the Trinity*, 111.

if they are three distinct entities or agencies that interact with each other to form a kind of divine committee.[16]

God is one, one agency with three ontologically distinct ways of interacting with the world. We speak of the Trinity because we have experience of God acting toward us, being with us, in three distinct ways. We ought not begin speculating about what God would be or must be like apart from God's relation to us and our world, because, frankly, we have no basis for this sort of trinitarian speculation about the inner life of God. The immanent Trinity *is* the economic Trinity.

Christology

My primary aim in this book has been to develop a revised doctrine of God, not a new Christology. But I have tried to formulate my understanding of God and God's action on a christological basis; that is, I have used the teaching, life, death, and resurrection of the historical Jesus Christ as the religious basis for grounding a theological interpretation of God and a theory of how God acts. My aims oblige me to give at least the sparest of indications—though I can here do no more than that—of what implications my revised Whiteheadian understanding of God might have for the classical christological problems.

Using a different metaphysical basis than the tradition did for understanding the presence and action of God in Jesus by itself resolves several of the more severe problems. The classical philosophical categories employed by the tradition expressed a substance metaphysics that made it extremely difficult to understand how God could be present in Jesus Christ, since this metaphysics had no way of understanding how two "substances" could both

---

[16] As just one example, see Denis Edwards, *The God of Evolution: A Trinitarian Theology* (Mahwah, NJ: Paulist Press, 1999), 21–24, 26–28, 31–33. I do not mean to single Edwards out; his speech regarding the inner life of God as "Persons-in-relation," as "mutual love" or "mutual friendship" between the three divine Persons, and so on is typical of recent trinitarian speech. I sympathize with much of what Edwards has to say in his many books, but this sort of speech about the inner life of God trends too close to tritheism for my taste.

be present in and definitive of one entity. The Christian religious conviction about the presence of God in Jesus strains against the confines of this substance metaphysics. Whitehead's metaphysics abandons the notion of substance, replaces it with a processive and relational concept of actual entities, and is largely devoted to understanding how various entities (actual entities and possibilities or potentialities) can be present in actual entities.[17] Moreover, this "process" metaphysics, in its modal understanding of the divine attributes, is able to affirm both God's impassibility (in the absoluteness and transcendence of the Primordial Nature of God) and God's passibility (in the relatedness of the Consequent Nature of God). It therefore faces no contradiction to its affirmation of the divine perfection when it also affirms that God suffers. It is able to articulate in a coherent way the Christian religious conviction that it is God who suffers in self-sacrificing love for our salvation. In both these ways—its ability to speak intelligibly of God's presence in the human Jesus, and its ability to affirm the divine suffering involved in salvation—it is better able to express metaphysically the Christian religious experience of Jesus Christ than the classical metaphysics employed by the tradition ever could.

In Whitehead's philosophy, especially as I have revised it in my discussion of creation, God is present in every actual entity. The "life" of every actual entity is a participation in the life of God: "the world lives by its incarnation of God in itself."[18] If one accepts this, then the christological problem is to articulate a unique or more intensive presence of God in the historical Jesus Christ. I have already argued that the incarnation could occur only because of the divine initiative on the one hand, and because of the human cooperation of Jesus on the other. The New Testament tradition tends to express Jesus' human cooperation in terms of his perfect "obedience" and "sinlessness." "Obedience" is derived from the Latin *ob* (an intensifier) plus *audire* (to hear or listen). It connotes "hearing thoroughly" or "listening intense-

---

[17] See Whitehead, *Process and Reality*, 50: "The philosophy of organism is mainly devoted to the task of making clear the notion of 'being present in another entity.'"

[18] Whitehead, *Religion in the Making* (New York: Macmillan, 1926), 156.

ly," a listening so intense that it forms a full-hearted conviction and loyalty toward what has been heard or listened to.[19] In this sense we can suggest that God could dwell in a unique way in Jesus Christ because the human Jesus "heard thoroughly" or "listened intensely" to the call of God, so intensely and thoroughly that *his identity as a person was co-constituted by the Word of God*, the second Person of the Trinity.[20] Jesus' full human loyalty and conviction are given over completely to the presence of the Word of God in him. The New Testament conviction of Jesus' "sinlessness" (which appears as well in the Chalcedonian creedal statement as "consubstantial with us in all things except sin") expresses a correlative view, but with the emphasis on Jesus' action: at every moment of his life Jesus did the will of God. If Jesus' identity is co-constituted by his perfect obedience to the Word of God present in him, and his every action actualizes the possibility God wills (or desires to have actualized) for that moment, then Jesus Christ can be said to incarnate the Word of God in a unique way through his perfect cooperation with the immanence of God.

In this way the divine and the human are joined together in the unity of Jesus Christ's person. The "one person" here means the human person and the divine "Person" so completely identifying with each other that a unique unity of God and human is achieved without confusing or melding the human and divine "natures." One could argue that the "one person" is the human person, since it is the human cooperation that determines the actualization of the Incarnation. Yet that one person's *identity* is truly co-constituted by the divine "Person" and is entirely dependent on the divine initiative. The "communication of properties" here means that the divine identifies with the experiences of the

---

[19] See Jeffrey G. Sobosan, *The Turn of the Millennium* (Cleveland, OH: The Pilgrim Press, 1996), 45, 144; and, at greater length, idem, *Christian Commitment and Prophetic Living* (Mystic, CT: Twenty-Third Publications, 1986), 47–48; and idem, *Guilt and the Christian: A New Perspective* (Chicago: Thomas More Press, 1982), 42–45.

[20] See Cobb, *Christ in a Pluralistic Age*, 136–46, 163–73. My proposal, if worked out in more detail, would differ from Cobb's view, but I believe his articulation of this point to be a viable way of expressing the intent of the christological dogma in terms of a process metaphysics.

human so completely that they are truly God's own experiences, and the human identifies with and is faithful to the character of the divine so completely that God acts in and through Jesus in perfect unity. In God's immanence in Jesus Christ, God presents the specific call for the actualization of the kingdom of God in the concrete, historical situation: the love of enemies; compassion and mercy for sinners, the poor, and the oppressed; the call for an inclusive community that lives out of the divine love. In God's immanence in Jesus Christ, God also suffers the rejection, the passion, and the cross the human Jesus undergoes; God identifies with the human experiences of Jesus Christ. In God's immanence in Jesus Christ, the human Jesus identifies at each moment with the cause of God and proclaims it in his teaching, and in his actions he is faithful to the divine salvific character as he enacts the divine compassion, healing, forgiveness, vulnerability to rejection, and willingness to suffer for the salvation and redemption of the world.[21] In the resurrection the human Jesus Christ incarnates the divine transformation of the tragedies and evils of temporal finitude into surprising divine victories that offer new life and new hope.

I argued earlier in this book that much of the religious power of the central christological claim about the person of Jesus Christ resides in the implication that the suffering, death, and resurrection of Jesus Christ constitute the deepest revelation of God's self-sacrificing, salvific love for the world. But the official theology, because of the assumptions and implications of the classical metaphysics in which this doctrine was expressed, actually denied that God suffered (in the divine nature), even while trying to preserve that implication by stressing the unity of the divine and human natures in the one person of Jesus Christ. The result was the metaphysical incoherence of trying to affirm both the absolute divine attributes and the relative human attributes of the one person of Jesus Christ. This central incoherence in the fundamental christological affirmation of the Christian faith

---

[21] From a New Testament perspective, N. T. Wright expresses this idea—that the human Jesus incarnates God's presence and action—very well (see N. T. Wright, *Simply Jesus: A New Vision of Who He Was, What He Did, and Why He Matters* [New York: HarperCollins, 2011], esp. 167–89).

is troubling and has often been covered over by appeals to the mystery of God or the mystery of faith. In the modern period it has often been resolved (both publicly and privately) by denying the divinity of Jesus Christ. I suggest that a Whiteheadian metaphysics, able to distinguish between the absolute and relative functions and attributes of God, offers an important assistance to Christian theology in this regard.

Because Jesus Christ incarnates the relative aspect of God's interaction with the world (the Consequent Nature of God), the divine attributes involved in the incarnation are not the absolute ones of God's Primordial Nature but the relative ones: finitude, being conditioned or affected, having one's experience partially determined by the world, passibility. Because of this, there is no contradiction or incoherence between the attributes of the human and the attributes of the divine in the unity of Jesus Christ's person: the human is affected by the world and the divine is affected by the world; the human is capable of suffering and the divine is capable of suffering, and so on. If the tradition could find no coherent way of holding together the divine impassibility and the human passibility in the one person of Jesus Christ, a christological interpretation along the lines I have suggested does not face this problem. Nor is the humanity of Jesus Christ in danger of being wholly absorbed and lost in the absoluteness of the divine incarnate in him. Recognizing the relative attributes of God offers hope of resolving the metaphysical incoherence in the central christological claim of the Christian faith. This view also resonates deeply with the beautiful idea of God's humility, God's "emptying" of Godself in the incarnation.[22]

My suggestion here is even in accord with the tradition's insistence that it is the Son, the second Person of the Trinity, that is incarnate in Jesus Christ, not the Father. Since I have argued that Jesus Christ incarnates the immanence of the Consequent Nature of God, not the Primordial Nature, this suggestion is metaphysically in accord with the tradition's claim, and even (dare I suggest) renders it more intelligible. My suggestion appears to run into conflict with the tradition's condemnation of patripassianism (which most theologians today take to mean attributing suffering to the Father), because I have identified the first Person of the

---

[22] See Philippians 2:6–8.

Trinity as the transcendence of both the Primordial and Consequent Natures of God, or the transcendence of God as a whole
actual entity. This implies that even the "Father" suffers in the
unity of God. In response I would offer two thoughts. First, the
condemnation of patripassianism as a heresy was really not so
much condemning the idea of God as suffering as condemning a
temporalized modalism (Sabellianism or modalist Monarchianism) and a denial that the distinctions between the Persons of the
Trinity are ontologically real.[23] I have already affirmed that the
distinctions between the Persons of the Trinity are ontologically
real distinctions in God, and so my proposal is certainly not the
same as Sabellianism or modalist Monarchianism. Second, the
unity of God, the mutual coinherence or *perichoresis* of the three
Persons in the unity of God, really in any case implies that the
Father suffers. If we think of God as one entity, and the three
Persons as inseparably united in that oneness despite their real
distinction, what sense does it make to say that only the Son
suffers, but not the Father or the Spirit? Because of their *perichoresis* or mutual coinherence, all three Persons must share in the
experiences of the others (to use traditional language). I do not
think one can coherently attribute suffering to only one Person
of the Trinity and hold that the other two Persons do not suffer
as well. I believe such a claim actually compromises the unity
or oneness of God.

There is, obviously, much more work that would have to be
done to develop such a Christology thoroughly. But it seems to
me that if our Christology is to be faithful to what we experience
in Jesus Christ and faithful to the profound and ancient Christian
discipline of the *imitatio Christi* (the imitation of Christ), then we
must safeguard the full humanity of Jesus Christ and recognize

---

[23] See Jaroslav Pelikan, *The Christian Tradition*, vol. 1: *The Emergence of the Catholic Tradition (100–600)* (Chicago: University of
Chicago Press, 1971), 176–82. See also Marcel Sarot, "Patripassianism,
Theopaschitism, and the Suffering of God," *Religious Studies* 26, no. 3
(1990): 363–75; this is a very interesting study of the historical meanings of the terms *patripassionism, theopachitism,* and *impassibility* and
how they are often misused in contemporary theology. On the issues
involved in the historical condemnation of "patripassianism," see esp.
369–71.

the central importance of his human cooperation with God as crucial to the possibility of the incarnation and crucial as well to the possibility of Christian discipleship. The few indications I have given here, I believe, could be further developed into a christological doctrine that would do this while remaining faithful to the foundational Christian religious experience of encountering God's compassionate, self-sacrificing, salvific, and redeeming love in and through the person of Jesus Christ.

Conclusion

Eschatology and the Incomprehensibility of God

Throughout this book I have sought to work out a revised Christian understanding of God utilizing a modified Whiteheadian metaphysics. I believe that the resulting interpretation of the doctrine of God is faithful to the vision of God implied by the teachings and actions of the historical Jesus Christ, as well as compatible with the central claims of Christian religious experience. Although it differs from the received theological tradition in many ways, it can coherently express the intentions of the major Christian theological doctrines. This understanding of God is also surprisingly compatible with the contemporary scientific understanding of reality, as I have tried to show. And although I have not focused on this question, I hope my discussion has implicitly shown that this view of God can speak to the social and religious needs of our time and ground our commitment to working for the healing of human society, the cherishing of our fellow creatures, and the care of our earth. Even if we will never be perfect in accomplishing this, we can invest our lives and energies in working for the improvement of our world, because we understand that God has entrusted God's creation to us and awaits our cooperation, even as God continually sustains us, heals us, and leads us toward more beautiful and healing possibilities. This vision of God, I believe, can ground our hope in the midst of all the ambiguities of life in the contemporary world.

The story of God's dynamic interaction with the universe is not over. The Christian tradition teaches eschatological hope, based on the resurrection of Jesus Christ and the conviction that the cosmic importance of the Christ event will one day reach its completion. Traditionally, the doctrine of eschatology, or the "last things," concerned the return (or "second coming") of Jesus Christ, the resurrection of the dead, judgment, and the final establishment of the kingdom of God. Exactly what this might entail, what form it might take, is beyond our understanding. There are attempts to think about eschatology in the context of contemporary scientific scenarios about the ultimate fate of our universe,[1] but all such attempts are quite speculative.

The doctrine of eschatology, it seems to me, at root expresses a human commitment, a human hope, and a divine promise. The commitment is that we will dedicate ourselves to living under God's "rule," so that we might contribute to the building up of God's kingdom. The hope is that God will not abandon God's creatures to final death and destruction, but will save them. And the promise—for Christians based in the resurrection of Jesus Christ—is that God will in fact overcome all the tragedies of temporal existence and raise all to everlasting life and blessing. When we try to go beyond this commitment, hope, and promise in our understanding, we are involved in a great deal of speculation and must be quite humble with regard to what we can know. And yet one can indicate why the doctrine of God ultimately issues in this hope.

The religious and theological ground of eschatological hope is the revealed character of God and God's act in raising Jesus Christ from the dead. In recognizing God as the sole Creator of all things, the Jewish, Christian, and Islamic traditions recognize that every creature lives out of the power and being of God. Theologically, one might express this conviction by saying

---

[1] See, e.g., John Polkinghorne and Michael Welker, eds., *The End of the World and the Ends of God: Science and Theology on Eschatology* (Harrisburg, PA: Trinity Press International, 2002); John Polkinghorne, *The God of Hope and the End of the World* (New Haven, CT: Yale University Press, 2002); Ted Peters, Robert John Russell, and Michael Welker, eds., *Resurrection: Theological and Scientific Assessments* (Grand Rapids, MI: Eerdmans, 2002); Robert John Russell, *Time in Eternity: Pannenberg, Physics, and Eschatology in Creative Mutual Interaction* (Notre Dame, IN: University of Notre Dame Press, 2012); and Joseph A. Bracken, SJ, *The World in the Trinity: Open-Ended Systems in Science and Religion* (Minneapolis: Fortress Press, 2014), 217–45.

that all things participate in the divine life. If God's life is everlasting, and every created thing participates in that life, then it follows that God's infinite and everlasting life and love not only give life to all things, but also enfold all things and save all things. The tradition's affirmation of God's universal salvific will supports this view. Furthermore, according to the Gospels, Jesus himself, in the context of discussing the resurrection, said that God is the God of the living, not the dead.[2]

I firmly believe that God's universal salvific will must mean the ultimate salvation of *all* things, not just human beings. If one reflects in an eschatological context on the implications of what Jesus reveals about God in his teachings and actions, is seems to me that universal salvation of the cosmos once again speaks to us of an ultimate wholeness centered on Jesus Christ. Jesus' parables of finding the lost speak of God's universal salvific will and even of God's desire for wholeness and completion. And Jesus' own self-sacrifice reveals how God opens God's arms to embrace all suffering and to overcome sin and death for all.[3] The belief in the return or second coming of Jesus Christ really expresses the hope for the cosmic fulfillment or completion of what God has begun in Jesus Christ. Paul, or the author of the Letter to the Ephesians, speaks of God's "plan for the fullness of time, to gather up all things" in Christ, the completion of Christ's redemptive work (Eph 1:8–10). The earliest church saw the ultimate significance of Jesus Christ in this cosmic context: God enfolding all things in God's saving love through Jesus Christ. Eschatological hope is the conviction that ultimately God will be "all in all" (1 Cor 15:28).

There remains a final topic for reflection: the ultimate mystery and incomprehensibility of God. I have avoided this topic until now because, as one of my teachers once said, theologians tend to invoke the mystery of God precisely at the point where their theologies break down. The mystery of God is frequently

---

[2] See Matthew 22:32; Mark 12:27; Luke 20:38.

[3] N. T. Wright speaks of this as an essential part of Jesus' self-sacrifice and saving work (see N. T. Wright, *Simply Jesus: A New Vision of Who He Was, What He Did, and Why He Matters* [New York: HarperCollins Publishers, 2011], 183–89).

used as a cover for inconsistencies and incoherence in thought, an excuse not to think further. And so I invoke the mystery of God at the conclusion of my project, after I have done my best to present a consistent and coherent discussion of God. It is proper to invoke the mystery of God at the end, because the infinite creative source of all that is and the infinite love saving all that is cannot be grasped and understood by the limited and fallible mind of a human. I have used metaphysics to bring philosophical precision and depth to analyzing the implications of metaphors and ideas. But this metaphysics cannot be taken as a univocal description of God—this would be to deceive ourselves that we have understood God. As Whitehead said of the technical terms of his own metaphysics, "They remain metaphors mutely appealing for an imaginative leap."[4] The best metaphysics can do is to enlighten our ignorance to some degree. What Nicholas of Cusa confessed at the outset of his project—our ignorance of the infinite God—I confess at the end of my project and hope only to have made that ignorance a bit more educated, a bit more faithful to the God of Christian experience. As a Christian I believe our surest knowledge of God to be the person of Jesus Christ, and I have sought to serve this revelation as best I could. But in the end, all such efforts fail before the mystery of God.

We cannot understand the mystery of God. But we can feel the beauty, the beauty that evoked Jesus' devotion to his Abba, the beauty that makes the sun to shine and the rain to fall on the just and unjust alike, the beauty that feeds the birds and clothes the flowers and does not abandon a single sparrow falling to the ground. We can feel the beauty of mercy, compassion, and forgiveness. And we can feel the tragic beauty revealing itself in the cross of Jesus Christ and offering new life and healing and hope in the resurrection.

The one statement about God in the New Testament that summarizes all we know of God through Jesus Christ is in 1 John 4:8, 16: "God is love." We live out of this love; we live *because* of this love; we are healed and saved in this love. We

---

[4] Alfred North Whitehead, *Process and Reality: An Essay in Cosmology*, corrected ed., ed. David Ray Griffin and Donald W. Sherburne (New York: The Free Press, 1978 [1929]), 4.

cannot understand this infinite Love, this God, but we can know with our hearts. We can feel the Love at the heart of the universe, "the divine incarnational energy at the heart of cosmic evolution."[5] We cannot understand, but we can love in response—we can love one another; the wondrous universe in which we live; and the wondrous God who gives life to all, sustains all, and saves all. Only in striving to love as we are loved do we become worthy to be called children of the Love in heaven. Only in striving to love as we are loved do we allow to be born in us the image of the unseen God.

---

[5] Ilia Delio, OSF, *Making All Things New: Catholicity, Cosmology, Consciousness* (Maryknoll, NY: Orbis Books, 2015), xiv.

Recommended Reading

Barbour, Ian G. *When Science Meets Religion*. New York: Harper-Collins, 2000.

Bracken, Joseph A., SJ. *Christianity and Process Thought: Spirituality for a Changing World*. Philadelphia/London: Templeton Foundation Press, 2006.

———. *The World in the Trinity: Open-Ended Systems in Science and Religion*. Minneapolis: Fortress Press, 2014.

Delio, Ilia. *Christ in Evolution*. Maryknoll, NY: Orbis Books, 2008.

———. *The Emergent Christ: Exploring the Meaning of Catholic in an Evolutionary Universe*. Maryknoll, NY: Orbis Books, 2011.

———. *From Teilhard to Omega: Co-Creating an Unfinished Universe*. Maryknoll, NY: Orbis Books, 2014.

———. *Making All Things New: Catholicity, Cosmology, Consciousness*. Maryknoll, NY: Orbis Books, 2015.

———. The *Unbearable Wholeness of Being: God, Evolution, and the Power of Love*. Maryknoll, NY: Orbis Books, 2013.

Haught, John F. *Christianity and Science: Toward a Theology of Nature*. Maryknoll, NY: Orbis Books, 2007.

———. *God after Darwin: A Theology of Evolution*. Second edition. Boulder, CO: Westview Press, 2008.

———. *Making Sense of Evolution: Darwin, God, and the Drama of Life*. Louisville, KY: Westminster John Knox Press, 2010.

———. *Resting on the Future: Catholic Theology for an Unfinished Universe*. New York: Bloomsbury, 2015.

———. *Science and Faith: A New Introduction*. New York: Paulist Press, 2012.

Hosinski, Thomas E. *Stubborn Fact and Creative Advance: An Introduction to the Metaphysics of Alfred North Whitehead*. Lanham, MD: Rowman and Littlefield, 1993.

Macquarrie, John. *In Search of Deity: An Essay in Dialectical Theism*. The Gifford Lectures, 1983. New York: Crossroad, 1984.

Peacocke, Arthur. *Theology for a Scientific Age: Being and Becoming—Natural, Divine and Human*. Enlarged edition. Minneapolis: Fortress Press, 1993.

Polkinghorne, John. *The Polkinghorne Reader*. Edited by T. J. Oord. West Conshohocken, PA: Templeton Press, 2010.

———. *Science and Religion in Quest of Truth*. New Haven, CT: Yale University Press, 2011.

Re Manning, Russell, and Michael Byrne, eds. *Science and Religion in the Twenty-First Century*. The Boyle Lectures. London: SCM Press, 2013.

Whitehead, Alfred North. *Process and Reality: An Essay in Cosmology*. Corrected edition. Edited by David Ray Griffin and Donald W. Sherburne. New York: The Free Press, 1978. [Originally published by Macmillan, 1929.]

———. *Religion in the Making*. New York: New American Library, 1974. [Originally published by Macmillan, 1926.]

Życiński, Józef. *God and Evolution: Fundamental Questions of Christian Evolutionism*. Translated by Kenneth W. Kemp and Zuzanna Maślanka. Washington, DC: Catholic University of America Press, 2006.

Index

Alexandrian theology, 37, 136
analogy, way of, 47
Anaxagoras, 47
Anderson, Bryon D., 64 n1, 69 n8, 139 n12
Anselm of Canterbury, 41–44, 45, 47, 112
Antiochene theology, 37, 136
Aquinas, Thomas, see *Thomas Aquinas*
Arian controversy, 29–35, 175
Aristotle, 44, 47
Arius, 29–30, 33
Aspect, Alain, 71
attractor, 91, 92, 100, 101, 113, 142, 146
Augustine of Hippo, 35, 42 n1, 52, 157, 165
Augustinian tradition, 42, 112, 113

Barbour, Ian G., 70 n11, 71, 110 n9
basin of attraction, 92, 100, 101, 113, 142, 146
Bell, John, 71
biology, 81–103
Bohr, Niels, 70
Borg, Marcus, 16 n20
Bowler, Peter J., 88 n12
Bracken, Joseph A., 176 n1, 177 n2, 184–85, 194 n1
Brown, J. R., 68 n7, 70 n12
Browne, Janet, 81 n2
Byrne, Paul M., 107 n5

Calvin, John, 157, 165
Cambrian explosion, 95

catholicity, xiii-xiv, 23, 50, 160
causality, 55
hierarchical, 108
causes, secondary, 45, 133
chaos, 92
theory, 92, 111, 113
Chalcedon, Council of, 37–39
dogma of, 124, 135–36
Chargaff, Erwin, 89
Christ, cosmic, 23–25, 29, 51, 61, 194–95
Christian tradition, 20, 23, 26, 133, 157, 165–66, 169, 171, 173, 181–83
Christology, 40, 132, 175, 186–92
Clement of Alexandria, 165
Cobb, Jr, John B., 1 n1, 172, 177, 188 n20
co-creators, God and universe as, 116, 117, 122, 129
Cohen, Jack, 91 n19, 91 n20
communication of properties (in Jesus Christ), 53, 188–89
complexity theory, 89–93, 100–102, 111, 113, 142–44
consciousness, 115
Constantine, 29
Constantinople, Council of, 34
Constantinople, Third Council of, 136
Conway Morris, Simon, 96, 97, 113, 146
Cooke, Bernard J., 3–4
Copernicus, Nicholas, 54
Copleston, Frederick, 46 n15, 108 n6
cosmic background radiation, 66–67

cosmic Christ, see *Christ, cosmic*
cosmology, 63, 65–68, 72–75, 109
cosmos, see *universe*
creatio ex nihilo (creation from
    nothing), xiv, 106–10, 118, 121
creation, see *God, as Creator*
creation, doctrine of, 106–22, 123,
    127, 132
creation, narratives of (in scripture),
    85–86, 109
creativity, 114 n17, 118, 119 n24,
    122, 168–69
Crick, Francis, 89, 89
Crossan, John Dominic, 16 n20
Crouzel, Henri, 26 n6, 27 n9
Crutchfield, James P., 91 n19
Cyril of Alexandria, 37

Daley, Brian E., 26 n6
dark energy, 67
dark matter, 67
Darwin, Charles, 81–86, 89, 102,
    103
Darwin, Emma, 82
Darwin, Francis, 83 n5
Davies, P. C. W., 68 n7, 70 n12
Davis, Leo Donald, 29 n12, 34
    n18, 37 n24
Dawkins, Richard, 106 n1
Delio, Ilia, xiii, 23, 122, 197 n5
Dennett, Daniel, 106 n1
design (in nature), 84
Desmond, Adrian, 81 n2
determinism, "soft," 100–102,
    143–44
Dicke, Robert, 66
Dirac, Paul, 69
divine attributes, see *God, attri-
    butes of*
divine operations, unity of, 34
DNA, 88–89, 99
Duns Scotus, John, 46
dynamic systems, see *systems,
    dynamic*

ecology, 98
Edwards, Denis, 186 n16
Einstein, Albert, 64–65, 68–71, 75

Eldredge, Niles, 96
emergence, 92, 98
energy, 64–65, 68, 72–73, 75–77,
    114, 120–22, 128, 160
law of conservation of, 125, 141
Ephesus, Council of, 37
Erasmus, 54
Erwin, Douglas H., 95 n27
eschatology, 127, 149, 193–95
ethics, 86
eukaryotic cells, 94
evil, problem of, 102, 168–71
evolution
    and religion, 82–88, 98–100,
        144–47
    by natural selection, 81–83,
        84–85, 92–93
    cosmic, xiv
    modern synthesis of, 88
    Roman Catholic response to, 86–88
existence as participation in being
    of God, 41–45, 49–50, 58,
    76–77, 119–22, 133, 147, 166,
    169, 187
experience, religious, 58–59, 61,
    105, 130, 138, 146, 175, 176,
    181, 187, 192–95

Farmer, J. Doyne, 91 n19
Ferris, Timothy, 66 n2, 72 n15
Ford, Lewis, S., 166 n20
Franklin, Rosalind, 88–89
free will, 115, 117
freedom, 100–102, 114–17, 118–
    19, 129, 132, 143, 145, 169

Galileo, 54
Gamow, George, 66–67
genetics, 88
Gerrish, Brian A., 60 n51
Gilkey, Langdon B., 51 n31, 118,
    123 n1
Gilson, Etienne, 42 n1, 46 n15, 47
    n17, 48
Gnosticism, 107
God
    acting in and through natural
        processes, 3, 10, 126, 134

action of, 123–47
action of as hidden, 12–14, 45–46, 61, 99, 126, 134–35, 140
action of as non-coercive, 14–16, 130–31, 133
arguments for existence of, 44–45, 75–76, 105–6, 121
as Abba (Father), 2, 120
as coincidence of opposites, 48–49, 157, 159
as Creator, 87, 98, 107–8, 110–17, 129, 149–50, 153–58, 169, 178, 194
as empowering, 115–17, 130–31
as Judge, 5, 126, 161–63
as Love, xiv, xv, 164, 165, 166, 170, 171, 178, 196–97
as merciful, forgiving, and compassionate, 2–7
as Redeemer, 107
as Triune, see *Trinity*
attributes of, 30, 42, 151, 152–58, 161, 187
care of for non-human life, 9–12
Consequent Nature of, 150–60, 162, 178, 179, 183–84, 187
creativity and, 114 n17, 118, 122
dwells in the universe, xiii, 50, 119
dynamic interaction of with the universe, 97, 114, 116, 127, 150, 158–60, 164, 193
existence of, 105
freedom of, 107, 146, 152, 156
hiddenness of, 52, 53–54, 99 (see also *God, action of as hidden*)
humility of, 103, 117–19
immanence of, 36, 147, 178–81, 183, 188–89
in the actions of Jesus, 16–21
in the teachings of Jesus, 1–15
incomprehensibility of, 195–96
Kingdom of, see *Kingdom of God*
knowledge of, 161–62
mystery of, xiii, 168, 195–96
power of, 5, 14–15, 16, 20, 117–19, 126, 130–33 (see also *omnipotence*)

Primordial Nature of, 112–19, 127, 143, 151, 152–58, 161, 162, 178–80, 183, 187
self-emptying of (*kenosis*), 103, 119, 190
self-limitation of, 117–19, 132–33, 146, 169–70
suffering of, 40, 53, 155–56, 187, 189
traditional doctrine of, 1, 83, 85, 97
transcendence of, 36, 107, 147, 172, 177–79, 183–84
universal salvific will of, 9, 11, 126, 149, 163, 166, 195
Word of, 24–25: incarnate in Jesus Christ, 29–32, 35; relation of to God, 29–32
Godzieba, Anthony J., 176 n1
Gould, Stephen Jay, 57 n43, 96, 97
Gray, Asa, 82, 144
Gregory Nazianzus, 26 n6, 165
Gregory of Nyssa, 26 n6, 34, 165
Griffin, David Ray, 168 n21
Grillmeier, Aloys, 37 n24

Harris, Sam, 106 n1
Hartle, James, 73
Haught, John F., 103, 106 n1
Hawking, Stephen, 73, 108 n7
Hegel, Georg W. F., 55
Heinrich, Bernd, 10 n9
Heisenberg, Werner, 69, 70
Henig, Robin Marantz, 88 n13
Heschel, Abraham, 3, 180 n9
Hitchens, Christopher, 106 n1
Hitler, Adolf, 166
Hodgson, Peter C., 176 n1
homoousios (of the same substance), 32–33
Hubble, Edwin P., 65, 66
Hume, David, 54–58, 137–38
Huxley, Thomas Henry, 56 n39, 83
hypostasis, 31, 34
hypostatic union, 37

immutability, divine, 30, 36, 39, 40, 51–52, 152, 155

impassibility, divine, 30, 36, 39, 40, 52, 152, 155–56, 187, 190
indeterminacy, 100
information, 141–42
interconnectedness, 78–79, 98–99
Irenaeus of Lyon, 25–26, 165
Isham, C. J., 73 n18
Islam, 176, 194

Jacob, Francois, 90
Jenkins, Philip, 29 n12
Jeremias, Joachim, 8 n5, 13 n13
Jesus Christ, 119, 125, 136, 149, 150, 154 n7, 157, 160, 162–63, 165, 167, 171–73, 174, 179–80, 186–92, 193, 195, 196
    actions of, 16–18, 124, 135, 149
    as revelation of God, xiii, xv, 1, 165, 171, 196
    as incarnation of God, xiv, 35–40, 119, 124, 181, 186–91
    as key to understanding God, 40, 124
    as Redeemer or Savior, 179
    association of with "sinners," 17–18
    cross (or crucifixion) of, 21, 131, 133, 156, 170, 196
    divinity of, 36–39, 186–91
    humanity of, 36–39, 186–91
    obedience of, 187–88
    resurrection of, 20–21, 140, 163, 193, 194, 196
    sinlessness of, 188
    teachings of, 2–15, 120, 124, 126, 134, 149, 158, 164, 166
    uniqueness of, 171–73, 187–89
Jewish tradition, 2, 3, 10, 16, 19, 23–24
John Paul II, Pope, 87
John Scotus Erigena, 165
Judaism, 176, 180–81, 194
judgment, divine, 5, 8–9 (see also God, as Judge)
Jungel, Eberhard, 176 n1

Kant, Immanuel, 55, 56–57, 58, 105–6

Kasper, Walter, 175 n1
Kauffman, Stuart, 90–93, 94 n25, 100–102, 113, 142–43, 146
Kelly, J. N. D., 29 n12, 31 n13, 32 n14, 33 n16, 34 n19, 35 n21, 37 n24, 38 n25
Kelsey, David, 110 n9
Kendzierski, Lottie, 107 n5
Kepler, Johannes, 54
Kingdom of God, 6–7, 11, 16, 119, 126, 127, 135, 156, 167, 173
Knowles, David, 44 n4

LaCugna, Catherine Mowry, 176 n1
laws of nature, 137–39
Lee, Bernard L., 177–80, 182
Lemaitre, Georges, 65–66
life, origin of, 81, 89, 93
Loewenich, Walther von, 52 n32
Lohfink, Gerhard, 16 n20
Lonergan, Bernard J. F., 161 n15
Luther, Martin, 51, 52–54, 157, 165

Macquarrie, John, 49 n26
Maimonides, Moses ben, 44 n4
Malina, Bruce J., 2 n2
many-worlds theory, 74, 109
Marcion, 107
Marshall, Michael, 81 n1
Margulis, Lynn, 94
Mary, Mother of God, 38, 39
mass extinctions, 95–96
Mayr, Ernst, 88 n12
McGrath, Alister E., 52 n32
Mendel, Gregor, 81, 88
metaphysics, Greek, 153, 154, 175, 189 (see also philosophy, Greek)
miracles, 55, 137–40
modalism, 181, 191
Moltmann, Jurgen, 176 n1
Monarchianism, 191
Monod, Jacques, 90
Monophysite controversy, 37–38
monotheism, 107, 118
monothelitism, 136
Moore, James, 81 n2

natural selection, see *evolution by*
natural theology, 58, 84
Nestorius, 37
Newton, Isaac, 64, 83
Nicea, Council of, 32–33
Nicene Creed, 32–33
Nicholas of Cusa, 46–51, 54, 79, 119, 121, 157, 160, 165, 196

omnipotence, 117, 130–32, 133, 168
omniscience, 161
ontological principle (Whitehead's), 111
order, 92, 98, 100, 102, 111–12, 116, 122, 127
Origen, 26–28, 31, 165
original sin, 86
oscillating universe theory, 66, 67–68
ousia (being), 31–34
Overbye, Dennis, 66 n2, 72 n15

Packard, Norman H., 91 n19
Pais, Abraham, 64 n1
Paley, William, 84
panentheism, 49, 107, 160
Pannenberg, Wolfhart, 160 n12
parable of the
    Leaven (Yeast), 13, 135
    Lost Coin, 7, 150
    Lost Sheep, 7, 150
    Mustard Seed, 12–13, 134
    Prodigal Son, 4–6, 120, 131, 150, 163, 166
    Seed Growing Secretly, 134
    Sower, 134
    Talents, 135
    Two Sons, 135
    Vineyard Workers, 6–7, 166
    Wheat and Weeds, 8–9, 20, 134, 163
patripassionism, 190–91
Paul, Saint, 24, 52, 119, 195
Pelikan, Jaroslav, 27 n6, 29 n12, 33 n17, 37 n24, 42 n1, 46 n15, 53 n34, 57 n42, 106 n2, 191 n23

Penzias, Arno, 67
perichoresis, 34, 183, 191
Peters, Ted, 110, 176 n1, 194 n1
philosophy, Greek, 23, 40, 106–7
    (see also *metaphysics, Greek*)
physics, 63–79
Pius XII, Pope, 86
Planck, Max, 68, 69
Plato, 36
Platonism, 31 n13, 32, 106–7
Podolsky, Boris, 71
Polkinghorne, John C., 69 n7, 117, 132, 194 n1
possibilities, role of, 77–78, 99–102, 141–42
    God and, 111–17, 127–28, 134, 141–42, 145–46, 152
    novel, 116, 145, 146
power, divine, see *God, power of*
predestination, 51, 52, 54, 157
Prestige, G. L., 31 n13
Prigogene, Ilya, 89–90
prokaryotic cells, 94
providence, divine, 85, 123–47
punishment, divine, 5, 27–28
    eternal, 27–28

quantum cosmology, 72–74
quantum entanglement, 71–72, 78–79
quantum theory, 41, 68–72, 75, 78–79, 115, 138
quantum vacuum, 72, 109

Rahner, Karl, 176 n1, 181, 182
Raup, David M., 95 n27
Reformers, 51–52
relatedness of all things, 65, 71–72, 78–79, 98–99, 160
relativity, theory of, 64–65, 68, 78–79
relativity, Whitehead's principle of, 178
religion and science, see *science, and religion*
Re Manning, Russell, 124 n2
revelation, 59, 124, 136–37, 150, 158, 170, 181
Rolston III, Holmes, 74 n19

Rosen, Nathan, 71
Russell, Robert John, 194 n1

Sabellianism, 191
Sachs, John R., 26 n6, 27 n7 & n9, 28 n11
Sagan, Dorian, 94 n26
salvation, 7, 9, 11, 52, 97–98, 149–73
    universal, 9, 11–12, 25–29, 164–68, 195
Sanders, E. P., 16 n20
Sarot, Marcel, 191 n23
Schleiermacher, Friedrich, 54, 55, 57–61, 63, 172 n22
Schüssler Fiorenza, Elizabeth, 18 n22
Schrödinger, Erwin, 69, 138
science, 1, 23, 55–58, 61, 63, 106, 109, 121, 125,140, 142 (see also *biology, complexity theory, physics, quantum theory*)
    and religion, 57, 60–61, 78, 87, 123, 140–47, 194
scientific revolution, the, 54
scripture, as inspired and inerrant, 86
Shaw, Robert S., 91 n19
singularity, cosmic, 68, 75
Smith, John Clark, 26 n6, 27 n8
Sobosan, Jeffrey G,, 188 n19
soteriology, 149, 171–73
soul, immortal, 85, 87, 99, 114
Spielberg, Nathan, 64 n1, 69 n8, 139 n12
Spirit of God, 180–81, 183–84
Stalin, Joseph, 166
state space, 91, 101
Stengers, Isabelle, 89 n15
Stewart, Ian, 91 n.19 and n20
Stoicism, 31 n13
stromatolites, 93–94
substantia (substance), 31–34
Suchocki, Marjorie Hewitt, 164 n19, 169 n21, 177 n2

suffering, 83–85, 99, 102–3, 117
super-symmetry theory, 68
systems, dynamic, 92–93, 100–101, 142–44, 146

Tertullian, 31
Thomas Aquinas, 44–46, 47, 76, 107–8, 133, 155, 157, 162 n16, 165
Tillich, Paul, 110 n9, 118
Trinity, the, xiv, 29–36, 39, 40, 175–86
    economic, 31, 176, 177, 181–82
    immanent, 31, 177, 181–82
    Persons of, 31, 177, 183–84
Tryon, Edward, 73 n16

uncertainty principle, 70
universe, 1, 50, 51, 52, 158–59, 167, 181
    expanding, 65–68, 72
    fine-tuning of, 74
    origin of, 66, 68, 72–73, 74, 76, 121

value, God as ground of, 43, 112–13
Vilenkin, Alexander, 75
Vollert, Cyril, 107 n5

Wade, Nicholas, 94 n24
Wallace, Alfred Russel, 81
Watson, James D., 88, 89
wave-particle duality, 69
Welch, Claude, 60 n51
Whitehead, Alfred North, xiv, 8–9, 36, 50 n28, 110–18, 119, 127–28, 139, 141–43, 147, 150–61, 163–5, 168–69, 178, 183, 187, 196
Wilson, Robert, 67
Wingren, Gustaf, 25 n2
Wright, N. Thomas, 25 n2, 189 n21, 195 n3

Zacchaeus, 150